WITHDRAWN

THE CONVERSION OF THE JEWS
AND OTHER ESSAYS

The Conversion of the Jews and Other Essays

MARK SHECHNER

Professor of English
State University of New York

St. Martin's Press   New York

First published in the United States of America in 1990

Printed in Hong Kong

ISBN 0–312–04619–7

Library of Congress Cataloging-in-Publication Data
Shechner, Mark
The conversion of the Jews and other essays / Mark Shechner
p.   cm.
ISBN 0–312–04619–7
1. American literature – Jewish authors – History and criticism
2. Jews – United States – Intellectual life   I. Title.
PS153.J4S49   1990
810.9′8924 – dc20   89–29460
                                                      CIP

To Anne and Sarah

Contents

Acknowledgments
and Notes for Contents

Earlier versions of these essays appeared in *Partisan Review, Salmagundi, Nation, New Republic, New Review, American Literary History,* and *Modern Jewish Studies Annual.* "Jewish Comedy and the Contradictions of Culture" appeared in *Jewish Wry: Essays in Jewish Humor,* edited by Sarah Blacher Cohen, Indiana University Press, 1987, and "Isaac Rosenfeld's Passage" was first published as the introduction to the reprint of Isaac Rosenfeld's novel *Passage from Home,* Markus Wiener Books, 1988. My gratitude to all editors and publishers for their gracious permission to reprint these essays in this volume. More detailed information on the essays is given below:

"The Conversion of the Jews." An earlier version of this essay was delivered as a talk before the Association for Jewish Studies in Boston, Decemberr 1986.

"Isaac Rosenfeld's Passage." Introduction to the reprint of Isaac Rosenfeld's novel *Passage from Home* (New York: Markus Wiener Books, 1988).

"Saul Bellow and Ghetto Cosmopolitanism." First appeared in *Modern Jewish Studies Annual,* 2 (Winter, 1979). Revised and reprinted in P. Shiv Kumar (ed.), *Saul Bellow: A Symposium on the Jewish Heritage* (Warangal, India: Nachson Books, 1983).

"Jewish Comedy and the Contradictions of Culture." Appeared in *Jewish Wry: Essays in Jewish Humor,* edited by Sarah Blacher Cohen (Bloomington: Indiana University Press, 1987).

"The Survival of Alan Ginsberg." Review of Ginsberg's *Mind Breaths: Poems 1972–1977*; Ginsberg, *Journals: Early Fifties, Early Sixties,* ed., Gordon Ball; *As Ever: The Collected Correspondence of Allen Ginsberg and Neal Cassady,* ed., Barry Gifford. *Partisan Review,* 46:1 (1979). Reprinted in *On the Poetry of Allen Ginsberg,* edited by Lewis Hyde (Ann Arbor: The University of Michigan Press, 1984).

"Bernard Malamud, or the Return of the Repressed." Review of

Bernard Malamud, *Dubin's Lives*. Nation, 228:10 (17 March 1979).

"Malamud: The Still, Sad Music." Review of Bernard Malamud, *The Stories of Bernard Malamud*. *Partisan Review*, 51:3 (1984). Reprinted in *Critical Essays on Bernard Malamud*, edited by Joel Salzberg (New York: G. K. Hall, 1987).

"A Portrait of Delmore." Review of *Portrait of Delmore: Journals and Notes of Delmore Schwartz*. Edited and introduced by Elizabeth Pollett. *Partisan Review*, 54:3 (Summer, 1987).

"Where's Papa." Review of Ernest Hemingway, *Selected Letters: 1917–1961*. *Partisan Review*, 49:2 (1982).

"The Truants." Review of William Barrett, *The Truants: Adventures Among the Intellectuals*. Nation, 234:8 (27 February 1982).

"Gates of Eden." Review of Morris Dickstein, *Gates of Eden. The New Review* (London), 41:4 (August, 1977).

"Elusive Trilling." Part I, Nation, 225:8 (17 September 1977). Part II, Nation, 225:9 (24 September 1977).

"Criticism and Culture." Review of Mark Krupnick, *Lionel Trilling and the Fate of Cultural Criticism*. Nation, 242:21 (31 May 1986).

"In Defense of the Imagination." Review of Robert Alter, *Defenses of the Imagination: Jewish Writers and Modern Historical Crisis. Nation*, 226:18 (13 May 1978).

"The Partisan." Review of Philip Rahv, *Essays on Literature and Politics, 1932–1972*, edited by Arabel Porter and Andrew Dvosin, and *Images and Ideas in American Culture: The Function of Criticism. Essays in Memory of Philip Rahv. Nation*, 227:16 (11 November 1978), and 227:17 (18 November 1978).

"Ambition and the American Scholar." Review of Joseph Epstein, *Ambition. Nation*, 232:2 (17 January 1981).

"Three Honest Men." Review of Philip French (ed.), *Three Honest Men: Edmund Wilson, F. R. Leavis, Lionel Trilling. New Republic*, 186:7 (17 February 1982).

"An American Procession." Review of Alfred Kazin, *An American Procession. Nation*, 238:24 (23 June 1984).

"The Last Trotskyist." Review of Alan Wald, *The New York Intellectuals. Salmagundi* (Winter, 1988).

1

The Conversion of the Jews

1

It is a fact, everywhere acknowledged and now even canonized in the histories, that between roughly 1945 and 1960 the terrain of American literature underwent a radical change, and that Jewish writers, critics, and intellectuals played an essential role in that change. In a phrase, American fiction was Europeanized, and it was Jewish writers and thinkers, in touch with European trends, who bore some responsibility for the new directions in American writing. To document that I could simply enumerate the names of those novelists, poets, playwrights, and critics who starred on the American literary stage during this period, or list the journals, starting with *Partisan Review* and *Commentary*, that became the vehicles of a new sensibility, but since that list could go on for pages and there is no end of list-making, I would prefer for the moment to dispense with the roll call and examine the proposition, rather than defend it. What I want to explore in brief is the question of where this Jewish presence came from, what it consisted of, and why it should have flourished just when it did.

One immediate answer is the obvious one: it was bound to happen. The children and grandchildren of butchers, grocers, fish peddlers, junk dealers, garment workers, and even the occasional rabbi, came of age all at once in a kind of Jewish baby-boom and elbowed their way into the cultural arena by the force of their ambition and the keenness of their intellects. Demographically, I would venture to say, the garment industry in this century has given birth to more writers, scholars, critics, and professors than any other American profession, including the ministry. Like the illegal immigration into Palestine after World War II that broke the back of the British mandate, the Jewish literary arrival had certain features of a mass movement, and nothing short of an American version of the Nuremberg Laws was going to stop it. Given the special Jewish

1

affinity for literacy and learning, Jews in any society will rise into elite literary circles when granted the opportunity. As "people of the book," Jews were once people of Torah and Talmud, but since the Enlightenment they have become the people of whatever book they may become acquainted with, and it is no more strenuous to see the novel as a contemporary Torah than to see the law firm as a modern variant on the Bet Din or Rabbinic court.*

Moreover, the rise of Jews into artistic and intellectual circles in America can be correlated with the improvement of their economic fortunes, as the children of businessmen and workingmen, in waves of cultural ascent, percolated upwards into the arts. With money made in business came the leisure of the children to paint, sculpt, dance, act, play, compose, write, weave, or throw clay. That's what comes of all those expensive lessons. This rise in station also corresponded with the post-war opening of doors. After the Shoah it was inevitable that social barriers would wither away, especially the reprehensible quota systems that permitted only so many Jews into the elite universities, the medical and law schools, the tenured faculties, and the English departments.

So, we might think of the rise of the Jewish novelist as basically that, a rise, an arrival, an emergence, a maturation, the literary harvest of a social growth. And to a great extent, it was exactly that. But if we have learned anything at all from history it is that all complex events are, to borrow a phrase from Freud, "overdetermined," the resultant of many forces in sudden intersection. The arrival of the Jewish writer at the heart of American letters was precisely such an event, and conditioned as it may have been by simple social factors, it also displayed features that are not so neatly explained. One is the explosiveness with which so many talented Jews rose to the top. To a native New Yorker, the literary scene in 1945, especially as viewed through the "little magazines," must have looked like Ellis Island just after a boat had docked – all these gabbling, animated, contentious Jews where just moments ago there had been only a few. The other feature is less tangible, less social, more literary, and concerns the systematic differentness of the literature produced by Jews after World War II from that produced before it. It is more

---

* When I was a child in New Jersey, our family knew a lot of Jewish bookmakers – "bookies" – and I now cannot help but wonder if there wasn't a kind of inverted Talmudic scholarship that involved their enterprise. Certainly I heard more than a little *pilpul* in their professional deliveries.

contemporary in its gestures: at first brooding, introspective, studiously melancholy, occasionally neurotic, painfully self-conscious, slyly Russian, a far cry from the kind of work Jewish writers were producing before the war, which was closer to the habits and manners, the exuberance and social panorama of classic American realism. Before the war there were the likes of Abraham Cahan, Anzia Yezierska, Sholom Asch, Michael Gold, Clifford Odets, and Daniel Fuchs producing novels and plays in the native realist mode and, in the case of Odets, writing American drama as though it were Yiddish theater. In all their writing, dollops of social realism swam in bowls of sentiment like sour cream in borscht. Only Henry Roth's tormented and symbolistic *Call it Sleep* and the surrealist novellas of Nathaniel West anticipated the emerging modernism.

With Saul Bellow and *Dangling Man* in 1944, however, a new writing appeared to be at hand, one that was more technically advanced, more inner-directed and self-conscious. It took other writers a few years to catch up with Bellow's sultry interiority and cunning stylistics, but by the mid-fifties Bernard Malamud, Isaac Rosenfeld, Norman Mailer, and others could be seen grappling with the subtleties of literary form and the intricacies of the human spirit. (The technical advance represented by this writing was not so thoroughgoing as to make it appear strikingly modernist. As Bellow himself would later complain, his first books were rather cautious performances. More significant was the turn inward and the discovery of the heart as the battlefield of history.) Other words beside emergence might characterize this moment – this twenty-year moment from 1945 to 1965. *Breakthrough* is one of them, implying the release of pent up energy and the collapse of obstacles. Another is *renaissance*, suggesting a renewal, a resurrection, a rebirth.

The number of Jews entering American letters after the war may have been socially determined but social considerations tell us nothing about the impact of their writing. There were almost as many Jewish novelists and poets at work in America in the 1930s as there were in the following two decades, though the impression they made on American letters was nowhere near as great. To understand that, we have to look at the inner dimensions of the fiction – the spiritual conditions that produced it and are reflected so vividly in it. The new writing comes into focus as a literature of turmoil and confusion, crisis and conversion, death and rebirth, conditions which determine its manner and sometimes its explicit themes. The new writers are all converts of one variety or another, and their writing is the testament of their conversions.

(I'm tempted to say that conversion constitutes the single most comprehensive "theme" of contemporary Jewish writing, though the word "theme" itself is ambiguous, and the same piece of litera- ture, cut into from different angles, will reveal different "themes," so that it may be advisable to reserve the word "theme" for an author's rather explicitly drawn concerns: the "theme," say, of life on the lower East side or the struggles between father and son, husband and wife, tradition and change, etc. Most of the time, the impulse to change is not so much a theme as it is a field of force, a property of the soul itself that draws the world around it into its own shape, much as gravity is said to shape space. It is the shape of dissatisfaction but also the shape of possibility. The Jewish writer, one tends to find, is always straining at the limits of his being. His dissatisfaction gives him motive, contour, and line.)

The Shoah had something to do with this – how could it not? A culture to which one was attached by history, by blood, and by tendrils of emotion had been destroyed, and a part of oneself had died with it. Though many of these writers and intellectuals were estranged from Jewish culture, having grown up with the socialist rejection of religious Judaism, they were not insensible of the fact that only an ocean divided them from Auschwitz and that but for an accident of birth and the vagaries of immigration they themselves were the victims of the Final Solution. Yet it is a curious fact that the first generation of post-war writers did not write much about either the Shoah or the founding of Israel. The Shoah was a hidden wound, shrouded in darkness and suffered in silence, felt everywhere but confronted virtually nowhere. In similar fashion, Israel was not readily available to the American literary imagination – certainly not to writers who had not experienced it directly – but it had lodged in the heart, in some deep chambers from which it could exert a tug, a gravitational pull, upon other centers of the mind. I would suggest that the Jewish writers, though pointedly ignoring these great events as themes for their fiction, were symbolizing them in the lives they lived and the moods they expressed in their writing. Death and rebirth were very much the implied subjects of their writing, and if their explicit themes were commonly local, domestic, and far removed from the catastrophic and the monumental, the deeper tonalities of their fiction were profoundly determined by these events. It was not for nothing that Bernard Malamud called his 1961 novel *A New Life,* and though the scene of renewal was just a small town in Oregon, the idea of the new life had resonances far beyond the fields and meadows of the Willamette Valley. To take yet another phrase from Freud that is particularly apposite here, something like a displacement of affect took place; feelings about unspoken and unspeakable subjects were displaced onto the overt themes of Malamud's writing.

But if the great dramas of death and rebirth provided the mood and the music of post-war Jewish writing, yet another great drama affected intellectuals more directly and provided the explicit crisis: the collapse of the revolutionary dreams of their youths. (This was rather more the case with critics and literary intellectuals than it was with novelists, but since it is a paradigm of experience that touches in some way a generation as a whole, I'll let it stand. It is not irrelevant to an understanding of Bellow, Mailer, and Lionel Trilling in his brief career as a novelist.) A number of the writers who continue to matter to us had grown up with visions of socialism (or communism or Trotskyism) dancing in their heads like sugar plums and after the War threw in the revolutionary towel and sought their dreams of redemption elsewhere. Their careers traced out an arc of commitment, recoil, and conversion. The ex-Communist or ex-Trotskyist or ex-Socialist or even ex-liberal was the typical Jewish figure of that generation.

The post-war generation of Jewish writers and social thinkers had been nurtured in the hothouse climate of social unrest and revolutionary zeal of the thirties. Throughout the 1930s, event after event came along to spoil dreams of an ideal socialist order, capped off by the revelations that the Soviet Union had failed utterly as the embodiment of Man's Hope. In the climate of crisis that came in the wake of these revelations, writers and intellectuals faced the dilemma of how to bury their revolutionism while preserving their iconoclasm. It was in the effort to resolve that dilemma that a remarkable history of personal changes took place, shaping the careers of a generation and leaving a profound mark on our literature and our thought. Both the critical intelligence and the creative impulse flowered during the twilight of American Marxism, as the conversion of intellectuals from sectarians to individuals released geysers of creative and intellectual power.

Most of the major Jewish writers of this era brought their careers to a point at the moment of abandoning old faiths. But the writers who generated the most excitement were not simply those who changed their minds, but rather those who transformed themselves through ordeals of conversion and redemption. From Isaac Rosenfeld's 1946 novel *Passage from Home* and Lionel Trilling's novel *The Middle of the Journey* (1947), to Saul Bellow's *The Adventures of Augie March* (1953) and *Henderson the Rain King* (1959) and especially his play *The Last Analysis* (1964), Allen Ginsberg's *Howl* (1956), Norman Mailer's *Advertisements for Myself* (1959) and, a generation later, Philip Roth's *Portnoy's Complaint* (1967), a single note rings clear from book to book: I am not, I can no longer be, the man I was. It is not to be wondered that when these writers took stock of their situations, many discovered in psychoanalysis or other psycho-therapies formulas for their shock and substitutes for the principles of social redemption they could no longer support. As releasing agents for the imagination and as guides to the American ethic of self-improvement, therapeutic ideas became both guides to the perplexed and bridges to the New World. The Jewish writers' books were allegories of crisis and change that, by a logic that is as strange as it is fascinating, were their generation's tickets to the American heartland.

2

By way of illustration, I'll content myself here with just one instance that will stand, I think, for some larger movement. What are we to make of a writer who started out in the thirties with the Spartacus Youth League and the Young People's Socialist League during its brief phase as a revolutionary Trotskyist organization and wound up thirty years later humoring the public with the antics of Moses Herzog, failed scholar and cuckolded husband, who goes about half-dazed in a striped jacket and straw boater trying to understand how he lost out?

I'm speaking of course of Saul Bellow, a prime case in point of the artist as convert, whose labors at self-transformation, self-transcendence really, provide the basic impulse and drama of his writing. Bellow came onto the scene in the 1940s as a writer of depression. *Dangling Man* in 1944 and *The Victim* in 1947 are depressed and depressing books. Perhaps to match his mood or to symbolize the times, the young Bellow – he was twenty-nine in 1944 – had apprenticed himself to Fyodor Dostoevsky and tailored his imagination to the poetic half-light of Czarist St Petersburg, taking the plot of *The Victim* from Dostoevsky's novella, *The Eternal Husband*. The impulse to Russianize the imagination was thoroughgoing; not only was it a rule of style, it was the very character Bellow and his friends, the Chicago Dostoevskians – Isaac Rosenfeld and Oscar Tarcov – assumed in the 1940s when they embarked for New York to seek their fortunes. These attitudes hardly need justifying: 1944 was a tragic year world-wide, especially if you were Jewish, and to assume a depressive literary posture was to do no more than respond to the times.

What strikes me now as noteworthy about both *Dangling Man* and *The Victim* is not their plots, which could have been anything at all that suited Bellow's state of mind, but their rhythmic and melodic architectures: their keening timbres and languorous cadences – in short, their funereal music. These books are adagios, not allegros, surely not scherzos. This is both intentional – at twenty-nine Bellow was a coming master of his narrative medium; and involuntary – he was writing out of a powerful sense of despair. Behind this despair lay both the Shoah – unspoken but symbolized – and a shattered vision, a lost optimism and innocence.

Upon finishing *The Victim*, Bellow embarked on an ambitious novel to be titled *The Crab and the Butterfly*. The novel was suppressed and we know little about it except for a fragment that was published separately in 1950 as "The Trip to Galena." We can only surmise why Bellow suppressed the novel, and my guess is that it cut too close to the bone and gave too much away. Many elements that would be properly distanced and impersonalised in *The Adventures of Augie March* were presented in too raw a form in the uncompleted novel. "The Trip to Galena" provides us with clues about what that might be. It is the frantic monologue of one Weyl, a patient in a mental hospital whose tale of a trip to Illinois decomposes into a ramble, spinning off a froth of metaphysics: wild speculations on shoes and garters, murder and mass murder, conduct and the depths of life. Weyl is a manic-depressive who bursts out of his iron lethargy while telling his story to a fellow patient and sinks in again once he is finished. In the midst of his mad ramblings occur some lines that are symptomatic of what Bellow was trying to do in *The Crab and the Butterfly* and *Augie March*.

You heard me tell my old aunt a while back when she asked me what I wanted, that I didn't want to be sad any more. I meant it to the letter. That being sad is being disfigured, and the first reply I feel like making to it is a good fast kick in the wind.

The key phrase is, "I didn't want to be sad anymore." By 1953, when Bellow published *Augie March*, his public disposition was anything but sad: it was upbeat, uptempo, boosterishly American. He had turned in his dirges for rhumbas, exchanged his Shostakovich for Xavier Cugat. "I am an American, Chicago born." In its rambling free-style structure it is boyishly American, resembling in its high spirits, its vivid adventures, its larger-than-life characters, nothing so much as *The Adventures of Huckleberry Finn*. So promotional was the design of the book that a few critics were prone to take it for Bellow's rejection of his own past and a statement that henceforth he could no longer be counted among the alienated.

Augie March was a classic conversion book – a testimonial to a new faith – the first of several Bellow would write, exhibiting all the classic symptoms of a testimonial: the overstatement, the note of protest, the uncommon vividness. That conversion had both public and private meanings. Publicly, it was a testament of de-Russification and acceptance of the terms and conditions of being an American at last. It was a public burning of Old World manners: the gabardines of alienation and mourning that had been draped like a caftan over his previous books. Bellow had sat *shiva* long enough and was fretting to start life anew. The early 1950s were, moreover, the time for such affirmations, and *Augie March* in 1953 comes a year after a famous symposium conducted by *Partisan Review* magazine in which 25 writers and intellectuals, many of whom had once identified with radical causes, sang hallelujah to "Our Country and Our Culture." There were three notable dissenters – C. Wright Mills, Irving Howe, and Norman Mailer – but by and large the symposium was a rousing affirmation of American life and values, as its sponsors had intended it to be.

And then, of course, in 1953, there was Israel, embattled but indisputably there, and while Bellow would not write of it until many years later, in *To Jerusalem and Back*, it was, one now imagines, yet another source of the high spirits that permeated *The Adventures of Augie March*. Its hero may have been American, Chicago born, but its author was a Canadian-born son of Jewish immigrants.

The cultural climate, the *Zeitgeist*, into which such a book appeared was not the whole story behind its spirit of revival, for the public posture was abetted by a program of spiritual self-transcendence. Some time late in the forties Bellow had become involved with a radical psychotherapy variously called Character Analysis or Vegetotherapy or Orgonomy. By any name it was the psychological doctrine and therapeutic program of Wilhelm Reich, the émigré German-Jewish psychotherapist who had been in the 1920s Sigmund Freud's most brilliant disciple and had wound up in the forties in rural Maine, dabbling in biochemistry and cosmology and issuing strident manifestos on the global sexual crisis. The root cause of communism and fascism, Reich thought, was a sexual plague whose origins lay in the "character armor" of modern man and whose symptoms were sexual repression and political oppression.

Reich's attraction for intellectuals in the 1940s lay partly in his scaling down the field of battle from the economic order to the individual body, where gains might be more easily achieved and monitored, and partly in his gospel of the orgasm as the key to mental and social hygiene. In part also it lay in his seeming ability to account for the failures of the Russian Revolution and of Left insurgency everywhere by singling out sex as the missing variable in prior calculations, thus, in effect, keeping revolutionary hopes alive. Sex, for Reich, *was* politics, and his rejection of adjustment in favor of revolutionary assault upon the superego, personal or social, and his clinical methods for relaxing muscular rigidity, dissolving psychic resistance, and storming the Bastilles of pleasure appealed to stymied radicals as adjustments downwards of the campaign against Wall Street that more traditional strategies had failed to carry through.

By the end of the 1940s, Reich's sexual researches had grown into a full-blown biological mysticism that connected the substances of life with the elements of the universe – orgones – which Reich claimed could be harnessed to produce erections, enhance orgasms, cure cancer, or make rain. Over such claims, Reich would eventually run afoul of the Food and Drug Administration, which indicted him on charges of medical fraud for a contraption he manufactured and sold as a health aid and cancer cure. These orgone accumulators were little more than plywood crates whose walls were packed with alternating layers of rockwool and steel wool to capture cosmic orgones and channel them into the human body. Patently absurd on the face of them, the orgone boxes did exert a certain fascination for those already taken with Reich's militant erotics, and among New York intellectuals Isaac Rosenfeld and Norman Mailer were known to have them. Reich was convicted in 1955 and sentenced to a federal penitentiary where he died of a heart attack in 1957.

Paul Goodman was probably the first to discover Reich for the New York intellectuals, but Bellow's friend Isaac Rosenfeld was soon to follow, and by 1946 or 1947 Rosenfeld had entered therapy and was touting Orgonomy to his friends. By the end of the decade Bellow was also involved in Reichian therapy, and while the public premises of *Augie March* may reflect the gathering optimism of the times, a portion of its private agenda is the Reichian "breakthrough" into new regions of emotional possibility. This political-therapeutic synthesis is fascinating to contemplate, suggesting as it does that the key to a closer identification with American life and values might be a better relation to one's genitals and through them to the primal power of the big bang.

The therapeutic ideal – to be born again – becomes explicit in Bellow's next two novels and a play in which some of the basic themes are exposed more nakedly than in his fiction. Without writing a book on the subject, one can scarcely do more than sketch out the barest outlines of these writings and the role they play in the political – therapeutic synthesis, and in the interests of economy I'll skip over Bellow's next novel, *Seize the Day*, except to point out that its most vivid character is a free-lance therapist/goniff/commodities trader named Tamkin who spouts Reichian lore while perpetrating a host of commercial swindles. The quintessence of therapeutic revivalism was *Henderson the Rain King* in 1959. You undoubtedly know that book as a spirited romp through an imaginary Africa inhabited by comical tribes called the Arnewi and Wariri, the latter of which are led by a charming medicine man named Dahfu, who shepherds his people through the rites for making rain and in his spare time administers a cure to Eugene Henderson. But *Henderson* is also a book for the cognoscenti, an out and out allegory of Bellow's own experiences in therapy.

Dahfu is Reich in blackface. He runs Henderson through a course of exercises designed to free up his choked emotions, culminating in a session with a captive lioness who teaches him the arts of physical spontaneity, deep breathing, and whole-hearted roaring. After just a few days with the lioness, Henderson sends off an ecstatic letter to his forsaken wife, in which he claims to be bursting with life, with reality, and with the resolve to get home and, at fifty-five, enter med school. We may recognize in Dahfu's treatment a preview of Arthur Janov's primal scream therapy, and it is indeed some leonine version of the primal scream – call it the primal roar – that constitutes Henderson's cure and sends him home to his wife and his schooling.

After *Henderson*, this revivalism dropped out of Bellow's novels as he turned his attention elsewhere. By 1959, Reich had been dead for two years, and *Henderson* was a final homage, a send-off, an affectionate, comic farewell. But Bellow was not quite finished with conversion and redemption, for he had one more serious tussle with it in the play *The Last Analysis*, which was first staged off Broadway in 1964 and again in 1971. Both times it fared poorly on the stage, but the published versions – there are two of them – are readable, amusing, and good story-telling, if not always good theater. Again, considerations of economy prohibit anything but the sketchiest outline of the play, which revolves around the efforts of a broken down comedian to resurrect his career by staging his death and rebirth on closed circuit television before an audience of the American Psychological Association. He dies and is reborn out of a laundry hamper. It is an extravagant conception, portions of which are brilliantly conceived, though few actors, save absolute monsters of ego, could ever play the part. The play deals explicitly with death and rebirth, and while it treats them comically, as a kind of shamanistic vaudeville, it leaves little doubt that the basic proposition, that a man must be born again, is passionately meant.

Bellow's writing from *Augie March* in 1953 through *The Last Analysis* and *Herzog* in 1964, then, is fundamentally conversion literature, conversion away from his youthful Dostoevskianism and all that it implied: brooding, languor, guilt, alienation, a sense of life as bizarre and irrational and of the self as willful and perverse, toward a kind of Americanism, brimming with optimism, high spirits, a faith in work, destiny, futurity. The irony of such an Americanization was that it was facilitated by a discipline invented by a German-Jewish sexologist who by the end of his career had become a crackpot: a cancer quack, a rain maker, an egomaniac, and a UFO hunter whose youthful ideas about sex in culture had been eclipsed by his Quixotic charges into biophysics and his doomed quests for the cosmic Shangri-la. For a writer like Bellow, afflicted with the curse of irony, the only recourse in dealing with this phase of his life was to treat it as comedy and farce, even though it was the comedy of trying to stay alive and in command of his powers. The confusions and bewilderments this quest entailed have been part of Bellow's writing all along; he was in the 1950s and remains today far less rational or settled a writer than most people think, and I would argue that Bellow has been at his best as a writer when most desperate and uncertain. Fortunately for us that has been much of the time.

3

I write this introduction in a locale far removed from the main concerns of this book, in a house in the mountains above Kobe, Japan, some 2400 feet above Osaka Bay. The distance from America, from American publishing and American polemics, and from the books and journals that had inspired most of this writing to begin with, makes them feel just a trifle remote, even, given the vertigo of travel, as if they were not quite really of this world and wholly of my invention. Novels written by Jewish-Americans, I might add, are very much *à la mode* in Japan nowadays, and virtually every major university has a class devoted entirely to the writing of Bellow, Roth, and Malamud, and even, in one university I have visited, the writing of Abraham Cahan, Sholom Asch, and Anzia Yezierska. Black writers too are avidly read, at least in the universities, and one university even publishes a journal of Black studies. Astonishing. And yet as opposed to the fiction, which is decidedly a growth stock among Japanese students and scholars, the intellectual life in which that fiction took root is virtually unknown. When I talk to classes about the Jewish intellectuals and the history of the anti-Stalinist Left, I have the distinct impression that I am preaching strange doctrines, which, after a while, begin to sound strange to me.

That estrangement from one's own words and ideas is certainly one of the effects of removal from familiar precincts, and yet quite another, parallel, effect is an intuition about what is permanent in one's own concerns and what is transitory. Politics, past and present, tend to grow dim as distance reduces them to the dimension of the printed page or the TV screen. But issues of identity and change grow bold, even urgent. Surrounded by otherness, as I am here, a vital and intoxicating otherness at that, one understands keenly its allure, and it is not entirely by accident that I find myself just now absorbed in the writing of Lafcadio Hearn, the Irish cum American writer who bounced around the world for most of his life and wound up settling here in Japan, where he learned the language, adopted the culture, took a Japanese wife, and even assumed a Japanese name, Yakumo Koizumi.

The brand of self-transformation I find myself describing in these essays often came accompanied by politics, which so often overshadowed the personal transformations and masked the deep fault lines in the geology of the self. It has been most often written about as a politics, rather than as a phenomenology, of the self, and so finds its way into the history books: the history of the Left, the history of the Little Magazines, the history of the anti-Stalinist radicals, etc.

But perhaps that is inherent in the histories of Jewish writers and intellectuals themselves: when all the polemics and the accretions of opinion are boiled away, what remain as a residuum are the fluctuations of the heart itself, that unstable and desperate organ that takes refuge in opinion precisely when it least knows what it wants. Elsewhere I wrote of the New York Intellectuals, whose political hegiras away from leftism have played so large a part in setting the intellectual agendas of our own day, "It wasn't so that they changed their minds as it was that they changed themselves."

Partly by happenstance and partly by design, the last three books I read before sitting down to this introduction turned out to be explicit conversion stories, in which the issue of Jewish identity is presented as a question: Richard Gilman's *Faith, Sex, Mystery*, the memoir of his conversion to Catholicism as a young man and his eventual retreat from active faith; Philip Roth's *The Counterlife*, in which the issue of Jewish identity is posed in terms of repertory theater; and Julius Lester's *Lovesong*, the story of his conversion *from* Christianity *to* Judaism. Lester's book is a curiosity piece in the sense that it seems to be *sui generis*, to fit into no common pattern of American experience that I am familiar with. The phenomenon of Jews admiring and wishing to emulate Blacks, of which Norman Mailer's essays "The White Negro" is only the most celebrated instance, is far more familiar than that of Blacks wishing to emulate – let alone actually become – Jews. But then Lester is a special case, having had a Jewish great grandfather, a German-Jewish peddler who made his way to Arkansas in the nineteenth century and married a freed slave. Lester is wont to think of himself, then, as having fulfilled a kind of destiny, a blood legacy or something equally mysterious and evanescent. (A question for the literary historians. Is Lester henceforth to be classified as a Jewish writer? A Black writer? These are delicious questions and they are not entirely trivial. I have little doubt that one reason a writer so gifted and productive as Lafcadio Hearn has disappeared from our history books is that he defies the categories.)

More familiar to me, and more in the line of what Jewish writers are likely to produce in our time, are the Roth and Gilman books. In the former, a sort of five-act repertory theater, Nathan Zuckerman and his brother Henry pass around identities and lives and even countries, trying out, as it were, the varieties of Jewish destiny and belief (and Roth being Roth, erotic frisson) as if the uncertainties of Jewish identity – the *problematics*, as a contemporary jargon would say it – made the theme and variations form the most suitable method for exposing its ambiguities (see the essay on *Zuckerman Unbound* in this volume). As for the Gilman book, it strikes me as being of a piece with its time – not the 1980s but the early 1950s – when a younger Gilman, raised as a tepid and non-observant Jew, had himself baptized a Catholic and tried for a while to bring his life into line with Catholic belief and ritual. The discipline would eventually prove to be too taxing and unrewarding to be maintained, and Gilman drifted slowly away into a state of lukewarm faith, in which his formal Catholic beliefs and his lingering Jewish identity learned to cohabit in a state of languid détente, neither having the potency, or the particular need, to dislodge the other. Such a conversion turned out to be rather more additive than substitutive; it was a gesture toward self-enhancement rather than self-rejection.

This all may seem a little strange to the American mind schooled in distinctions and the necessity for making them, but here in non-ideological, or rather post-ideological, Japan the idea that one can be of two faiths – here it is normally Shinto and Buddhist – and enjoy the benefits of both is taken for granted. I have even met Shinto-Christians, and while Christianity may balk at such laxity of self-definition, the Japanese mind seems to be quite at ease with it. Living in ambiguity here seems to be formalized, even a cultural norm, whereas Jews fall into it anxiously, as if it were a kind of purgatory, a penalty for having lived badly.

Conversion is by no means a uniquely Jewish drama. The churning heart and the fragile ego, the sense of incompleteness or of shame that lead one to change one's life are universally if not evenly distributed throughout the tribes of mankind. It is a commonplace scarcely worth repeating, except that we're prone to undervalue it, that the very drama of the modern novel itself is the drama of conversion. The imagination is engaged by the tropes of becoming. But the Jewish people, plunged suddenly into the modern world in the last two centuries and subject to assaults from without and upheavals from within, have been subject to the forces of conversion in greater numbers and with greater force than other cultures. Is not Zionism to be thought a conversion, a movement of the soul projected onto history and decked out with the paraphernalia of a social and historical force: ships, airplanes, organizations, ideas? Was not the Yiddishist movement that brought the extraordinary and short-lived flowering of Yiddish literature, drama, and culture to life in he early decades of this century not also a conversion, or perhaps the external sign of some interior rearrangement in the furniture of the soul? Was not the romance of Marxism and the withdrawal from it?

It would be a wonder if the trials of Jewish history were not reflected in Jewish literature and were not indeed the very heart and soul of it, not only in its themes but in its very character as a form of human expression: its nervousness, its vividness, its fluxions of emotion. This may, again, seem rather a commonplace though one fails to see much evidence of it in the endless stream of books, essays, and monographs that all too often treat Jewish writing as the voice of timeless verities and Jewish writers as particularly insightful into what is generically human or profoundly spiritual or broadly "humanistic" in man. The Jew, by virtue of being ancient, is endowed with the faculty of being "deep" or wise.

One doesn't want to dispute that entirely; if trouble doesn't bring wisdom, what does? And especially in an American literary culture dominated from time to time by a peculiar Anglo-Saxon depthlessness, the Jewish writer may in fact be drawing his water from deeper wells. It is not a position I'd care to press too hard against now: we do have – did have – Hawthorne, Melville, Whitman, and Poe a century ago to point the way toward the hidden vestibules of the Anglo-Saxon mind. Ah, but we also have the cult of Ernest Hemingway and its implication that fishing, hunting, drinking, and womanizing are the bedrock of the American soul.

Unfortunately, the ascription of depth seems to carry with it the implication of being "ancient", bearded, contemplative, sage and knowing, poised and humane, not, as the Jewish writer often appears to be, unhinged or fanatical. I would say of Bernard Malamud that in honor of all that seemed to be rabbinical in him, we have not yet fully measured the side of him that was unsettled, unsure of itself, and often confused; we may yet, I think, have to temper our admiration for him in order to gain a full appreciation of him. In books like *Pictures of Fidelman, Dubin's Lives* and *God's Grace*, Malamud took off the gabardines and donned some shocking outfits. So too, with Bellow, whose restlessness has been more conspicuous but which we've been a little hesitant to see in full, in tribute to his full complement of "humanistic" ideas, we have been a little loathe to take the turmoil in his books at face value: as being of their essence rather than as, say, tests of the Bellovian heroes' "humanity," an ascription that is sometimes hard to pin down in terms of actual behavior. Roth has presented a different case: a careening turbulence receding slowly into wise passiveness, in virtue of which he has not yet stood widely accused of wisdom or depth, though as the road of excess leads to the palace of wisdom, those charges are bound to crop up.

My take, then, on the literature that has been called, for want of a better term, Jewish-American, is that it is a decidedly Romantic, as opposed to Classical, literature: that it is egotistical, self-assertive, spontaneous and undisciplined (though often painstakingly composed to give the appearance of spontaneity and undiscipline), naked in its appetites, unembarrassed in its need, and sometimes more than a little bit fanatical in its demands upon the reader. Classicism is an ethos of *being*, Romanticism one of *becoming*, and it is the trials and exactions of becoming that Jewish writers in our time have excelled in expressing. That the possibility of transforming the self should be an integral, even basic, ingredient of such a literature should not surprise us; Jewishness itself, in all its variousness and possibility, is the great surprise. Our writers, in their alarm, their uncertainty, and their Protean changeability, are heralds indeed, bringing the strange news about our strange selves.

2

Isaac Rosenfeld's Passage

Every age has its theme words, its verbal icons and semantic beacons that footnote its history, highlight its conflicts, and trace, however hazily, the stream of its consciousness. In the 1940s, words that gained favor among a small but influential group of intellectuals were "crisis," "transition," and "alienation," this last of which was virtually a cult term among those homeless radicals who saw "life without dogma and without hope" as their fate and, making a virtue of necessity, their refuge as well.

Unlike key words of more militant eras, "exploitation," "struggle," and "masses" in the thirties, or "self-determination" and "participatory democracy" in the sixties, alienation was anything but a call to action. Though it came in many packages, of various Marxist, existentialist, and psychiatric origin, alienation came into common use as a term of negation, signaling a dual rejection of American life and the orchestrated insurgency and partisan dogmatism of the revolutionary left. By and large it was the password of the post-Marxist fraternity that had migrated from faction and dogma to homelessness and indecision, pronouncing as it went its standing antipathy to a bureaucratic and materialistic America and its born-again immunity to party and line. One version of the alienated's creed was that of the Daniel Bell, at the time a young sociologist and an editor at, of all places, *Fortune* magazine, who had been scarred by the faction fights on the left and disillusioned by the *cul de sac* into which revolutionary Marxism had led him. In 1946 he would broadcast his estrangement in this fashion:

> The intellectual knows too well the ambiguities of motives and interests which dictate individual and institutional action. He cannot surrender himself wholly to any movement. Nor can he make those completely invidious or utopian judgments regarding the nature and needs of man which the cynic and romantic make. He can only live without dogma and without hope. He can

only, as an intellectual, realize his destiny – and by consciously accepting it, rework it – through seeing the world, in Friedrich Schiller's phrase, as disenchanted.

Bell is a prime witness here, since this credo of alienation came at the end of a review of Isaac Rosenfeld's *Passage from Home*, which Bell read as a parable of post-Marxist nausea *and* Jewish uprootedness: a summary of "the phylogeny of a race in its search for moral independence . . . ." However, in taking Rosenfeld for a troubadour of alienation, Bell was doing little more than taking cues from Rosenfeld himself, who placed in the mouth of his hero, the fourteen-year-old Bernard Miller, avowals of desolation that rang with the lonely metaphysics of the decade.

> "I had come to know a certain homelessness in the world, and took it for granted as a part of nature: had seen in the family, and myself acquired, a sense of sadness from which both assurance and violence had forever vanished. We had accepted it unconsciously and without self pity, as one might accept a sentence that had been passed generations ago, whose terms were still binding though its occasion had long been forgotten. The world is not entirely yours; and our reply is: very well then, not entirely."

"The world is not entirely yours; and our reply is: very well then, not entirely." Behind such spiritual-heroic renunciations as this, and they were legion, lay the bitter experience of the Marxist Fall of the thirties (Spain, the Moscow Trials, the Stalin-Hitler pact) and knowledge of the Holocaust, of which Rosenfeld was painfully aware but his teenage hero innocent. Because of that, *Passage From Home* is both more than the vision of intellectual homelessness that Bell would claim it to be and less. It is more in the sense that as the story of a specifically Jewish childhood in pre-war Chicago it possesses the savor and grit of a particular ethnic milieu that no metaphysics of alienation can possibly account for. But it is less inasmuch as the shocks and disenchantments registered in its language have not yet descended upon its characters; the great public unmasking of Stalin, which was a profound event for Jews of radical temperament, was still around the corner, and the death camps were still up the road. Fourteen years old some time in the early 1930s – the year in *Passage From Home* is not precisely given – Bernard Miller knows only the agonies of his own childhood, not the horrors of his generation. It is the book's singular weakness that its author bears the sorrows of Judea in his heart while his main character knows only the sorrows of the young Miller.

Passage From Home tells the story of a summer in the life of Bernard Miller, who at fourteen flees his father's house in a quest for adventure and knowledge, which he hopes to find in the company of his Aunt Minna, whose Bohemian life gives tantalizing promise of thrilling, possibly sexual, adventures. On visits to her apartment, where he frequently turns up unannounced, he makes amorous advances to his aunt which she peremptorily rejects. At last, in order to gain entry to Minna's life, Bernard stages an introduction to "cousin" Willy, a hillbilly and migrant from the South who had been married to his cousin Martha, who had died three years before. Bernard's motives are murky, though they seem to involve an erotic attachment to Minna as well as a need to escape the house of his father, a fussy, sour autocrat.

The introduction, awkward and comical at the outset, is a success, and it is not long before the unemployed Willy moves in with Minna to form precisely what Bernard, playing teenage *shadkhen*, has been angling for: an alternative household for himself. A family quarrel, instigated by Minna's unexpected appearance at his father's birthday party, gives Bernard the opportunity to storm out of the house in Minna's wake and attach himself, unbidden, to her and Willy. With its books, its records, its casual untidiness and simple utilitarian furnishings, Minna's apartment is everything his home is not, seeming at first blush to offer the passion and freedom that his young manhood demands.

> The pictures on the wall, their wild, broken colors and unrecognizable forms, took on meaning and welcomed me. Here dwelt that spirit which we barred from our lives, and in its freedom it was friendly, not raging, and not destructive, but liberal. This was its natural home.

The romance of Bohemia starts to sour, however, as Bernard takes up residence on a cot between the table and the sink, amid the dirty dishes and the cockroaches. Art, freedom, and eros have sunk their roots in disorder, and Bernard's delicate senses, schooled in fastidiousness, are repelled by the untidiness of this emancipation. "I went to the sink to wash under the tap, but saw a roach scurrying across the drainboard and drew back, nauseated. The moment of nausea was in the nature of a perception and the kitchen suddenly became for me a room of utter disorder, the paint flaking over the sink, the wall behind the stove streaked with dirt and grease." As for the erotic, there are quarrels in the dark and the fearsome sounds of drunken coupling – alcohol! – from behind closed doors.

Bernard's escapade with Minna turns out to be a training in disillusionment, as one by one the veils of romance peel away from Minna's life like paint from a tenement wall. Bernard looks upon Minna and Willy naked and sees only nakedness, not revelation. His cot is lousy with bedbugs that commute nightly across his body. The lovers quarrel. The odd ménage is finally shattered when Minna and Willy separate, as Willy turns out to be a freeloader who has been using Minna for a meal ticket, and Minna herself proves to be married to another man, a Jewish cabaret owner named Fred Mason with whom, for secret reasons, she cannot live. And the separation is effected cruelly, at a party that Minna and Mason throw for the purpose of humiliating Willy and driving him away.

Summer over, his options closed, Bernard boards the streetcar and heads ruefully home, to his stepmother's cleanliness and order, his father's silence and disapproval. "'So you're back,'" is all his father can muster as he enters. "In my embarrassment I avoided him, keeping my eyes averted to the floor, and while I still expected him to speak to me, it seemed to me that he, too, was staring at the floor. I saw him turn and leave and go to the front room. There, I knew, he would stand at the window, looking out." Avoiding the "cliché of the resolved mood," as Rosenfeld once called it, the novel leaves its themes unresolved: Willy fades away, Minna's history with the family remains unexplained, father and son are no closer at the end than they had been at the beginning. The novel is as untidy as Minna's kitchen. The passage from home leads only back home, but to what? To vexation and bewilderment, to a father at the window looking self-consciously out, to a son at the door peering self-consciously in.

This is admittedly a thin plot, poignant at moments of separation and return but no more so than a hundred novels of domestic travail before and since. What summons us back to this novel, however, is not its plot but the ambience in which it is carried out: a Jewish world in crisis in which the conflicts of father and son, more than just household spats, are symbols of a revolution in culture and belief that was changing American Jewry from a transplanted old world culture to something distinctly new and American. The mood of the book and its historical moment transcend the story and transform it into something more capacious than a mere record of Bernard Miller's experiences.

Passage from Home is a litany of the woes that were festering in Isaac Rosenfeld's heart as he wrote it, and with the solemnity of David at psalms he wrote about his childhood as if by incantations of regret he could exalt the miseries of a Chicago boyhood into world-historical rites of passage. That was not so vain an ambition, since the conflict between Bernard and his father is, in one sense, just a summer stock rendition of the same drama that was being played out everywhere in Jewish life: the drama of culture and family in crisis. As documentary, *Passage from Home* takes its place as a fairly typical novel of Jewish life as we have come to know it since vernacular Jewish fiction began to be written a century ago. From Mendele Mocher Sforim's *The Travels of Benjamin III*, in which Benjamin deserts his wife to go off in search of the Ten Tribes, to the novels of Saul Bellow and Philip Roth, where the family is already a museum piece and the Jewish man is usually found casting off his first (or second or third) *shikse* amid much wailing and gnashing of teeth, the decline of the Jewish family under the impact of modern conditions seems to be the most hackneyed of Jewish themes.

The Jewish family *in extremis*, then, was already a cliché by the time Rosenfeld got around to it, and indeed some of the bitterest portrayals of it are to be found in the domestic storm and stress literature of the 1920s and 1930s: in the explosive battles of father and daughter in Anzia Yezierska's *Bread Givers*; in the blows visited by father upon son in Henry Roth's *Call It Sleep*; in the omnibus bickerings and betrayals that mark Clifford Odets' *Awake and Sing*. In such company, *Passage from Home* seems to be a routine dramatization of Jewish civilization and its discontents, the son longing to take flight from the father, the father distant and inscrutable, given to sudden rages and bursts of rejection. But in *Passage from Home*, a book published twenty-one years, and thus a generation, after Yezierska's account of a young woman's bid for liberation from the family, the father's world is already a threadbare remnant of the Jewish tradition. In *Bread Givers*, at least, the father is a student of Torah, his iron dominion over his daughters sanctioned by his role as the keeper of law and preserver of memory. It is not an appealing picture of the Jewish tradition, since the father's immersion in study appears to be a mask for self-interest, but it is one in which the traditional elements of the family are initially in place, even if they must be shattered for the next generation to breathe freely. By contrast, the Jewish world in *Passage from Home* is already a decomposed one in which the father's tyranny has been divorced from any semblance of religious authority. He has inherited the Hebraic strictness of conscience but nothing of its piety and harmony. An American, Chicago born, he knows – to borrow a formula from Abraham Joshua Heschel – the danger and gloom of this world but not the infinite beauty of heaven or the holy mysteries of piety. Where Yezierska's father sat wrapped in phylacteries, Rosenfeld's sits wrapped only in sadness, and the son's revolt is infused with pity for the father and a nostalgia for a past with which he has no contact except through the grandfather.

It is precisely in this that *A Passage from Home* departs from the routines of Jewish revolt literature, for it is not toward the shabby avant-gardism of Minna's walkup that Bernard is finally impelled, though he does not understand this at once. The zone of enchantment, rather, is in the past, which has been there all along. Sent to his grandparents for a refresher course in "the Jewish spirit," Bernard does a tour of the old neighborhood with his grandfather. In his daily life, the grandfather is a petty man, a maestro of grievance and vanity, and as he leads Bernard through the streets of the old Jewish section, descanting on this one's fortunes and that one's bankruptcies, Bernard is repelled by this "poor, overdone figure of an old man, [with] his endless complaints and ironies, his arrogance, wit, familiarity, his pinchings and pettings, angers and cranks, his constant, unalleviated *shlepperei*".

Yet on these walks, as nowhere else, Bernard's senses are stirred and the novel vibrates with the color and vividness of those teeming streets in which the Jews first settled upon their arrival in America. The return to the old neighborhood calls to mind the grandfather's old grocery store, a sad kennel of a shop that had gone bankrupt and has since been spruced up and made profitable by a new owner.

> Flat tins of sardines he had in profusion – little oval cans, key attached, wrapped in wax paper with red labels pasted on, bearing the portrait of a Norwegian king. A tub of butter stood in the window of the ice box, tilted toward the customers. Eggs lay in a trough behind the counter and in unopened crates on the floor. The ice box leaked, and the scattered sawdust always turned damp and gave off a sour odor.

A little epiphany of old world defeat amid new world abundance, it was more a state of mind than a business, a piece of stirring, history-laden *shlepperei*, like the grandfather himself. Eventually, this *Spatziergang* leads to the home of Reb Feldman, an aging *melamed* at whose house a small band of Hasidim gathers to drink tea, play chess, kibbitz, and trade theses and conundrums from Talmud and Torah, while in the corner, propped on a divan, lies the *melamed*, a man with a puffy face, a black beard, and rings on his fingers. Like the grandfather's ancient store, this apartment, reeking of age and decay, also throbs with passion. Here, amid the shabbiness and the pilpul, the chess and the tea, the stained fingers and the earlocks, something quite magical is taking place, the transubstantiation of Jewish law into sacred music. Without any visible cues from Reb Feldman, the gray room begins to ring with divinity.

> In a corner of the room sat two men playing chess. I had not noticed them when I came in. Their light was poor and, as they bent over the board, they themselves seemed like nothing so much as chessmen, knights with narrow, pendulant faces, carved out of bone to which skin and hair still clung. They did not speak to each other, but occasionally one struck up a melody in which his partner joined, humming and intoning the syllables, "aie, dai, dai, dai, dai – yam, bim, bom." Together they would nod over the melody, sharing and extending it, turning their hands in and out at the wrist, their elbows planted before them on the table. During pauses in the discussion one could hear them, and the melody also seemed to be issuing in an undertone from the remote and ponderous Feldman, as well as the men at our table, a slight weaving rhythm catching their heads.

What Bernard hears is the *niggun*, the little melody that underlies every Jewish prayer, suddenly arise in a wave of song and fill the room. Here, off to the corner of the novel, is its center, a sanctuary of light within Judaism in which the young man experiences the joy and the community he fails to find at home. Here is the living heart of ecstatic Judaism in exile, playing out its last days as an ancient, minor cult in the houses of Chicago.

Seeing the light among these men, Bernard vows to seek it in himself:

> For, as at Feldman's house, when I had seen a moment of understanding pass before a group of old men and had felt that this represented what was best in their lives and in Jewish life, so I now felt that possession of such understanding would be the

very best of my own life, and knowing the truth, itself a kind of ecstasy.

But this is an ecstasy from which Bernard is locked out, the keys to it having been lost by his father. His own sundering from his father, indeed, is a replica of his father's sundering from his roots, and it is his artist's birthright: "tradition as discontinuity," to take a phrase from Irving Howe. Bernard's fate lies no more with Reb Feldman than it does with Aunt Minna. For better or for worse, he is sentenced to America and alienation.

Rosenfeld didn't set out to write a parable for his age. He wrote rather to soothe his own lacerated heart and purge it of its poisons. In so doing, however, he drew a profile of contemporary Jewish life in which the decomposition of his own family took on a certain collective meaning. The passage from home was the standard experience of Jewish boys of his generation, a collective emigration of the spirit away from the uncertain Judaism of their parents, which was especially agonizing for having to be undertaken alone. Like other adolescents of his time, Bernard Miller has two Bar Mitzvahs: the ceremony in which he takes his place as a man in the Jewish community and the trial by ordeal that initiates him into the actual terms of his life – the strangeness of his relation to Jewish tradition, the pain of his relation to the world, the hardness of his transactions with himself.

Moreover, as a typical post war world-disenchantment book, *Passage from Home* shared the climate of diffuse indolence that was endemic to books of the age, from Bellow's *Dangling Man* (1944) and *The Victim* (1947), to Lionel Trilling's *The Middle of the Journey* (1947), Delmore Schwartz's *The World is a Wedding* (1948), and Arthur Miller's *Death of a Salesman* (1949), to name just a few. In all these, excepting Trilling's novel, in which the politics are in the foreground, the critical events usually transpire in the parlor or the kitchen where the explicit drama is a domestic one. But in all, too, the nimbus of history looms just beyond the scrim of consciousness, unremarked by the characters, but casting a shadow of menace over them all, like a motion picture sound track. "This is the experience of the generation that has come to maturity during the depression," wrote Delmore Schwartz in 1944, "the sanguine period of the New Deal, the days of the Popular Front and the days of Munich and the slow, loud, ticking imminence of a new war." Schwartz was speaking of *Dangling Man*, but he might have said the same of any of these books that, written in the 1940s, testify to the agonies of recent history.

Brilliant as its moment was, however, alienation would probably have left a dimmer trace had it not found embodiment in a style through which it gained a kind of embalmed second life. The alienation of the Jewish intellectuals was a distinctly literary affair, something like the romantic despair of eighteenth-century Germany when *Werther* was the rage and young men in blue coats and yellow vests went around reading *Ossian* in tribute to the century's first martyr to bourgeois normality. To Rosenfeld and a few others, most notably his high school friend and literary comrade-in-arms, Saul Bellow, alienation meant Dostoevsky, and *Passage from Home* is as much the Dostoevskian novel in American garb as were Bellow's novels of that era: *Dangling Man* and *The Victim*. For both, respectively child (Bellow) and grandchild (Rosenfeld) of Russian Jews, Dostoevsky called up the romantic strangeness of a world they knew only through legend and literature but could feel in the strained atmospherics of their own homes. For both too, the pre-revolutionary Dostoevsky came to be a symbol of their own post-revolutionary malaise. By pointing the way to levels of the problematic beyond the agit-prop commonplaces of the 1930s and by being the prophet, as they saw it, of the decline of the Russian revolution into Stalinism, Dostoevsky became the muse of their apostasy from politics. Rosenfeld and Bellow were even known in New York as "the Chicago Dostoevskians" for the somber and "Russian" mood they sought to capture in their early writing and for their heroes, inhabiting imaginary Saint Petersburgs and acting out mute and desperate yearnings in their searches for redemption through self-abasement. In his journals, Rosenfeld touted Dostoevsky's underground man as his "patron saint," declaiming, "I hold to the conviction – it amounts to something of a theory – that embarrassment represents the true state of affairs, and the sooner we strike shame, the sooner we draw blood."

The libretto of *Passage from Home* was set to Dostoevskian melodies, as Rosenfeld set about striking shame in the hope of drawing blood. The character of Bernard is a clear bid to plumb the emotions to their root in order to expose the illness that in his Dostoevskian days he would see as shame but in a later, Reichian, moment would think of as a sexual plague. Stalking his Aunt Minna in the streets, placing his ear to her door, walking in on a naked, sleeping Willy and Minna, Bernard compulsively places himself in humiliating positions as though exposure and shame were precisely what he was seeking. His relations with his father especially are exchanges of embarrassment and guilt, the father tormenting the son out of impotent love, the son denying the father, whose love he can approach only through torment. " . . . I felt guilt not only in my own behalf; it was for his guilt, too, that I was being punished. I bore his guilt as I bore the equal burden of his love. I was his son, and bound to suffer." In such families, natural expressions of human affection are prohibited, and love comes only in the form of stratagems.

Bernard is not the book's lone undergroundling. There is also Fred Mason, Minna's secret husband, whose appetite for humiliation is so voracious as to mark him as a virtual distillate of the underground character. Unpredictable, self-mocking, wounded to the core by Minna's refusal to live with him and yet ready to do her bidding on an instant's notice, he is a neurotic whose Jewish identity, cut off from ritual, belief, and community, expresses itself only in symptoms. In such a dead-end Judaism, the Jewish character is robbed of all that is distinctive and positive and reduced to being little more than a breed of disablement. Bernard sees Mason as a mystic who "spelled out the invisible truth from the letters of the invisible world. (In his own fashion, I suppose, one might call him a mystic – a mystic who elevated not holiness but vulgarity to a fantastic principle.)" And it is precisely in his extremity, in the perfection of his alienation, that Mason takes on meaning, for he is Bernard's own mirror on the wall, the man in whom the distortions of the heart that are just incubating in Bernard have grown florid and monstrous.

Passage from Home was an auspicious debut for a young writer; just twenty-eight years old in 1946, Rosenfeld had a bright career before him. Two years earlier he had published a striking first story, "The Hand that Fed Me," in *Partisan Review*, and a year later had won a *Partisan Review* award with his second story, "The Colony." With *Passage from Home*, he would appear to have been launched upon a major career, and by some measure he was. At the time of his death of a heart attack in 1956, just ten years after *Passage*, he had published some twenty short stories and well over one hundred essays and reviews. Though not so dramatic a success as Bellow, who by 1956 had *Dangling Man, The Victim, The Adventures of Augie March*, and *Seize the Day* under his belt and was well on his way to becoming America's leading novelist, Rosenfeld was a writer to be reckoned with, a regular presence in the pages of the *Partisan* and *Kenyon* reviews and, especially, *The New Republic*, where for a while he was an associate editor.*

However, though Rosenfeld would later write a clutch of brilliant stories, his promise as a fiction writer was never fulfilled, and it is the reviewer and critic in Rosenfeld – the New York intellectual – who is now most commonly remembered. Much of his subsequent fiction lacked either the immediacy of "The Hand that Fed Me" or the sustained tension of *Passage*; it is abstract and allegorical, modeled more on Kafka than on Dostoevsky, and conscious of making a metaphysical statement. His second novel, *The Enemy*, was to prove unpublishable, and an Indian novel, *The Empire*, was abandoned after years of work. He outlined at least two other novels, set respectively in Russia and Greenwich Village, but neither went beyond the stage of notes. As the 1940s drew to a close, Rosenfeld came to believe that his talent was biologically frozen and that to continue writing he would first have to free it up and restore its flow. His immersion in Wilhelm Reich's theories of the "orgonomic" basis of life persuaded him that his writer's block signified a sexual inhibition, and he spent much of the late forties locked in protracted combat with the more rigid and prohibitive sectors of his own character.

For Rosenfeld, who trusted only latent contents, what lay beneath the American dream of individual fulfillment was the life of quiet desperation, and he set his face implacably against it, abominating it in his Reichian fashion as the emotional plague. In the struggle between civilization and instinct, he aligned himself with instinct, and set out in quest of remote inner landscapes where the beleaguered ego could take luxuriate among the flowers of the libido in a state of grace. He bet everything on the chances for self-renewal, on breaking through to his animal nature. "A scientist experimenting on his own sexual possibilities for lack of someone else," remembers

---

* There are several selections of Rosenfeld's essays and stories. For essays and reviews, see Isaac Rosenfeld, *An Age of Enormity: Life and Writing in the Forties and Fifties*, edited and introduced by Theodore Solotaroff (Cleveland: The World Publishing Company, 1962). A selection of Rosenfeld's best stories can be found in *Alpha and Omega: Stories by Isaac Rosenfeld* (New York: The Viking Press, 1966). A recent collection combining some of both with selections from Rosenfeld's journals is *Preserving the Hunger: An Isaac Rosenfeld Reader*, edited and introduced by Mark Shechner (Detroit: Wayne State University Press, 1987).

Alfred Kazin, "Isaac drove himself wild trying to make his body respond with the prodigality promised by theory." And yet this Sybaritism was always concept-ridden, more postulate than practice, and over time his failure to transform his life into the image of his principles damaged him.

Unlike other Jewish intellectuals of his generation, Rosenfeld never made his peace with America. Rather, he followed a code of personal conduct that looked like unswerving downward mobility, recoiling from the icy touch of success that lurked everywhere around him in the late 1940s. In 1949, after a dispiriting visit to the offices of *Commentary*, where his work was no longer held in esteem (in part because of a brilliant and scandalous essay, "Adam and Eve on Delancey Street," which almost cost editor Elliot Cohen his job), and where, as he saw it, his contemporaries – Nathan Glazer, Irving Kristol, and Robert Warshow – had already taken the decisive turn toward accommodation with the middle-class, he lamented, "Alas, alas. Youth is fleeting. The young men locked in office, locked in stale marriages and growing quietly, desperately ill."

In time his Bohemianism resolved itself in asceticism, as he took up forms of marginal existence that bore the stamp of the ghetto. Long before the 1960s made a sacrament of elective poverty, Rosenfeld became a *Luftmensch* by design. "He did not follow the fat gods," Saul Bellow said of him after his death. "I think he liked the miserable failures in the Village better than the miserable successes Uptown, but I believe he understood that the failures had not failed enough but were fairly well satisfied with the mild form of social revolt which their incomplete ruin represented." Under a self-imposed injunction to simplify in order to purify, he jettisoned the excess baggage of the conventional life: steady work, a profession, and in the long run, even his family and his fiction.

In the early fifties, Rosenfeld withdrew from the nexus of modernist literature and postrevolutionary politics that prevailed at *Partisan Review* and moved away from New York, first to a teaching post at the University of Minnesota and three years later to the University of Chicago. In Chicago, recalls Bellow, "the disorder had ended by becoming a discipline."

> In the intricate warren of rooms called the Casbah and on Hudson Street it was simply grim. Toward the end of his life, on Woodlawn Avenue in Chicago, he settled in a hideous cellar room at Petrofsky's where he had lived as a student. The

sympathetic glamour of the thirties was entirely gone; there was only a squalid stink of toilets and coal bins here. Isaac felt that this was the way he must live.

And yet, there are signs that in the final months Rosenfeld experienced a breakthrough of sorts or at very least a remission of conflict that showed up in his writing as a relaxed and genial manner, a mellow *adagio* in his rhythms. One of his best stories, "King Solomon," was written during this period as was the draft of an essay, "Life in Chicago." Rosenfeld's King Solomon is a foppish old Jew, an overweight, cigar-smoking, pinochle-playing monarch who can barely recall his former wisdom but is still beloved by young girls who come from all over Judea – or is it Brooklyn? – to lie beside him and place their hands upon his breast. At the age of sixty he is courted fiercely by an overblown, bejeweled Queen of Sheba who, for all her wiles, cannot arouse him from his pinochle. But there is little tension in this: Solomon's pain is only a wistful, geriatric melancholy. In both, Rosenfeld's themes are familiar but his agitation is gone. "King Solomon" is tender and ironic, and the Chicago essay is cool, urban sociology. We cannot say from the writing alone what brought these changes about or what engines of creativity were set throbbing by the new mood, though this writing gives evidence that Rosenfeld's lyric gifts were very much intact. The last entry in his journal, written, perhaps, within days of his death, is poignantly affirmative, a call to life.

> This is what I have forgotten about the creative process, & am only now beginning to remember – that time spent is time fixed. One creates a work to outlive one – only art does this – & the source of creativity is the desire to reach over one's own death. Maybe now, if I want to create again, I want once more to live; & before I wanted, I suppose, to die.

Rosenfeld's heart attack cut short this affirmation and froze his career into its final shape – the brutal, downward curve of depression.

There was another side to Rosenfeld – the irrepressible humorist and man of spontaneous warmth. Rosenfeld – we should call him Isaac, as all did who knew him – touched people to the quick and was remembered tenderly for his humor, his passionate nature, and for, I believe above all else, the nakedness and innocence of his passage through the world. In a memorial eulogy, Bell spoke up for this other side, the side that did comic impressions of Dostoevskian characters and once wrote a Yiddish sendup of T. S. Eliot's *The Love Song of J. Alfred Prufrock* featuring such unforgettable lines as "Ich ver alt, ich ver alt, un der pupik vert mir kalt," (I grow old, I grow old, and my navel is growing cold).

> His great gift was for laughter, for joke-telling and fun, tempered always by the slight self-mockery so characteristic of Jewish wit . . . . He was boyish, prankish, yet never mean or narrow-spirited. People liked him instinctively, drawn by the open, engaging manner, recognizing his willingness to share rather than dominate.

By the turn of the decade, alienation had pretty much run out of rhetorical credit. In 1952, *Partisan Review* would run the symposium "Our Country and Our Culture," in which writers and intellectuals would queue up to testify, with a fair amount of uniformity, that a reaffirmation of America was under way and that "the American artist and intellectual no longer feels 'disinherited' as Henry James did, or 'astray' as Ezra Pound did in 1913." Saul Bellow would celebrate the moment in *The Adventures of Augie March*, which begins with the rousing "I am an American, Chicago born," and builds its case for the American century from there. And Bell, in *The End of Ideology*, his summary of his political hegira of the Fifties, would cease to speak of alienation as a force, as anything more memorable indeed than a footnote to Marxist philosophy.

Rosenfeld alone held firm to Bernard Miller's vision of the "empty space, which one might never hope to fill, stretched between person and person, between ignorance and knowledge, between one hand and the other," as he held firm to Bernard's cadenza of defiance: "The world is not entirely yours; and our reply is: very well then, not entirely." By the fifties, however, there was virtually no one left to pledge these renunciations with him. And yet, isolated though he was during these grim years, his death was a shock to those who had been touched by his wit and his charm, his fervor and his intensity, his warmth and humor, which was the cosmic humor of a man who had pondered long the absurdities of being. "Reflecting on his own death," Bell observed in his eulogy, "he might have said, 'C'est la vie,' and added wryly, "And you call this a *vie*?'"

3
Saul Bellow and Ghetto Cosmopolitanism

Consider Shapiro. "His nose was sharp and angry and his lips appeared to be smiling away their anger. His cheeks were white and plump, and his thin hair was combed straight back, glistening in the Rudolph Valentino or Ricardo Cortez style of the twenties." That gigolo's hair marks him as a dandy and a villain, while those lips, smiling through their anger, reveal him to be a man of mixed intentions. Like all the best people in *Herzog*, he is an uneasy composite, a walking (and talking) oxymoron, whose breeding is mobilized against his instincts. From all appearances, Shapiro is a man of manners, taste, and charm, and on this hot summer afternoon on the lawn in Ludeyville he clings obstinately to his professorial composure, refusing to even loosen his conservative necktie as he holds forth eloquently and flirtatiously with Madeleine Herzog on any subject under the hot sun: the Russian Church, Tikhon Zadonsky, Dostoevsky, Herzen, Soloviev, what have-you. He is a gentleman and a scholar until lunch is served, and then, under the spell of spice and vinegar, he is transformed.

> Saliva spurted to Shapiro's lips. Quickly he pressed his folded handkerchief to the corners of his mouth. Herzog remembered him as a greedy eater. In the cubicle they had shared at school, he used to chew his pumpernickel-and-onion sandwiches with an open mouth. Now at the smell of spice and vinegar Shapiro's eyes flooded, though he managed to keep his portly, good-humored, sharp-nosed, refined look as he pressed the handkerchief to his shaven jowls.

Shapiro has been set up for a fall; Saul Bellow, gentleman though he may be, is not one to let a character get by on good manners alone. Shapiro's performance is a Jewish joke, and pickled herring is the punch line. The intellectual has been exposed; the Yid stands revealed unmasked in all his greedy appetite, as a man who learned to chew with his mouth open. As the novels of both Bellow and Philip Roth demonstrate in such provocative detail, the best way to root out the essential Jew from behind his deep cover of intellectual armor is to bring him to the table and let him be a *chazer*. And, in case we should miss the point, Moses Herzog leans hard on the cultural accusation in one of his interior monologues. "You are too intelligent for this," he thinks at Shapiro. "You inherited rich blood. Your father peddled apples."

Another moment in another novel, *Humboldt's Gift*, finds Charles Citrine being shaken down for a gambling debt by Rinaldo Cantabile, a theatrical gangster with a furry mustache and an entirely operatic conception of what it means to lean on a man. To settle the debt, Citrine has agreed to meet Cantabile at the Russian steambath on Chicago's Division Street. Only once there, Cantabile turns out to be indeed a nervous extortionist, who, at the point of settling the score, loses control of his bowels and rushes urgently to the bathroom, dragging Citrine with him.

> The john entrance was doorless. Only the individual stalls have doors. I motioned him forward and was about to sit down on one of the locker-room benches nearby but he gave me a hard push on the shoulder and drove me forward. These toilets are the Bath at its worst. The radiators put up a stunning dry heat. The tiles are never washed, never disinfected. A hot dry urine smell rushes to your eyes like onion fumes. "Jesus!" said Cantabile. He kicked open a stall, still keeping me in front of him. He said, "You go in first."

Standing in the reeking stall beside Cantabile, "with the gun held in both palms, his hands between his knees, his eyes first closing then dilating greatly," Citrine fights to contain his humiliation by tuning out and resorting to a popular Jewish device for transcendence: sublimate upward and ponder "the human condition overall." He contemplates the primate analogues to Cantabile's behavior, "the rich repertory of visceral-emotional sensitivities in the anthropoid branch." In the Pale of Settlement, in such a predicament, with Cantabile cast in the form of a Cossack intent on pillage and pogrom, this might be a fearful moment, even one's last, but in Bellow's Chicago, Citrine's capture is no more than material for a musical "Godfather," as it might play in summer stock in the Berkshires.

In Bellow's hands, the comedy of the cloaca is not so different from that of the table; in either case the mechanism of comic release is the sudden shifting of planes, up or down, the undercutting of intellectual pretension by bodily needs or deep-seated ghetto habits, or, in Citrine's case, the strained efforts to achieve a minor transcendence a mind the depressingly, scatologically, ordinary. Here is what the philosophers call the "body-mind" problem exploited for its comic incongruities.

Only this isn't just a device borrowed from the philosophers of the Borscht Belt – Sam Levenson, Menashe Skolnick, Henny Youngman – who made hilarious comedy out of the Jewish gift for discrepancy, so much as it is a principle of the Jewish imagination itself in America, and, I submit, in the diaspora at large. It is a principle I call "ghetto cosmopolitanism," a quality of mind that arises out of the peculiar conditions of Jewish life and experience in exile, conditions that oblige the Jew to experience his very being in two different, even radically opposed, worlds at once.

The conception of a ghetto cosmopolitanism is most graphically illustrated for me by two epigrams. The first was coined by the British Arabist C. M. Doughty, and would appear to be the very model of Citrine's experience: "The Semite sits in a cloaca up to his neck, but his brow touches the heavens." The other is a remark of a family friend, an art collector who, when told of an opportunity to buy another Picasso, replied, "I'm up to my ass in Picassos already."

There is a decidedly American dimension to this pungent remark, for it is a by-product of American upward mobility: the language of the lower East Side is brought right up the elevator into the drawing rooms of Sutton Place and made to sound as if it originated there. Jewish comedy is largely a vertical comedy, a comedy of up and down, from, if you like, home furnishings on the top floor to discounted items in the basement. It is perfectly encapsulated in the story Wallace Markfield tells of Isaac Rosenfeld standing outside Sutton Place and calling up, "Hey ma, will you throw down a nickel?"[1] To Rosenfeld, the great unfulfilled genius of the *Partisan Review* circle in the 1940s and a mimic of considerable talent, *culture was comedy*, and he had the gift, common to Jewish comedians and mimics, of seeming most himself when imitating someone else. According to Bellow:

He tried on the faces of people in restaurants. He was great as Harry Baur in *Crime et Châtiment*, the inspector Porfiry

Petrovich, smoking cigarettes with an underhand Russian grip. He invented Yiddish proletarian poems, he did a translation of Eliot's *Prufrock*. a startling X-ray of those hallowed bones which brings Anglo-Saxons and Jews together in a surrealistic Yiddish unity, a masterpiece of irreverence.[2]

Delmore Schwartz, another tormented genius of the 1940s and the model for Von Humboldt Fleisher in *Humboldt's Gift*, encapsulated in his very character the ironies that attend upward mobility in America. He was chagrined and fascinated by the implications of his first name, and in his stories and poems rang the changes on it, giving his fictional alter egos such improbable names as Shenandoah Fish, Richmond Rose, Maximilian Rinehart, Cornelius Schmidt, and Hershey Green. In *Humboldt's Gift* he is Von Humboldt Fleisher, whose very speech is a breathless mishmash of the Russian and the American, the exalted and the shabby, the exotic and the familiar, the up and the down. "Orpheus, the son of Greenhorn," Bellow calls him. "He brought Coney Island into the Aegean and united Buffalo Bill with Rasputin. He was going to join together the Art Sacrament and the Industrial USA as equal powers." Schwartz himself boasted of being both an expert in Greek tragedy and a New York Giants' fan, and could exclaim in triumph that he was the only poet in America with power brakes, by which he meant that he was both sensitive and up-to date, both an exiled Jew and an American sport. Acutely sensitive to being born an outsider, he was excessively demonstrative in his embrace of American culture, and once boasted in a letter to the editor of *Partisan Review*: "I am . . . fulfilling the obligations of being an American in trying to be funny, just as, for the same reason in part, I am trying to be truly American in owning two used cars, in owning a TV set, in expecting everyone to love me, and in expecting everyone to admire my work and my 1949 Buick."[3]

There was panic behind such buffoonery and a touch of schizophrenia too, but it also proceeded from a distinctly cultural premise: Schwartz's indeterminate nature as ersatz American and nominal Jew, whose hyphenated identity was the juxtaposition of two inauthenticities. For centuries, certainly since the fall of the Second Temple, Jews have been specialists in bicameral thinking, cultural miscegenation, and intellectual hybridization, until the Jewish mind has come to resemble a warehouse of international bric-a-brac. It is what comes of crossing the border – any border

– every three generations or so, or, as happened all too frequently in the Old Country, of having the border cross you.

But what was delirium for Schwartz was raw material for Bellow. Born in Quebec, Canada's French-speaking province, of Yiddish-speaking parents who had only lately fled from Russia, he moved with his family to Chicago and the American heartland at the age of nine. Such an international background and such knowledge, by experience or legend, of the ghettos of three countries in three or four languages (Yiddish, French, English, and bits and pieces of Russian) are transfigured into a superior worldliness, a cosmopolitanism of the rarest kind, as familiar with the harsh side of international existence as it is with the privileged.

Now, to have multiple national identities is not so uplifting in itself, and is even, under the conditions of flight and disruption, a cause of great suffering. Cosmopolitanism by flight is no happy state of affairs, and for the immigrant generation even the freedoms of the New World were paid for in alienation and misery. But the deracination of the immigrants was passed down to their children as tradition, and, given the task of reconstructing a culture on what they had been given, the second generation founded a culture for themselves based on the contradictions and ironies of their situation. Where they were not defeated by the demands of a double existence, they were strengthened, gaining a freedom and a perspective that unitary cultures do not afford. "It is by loss of allegiance, or at the best by force of a divided allegiance to the people of his origin," observed Thorstein Veblen, "that [the Jew] finds himself in the vanguard of modern inquiry."[4] Though Veblen had in mind the Jews who had become eminent in the sciences, his observation applies no less to those who turned to art and culture, like the second generation intellectuals in America who were, at their most acute, masters of discrepancy and accomplished tight-rope walkers. Their greatest achievement as a generation was to have transfigured their chronic restlessness into a point of rest.

Saul Bellow is the leading exponent in our time of the second generation formula. It is a commonplace that his writing exhibits a certain symmetry that looks like an ambivalent balancing of worlds and moods; Irving Howe has described his style as "a yoking of opposites, gutter vividness with university refinement, street energy with high-culture rhetoric," and "a deliberate play with the phrasings of plebian speech, but often, also, the kind that vibrates with cultural ambition, seeking to zoom into regions of higher thought."[5] Allowing for our suspicion that Howe is really talking about his own habits of composition, we can see what he is driving at. For all its ingenious maneuvers, its attempts to create a new intellectual synthesis out of Jewish and American materials, Bellow's style, which is a paraphrase of his world view, is built on tensions rather than fusions, on keeping the ironies alive. This is particularly evident in *Herzog* where the juxtaposition of the Montreal slums against the Chicago near North Side is the very cultural point of the book. To be in bondage to the past is Moses Herzog's affliction *and* his truth; his sudden upwellings of "potato love" along with the drying up of his scholarship are rooted in his childhood. They are, we might say, childish. Herzog's compulsive backtracking – Madeleine looks upon it as backsliding – is a *reculer pour mieux sauter*, a regression in the service of ultimate sanity. His reflections on Montreal's Napoleon Street are the most lyrical and intense passages in the novel. In them, Bellow forces his powers of recollection to their limits to evoke the painfully vivid landscape of childhood.

> My ancient times. Remoter than Egypt. No dawn, the foggy winters. In darkness, the bulb was lit. The stove was cold. Papa shook the grates, and raised an ashen dust. The grates grumbled and squealed. the puny shovel clinked underneath. The Caporals gave Papa a bad cough. The chimneys in their helmets sucked in the wind. Then the milkman came in his sleigh. The snow was spoiled and rotten with manure and litter, dead rats, dogs. The milkman in his sheepskin gave the bell a twist. It was brass, like the winding key of a clock.

Such passages are devotional exercises; by infusions of childhood wonder and adult longing they achieve the "transcendence downward" for which Herzog yearns. The blocked scholar, no longer able to "zoom into regions of higher thought," gives himself over to reverie, to a therapeutic poignance, giving voice to the archaic, the sensitive, and shame-ridden parts of himself without entirely yielding to them, honoring recollection without wholly succumbing to it.

More boldly than Bellow's other books, *Herzog* imagines the encounter of distinct worlds, the clash of high principle and low motive, of present and past, of gold coast and slum, of worldly erudition and street savvy. We find in *Herzog* a sense of some sardonic anthropology at work, as though he were the comic Lévi-Straus of Jewish culture, tracing out an all-inclusive dialectic of the raw and the cooked among the inhabitants of Chicago.[6] Moses Herzog himself is the cuckolded husband as academic shlemiel, lost in a veritable syntopticon of ideas, up to his neck in the cloaca even as his brow makes a beeline for the heavens. Indeed, this metaphor becomes literal for a moment when Herzog, endeavoring to find peace away from his wife, takes up residence in the basement lavatory of his house in Ludeyville. "In summer the crickets liked it best, and so did Herzog. Here he loitered over a ten-cent bargain Dryden and Pope. Through a chink he saw the fiery morning of high summer, the wicked spiny green of vines, and the tight, shapely heads of wild roses, the huge elm in front, dying on him, the oriole's nest, gray and heart-shaped." Such ecstatic communion from down so deep! Herzog's rapture is a triumph of lavatory impressionism. The higher depths! And between couplets (of what, "MacFlecknoe"?) this Martin Luther of the Berkshires pauses to fuss with the chain. "He removed the top of the tank with a grating noise, and pulled the rubber fitting to release the water. The parts were rusty, stiff." Like Herzog's parts.

Several of Bellow's later books give the impression of emerging from the depths, or sinking into them, and along with it the sense of two worlds, a higher and a lower, vying for pre-eminence in a single, perplexed mind. These impressions are strongest in *Herzog* and *Humboldt's Gift* but it is a considerable part of Bellow's picture of himself to be the ghetto boy who has made good as a scholar, the tough kid at the Committee on Social Thought who covets esoteric knowledge the way a bookie covets inside dope.

That migration from the slums of Montreal or New York or Chicago into the American middle class that was the great social experience of the Jews of Bellow's generation has left its mark on their particular brand of irony, which we might call, to steal a metaphor from Philip Rahv, the irony of the Redskin becoming a Paleface. But that irony has a dimension that looks beyond the effects of social mobility toward something more traditional and basic, something woven into the very composition of Jewish life in the Ashkenazi communities of Eastern Europe. The experiments of Bellow and other Jewish writers in intellectual syncretism obey an ancient logic for which social climbing is just a contemporary imitation. It is the pattern of spiritual upward mobility that was endemic to the Ashkenazi Jews, and which was in sharp contrast to the bleak economic conditions of their lives. Bear in mind that the correlation between learning and class that we take for granted in America and which has characterized most of the peoples of Europe until recent times never applied to the Jews, who produced an intellectual type unique in Europe: the impecunious scholar. To be sure, Christianity did produce its mendicant orders, but the monk was a social exception, someone removed from the community of men to carry out his work in a world apart. The Jewish community had no tradition of monastic withdrawal to isolate learning from life; the scholar was a man in and of his community, even its typical figure, and was a familiar sight in the shtetls and urban enclaves of Eastern Europe well into this century. Amid the bleakest poverty, he prayed, studied Torah, and disputed the fine points of Talmud and Gemara with no more practical consideration than his yearning for justice and his obligation to God for having been given His word to uphold.

Out of such spiritual and intellectual dedication amid the harshest conditions arose a unique cast of imagination, which throve on the disparity between the material depletion of the ghetto and the spiritual wealth of the study house and mediated confidently between the debased and the sacred, the ordinary and the ceremonial, the world of man and the commandments of God.

Though degradation and transcendence were profoundly interwoven in their lives, the Jews strove to maintain a formal separation between them and had separate languages for them, as if to remind themselves that their daily cup of bitterness did not set limits on their spirituality. Thus they maintained two languages, Yiddish and Hebrew, the one the language of daily existence and the other the sanctified language of the Sabbath. The distinction was not rigid, and there was a broad region of overlap between the two: there were prayer books in Yiddish just as there was an infiltration of Hebrew into common speech. But despite these inevitable interpenetrations, the languages stood in symbolic opposition, leading to a condition that the Yiddish scholar, Max Weinreich, called "internal bilingualism,"[7] meaning that in the mind of every Jew the two languages stood for distinct and opposed realms of experience. Yiddish was the language of secular experience and the token of exile, Hebrew the language of both the Biblical past and the redemptive future. It was the language through which the Jew experienced his relation to God, to the line of Abraham, Isaac, and Jacob, and to the destiny of all Jews. In Yiddish he was a Yid, a *Zhid*; in Hebrew an Israelite. Out of such schism came the enormous melancholy of Jewish life and culture and the many strands of radical and revivalist yearning that swept through European Jewry in the eighteenth and nineteenth centuries: Hasidism, the Haskalah or enlightenment, labor Socialism, Communism, and Zionism. Each proposed to heal the split in the Jewish mind, and each included a linguistic program in its plan to redeem the Jews. The two languages did not create the split in the Jewish psyche; they bore witness to it. It was for compelling reasons that the national language of Israel had to be Hebrew, for once Jewish history was redeemed, the languages of exile *had* to be given up.

To the extent that this bilingualism still exerts pressure on the imaginative lives of American Jews, it is obviously not the historical bilingualism of the Ashkenazi diaspora. In America, the language of the synagogue is one with that of the street, English, and the single language suits well a social experience free of the extremes of the Old World. The paradoxes affliction a people "both vilified and Chosen" in one observer's words,[8] have been resolved, it appears, in the great Yankee stew of the American suburb. All tensions have not been released, but the coiled spring of Jewish life is no longer taut with contradiction and alienation; the normalization of the Jew in America is an accomplished fact. Yet, despite the softening of the contrasts in Jewish experience, some of our major writers, certainly Bellow, Singer, and Roth, continue to trade on internal paradox with spectacular success, suggesting habits of mind almost elegiac in their attachment to prior circumstances. All recast the mental acrobatics that were once needed to master the paradoxes of life as the very *aims* of thought. No longer found in the contrasts of exile, mental extremes are now invented. That would appear to be one reason why Bellow chose Delmore Schwartz to be the emblem of his generation in *Humboldt's Gift*, for in Schwartz's case a divided and decomposing inner life was always exploding into daring and vivid inventions, though in the end no amount of inventiveness could be shored up against his ruins. And while his neurosis, his terminal *nostalgie de la boue* bore the stamp of his culture and generation, his rapid surrender to it was the mark of too little personal culture; he inherited the perplexities of Jewishness but none of its resourcefulness. Isaac Rosenfeld inadvertently cast light on Schwartz's "case," as well as Bellow's and his own, in an essay on Abraham Cahan's *The Rise of David Levinsky*, in which he proposed a brilliant theory of why certain Jews are drawn to failure. Levinsky's character, observed Rosenfeld, was formed by hunger, and "because hunger is strong in him, he must always strive to relieve it; but precisely because it is strong, it has to be preserved. It owes its strength to the fact that for so many years everything that influenced Levinsky most deeply – say, piety, and mother love – was inseparable from it."[9] Hunger is his very essence, and for Levinsky to achieve gratification of his emotional needs is to betray the very ground of his being. In America, where the pursuit of happiness is a founding principle of the republic, this is a distinctly foreign sentiment; indeed, there is something decidedly Dostoevskian and Russian in such affection for the injured portions of the self. But it is a richly suggestive idea that tells us that "assimilation" does not come so easily as some suppose, and fear, and that in the Jewish mind there are powerful counterforces tucked away beyond the pleasure principle urging the Jew to cherish disadvantage and be true to the injuries under which his identity took form. The victories of social mobility, it suggests, are only apparent, and the Jewish imagination is subject to, strange to say, the lure of the ghetto. It tells us that we surrender the world of our fathers only at the cost of enshrining its image within us.

Surely that helps us understand the discrepancy between the wholesale advances in the position of Jews in America and the general refusal of any major Jewish novelist to treat success as an unambiguous social virtue. (The conspicuous exception in recent years is not a work of fiction but an autobiography, Norman Podhoretz's *Making It*, and the amount of obloquy it met with upon its publication in 1967 is some indication of how far it departed from the prevailing moral mythology of Jewish literature.) Surely that undertow of the past tells us something about the prevalence of the shlemiel and the luftmensh in our fiction, long after the businessman, the lawyer, and the *Realpolitiker* have become more representative figures. In *Humboldt's Gift* Charles Citrine ponders the paradoxes of wealth. "Yesterday I read in *The Wall Street Journal* about the melancholy of affluence. 'Not in all the five millennia of man's recorded history have so many been so affluent.' Minds formed by five millennia of scarcity are distorted. The heart can't take this sort of change. Sometimes it just refuses to accept it." His wife, Denise, complains that his fatal attraction to his roots is stubbornly regressive, and marks a failure of dignity, maturity, and taste.

De Gaulle made you a knight of the Legion of Honor and Kennedy invited us to the White House. You had a successful play on Broadway. *Now* what the hell do you think you're doing? Chicago! You hang around with your old Chicago school chums, with freaks. It's a kind of mental suicide, death wish. You'll have nothing to do with really interesting people, with architects or psychiatrists or university professors. I tried to make a life for you when you insisted on moving back here. I put myself out. You wouldn't have London or Paris or New York, you had to come back to this – this deadly, ugly, vulgar, dangerous place. Because at heart you're a kid from the slums. Your heart belongs to the old West Side gutters.

Citrine concedes her point, though he might have argued in extenuation that he is hardly unique. This isn't just a peculiarity of his any more than it is of Bellow's. Philip Roth, for all his up-to-dateness, is no more immune than Bellow to the return of the repressed and the lure of the ghetto. His compulsive visits to Eastern Europe, his fascination with Kafka, his publishing of "Writers from the Other Europe" for Penguin Books all bespeak the same racial undertow that draws Bellow to the past. As for Malamud and Singer, their writing speaks for itself. These writers, otherwise urban, sophisticated, and cosmopolitan, are secret sharers of a myth, of which they are but half-conscious, that the ghetto is the hidden nature of the world, and they are no more free to deliver themselves of that myth than they are to deliver themselves of their dreams.

NOTES

1. The story is told about Leslie Braverman in Wallace Markfield's *To An Early Grave,* a novel about the misadventures of a group of mourners on the way to Braverman's funeral. The novel is something of a *roman à clef* in which the deceased Braverman in based on Isaac Rosenfeld.
2. Saul Bellow, Forward to Isaac Rosenfeld, *An Age of Enormity,* ed. Theodore Solotaroff (Cleveland: The World Publishing Company, 1962), p. 13.
3. *Partisan Review,* 20:3 (May–June, 1953), p. 368.
4. Thorstein Veblen, "The Intellectual Pre-Eminence of Jews in Modern Europe," *Political Science Quarterly,* 34 (1919), p. 38. See Veblen's viewpoint reflected in Isaac Rosenfeld, "The Situation of the Jewish Writer," *An Age of Enormity, op. cit.,* pp. 67–69.

5.   Irving Howe, Introduction to *Jewish American Stories*, ed. Howe (New York: New American Library, 1977), p. 15. Howe is talking about "the American Jewish style" here, though it is clear that he has Bellow most prominently in mind, and has, in addition, been giving some thought, and credit, to his own rhetorical propensities.

6.   And it is not accidental to this connection that Lévi-Straus is himself a French Jew. See John Murray Cuddahy's remarks on Lévi-Straus in his *The Ordeal of Civility: Freud, Marx, Lévi-Straus, and the Jewish Struggle with Modernity* (New York: Basic Books, 1974), chapter 18.

7.   Max Weinreich, "Internal Bilingualism in Ashkenaz," collected in *Voices From the Yiddish*, ed. Irving Howe and Eliezer Greenberg (Ann Arbor: The University of Michigan Press, 1972), pp. 279–88.

8.   Stephen J. Whitfield, "Laughter in the Dark: Notes on American Jewish Humor," *Midstream* (February, 1978), p. 51.

9.   Isaac Rosenfeld, "David Levinsky: The Jew as American Millionaire," in *Age of Enormity, op. cit.*, pp. 276–77.

4

Jewish Comedy and the Contradictions of Culture

The oldest form of social study is comedy . . . . Comic irony sets whole cultures side by side in a multiple exposure (e.g. *Don Quixote, Ulysses*), causing valuation to spring out of the recital of facts alone, in contrast to the hidden editorializing of tongue-in-cheek ideologists.

Harold Rosenberg[1]

In a fantastical and funny story by Philip Roth entitled "On the Air,"[2] Milton Lippman, a talent scout, writes to Albert Einstein to ask if Einstein would agree to star on a radio program that Lippman hopes to negotiate with the networks, "The Jewish Answer Man." It will demonstrate to the world that "the Greatest Genius of all Time is a Jew." When his first approach to Einstein goes unanswered, Lippman bravely writes again:

Dear Mr. Einstein:

I can understand how busy you must be thinking, and appreciate that you did not answer my letter suggesting that I try to get you on a radio program that would make "The Answer Man" look like the joke it is. Will you reconsider, if the silence means no? I realize that one of the reasons you don't wear a tie or even bother to comb your hair is because you are as busy as you are, thinking new things. Well, don't think that you would have to change your ways once you become a radio personality. Your hair is a great gimmick, and I wouldn't change it for a second. It's a great trademark. Without disrespect, it sticks in your mind the way Harpo Marx's does. Which is excellent. (Now I wonder if you even have the time to know who The Marx Brothers are? They are four zany Jewish brothers, and you happen to look a little like one of them. You might get a kick out of catching one of their movies. Probably they don't even show movies in Princeton, but maybe you could get somebody to drive you out of town. You can get the entire plot in about a minute, but the resemblance between you and Harpo and his hair and yours, might reassure you that you are a fine personality in terms of show business just as you are.)

This is a splendid routine, taking Albert Einstein for a quiz show star and his Harpo-esque coiffure for a commercial logo. So fantastic are its premises that this comedy borders on the absurd, and indeed, as the story of Lippman's pilgrimage to Princeton unfolds, it takes on increasingly surreal dimensions. Consider the very incongruity of the proposition! Milton Lippman to join forces with Albert Einstein: the man who revolutionized our understanding of space and time to be managed and marketed by this *landsman*, this marginal hustler and jobber whose voice keens with the desperate wisdom that comes of 2000 years working bum territories: Egypt, Spain, the Pale of Settlement, New Jersey.

But why is this funny, and what, if anything, can we say is "Jewish" about it, besides the fact that Einstein and Lippman are both Jews and that a Jew, Philip Roth, has conjured up the entire phantasmagoria? For years now I have been gathering notes on "the Jewish imagination," prompted by a curiosity about Jewish culture and an appreciation of the role of humor and comedy in it, both as a typical product and as an expression of its deeper patternings. Indeed, I'm inclined to regard comedy as an index to culture, a *via regia* into the collective unconscious of a group no less revealing than dreams are of the individual unconscious, for in the comic, where all is essentialized and drawn in bold strokes, the basic terms of a culture are most available for inspection. Comedy discloses culture the way x-rays disclose bones or iron filings trace the force fields of a magnet, mapping its auras and trajectories, its nodes of energy points and its fingers of attraction. A culture's manners, values, fears, taboos, tempos, climates, and radiations constitute the very medium of comedy, and the comedian immerses himself in this medium in the spirit of an anthropologist immersing himself in an alien culture. The comedian's golden rule is, *the more familiar, the more strange.*

Some time ago I set out to write an essay on contemporary Jewish writers in America in an effort to determine whether there was anything decisively Jewish about the writers I was dealing with apart from their lineage and the cultural reference points in their books, and whether, in our current state of cultural homogenization, we could even distinguish between the fiction of Jewish writers or, speaking more cautiously, writers of Jewish descent, and that written by other Americans.[3] Is it possible, I wondered, to speak of a Jewish imagination without invoking universals, properties common to all people that just happened to be embedded in Jewish circumstances, or without citing the authority of the merely circumstantial – shtetls, rabbis, dybbuks, tailors, goniffs, cutting rooms, egg creams, chicken soup, or chicken fat – details that dissolve every generation or two as the circumstances and locales of Jewish life alter.

If geographical sign posts and social manners do not of themselves define a "Jewish" imagination, what about themes: the ethical imagination, the Bible, the exile, the wrath of Jehovah, the covenant, pogrom, the holocaust? What of moods or tonalities, like lamentation? Here we would seem to be on firmer footing, since there is scarcely an expression of the Jewish imagination for the last 2000 years that was not drenched in the basic premises of Jewish life. And yet even here we're bound to note that these premises, persistent though they be, are also perishable. The exile, for the time being, is over; the covenant has lost its authority for most modern Jews, and though pogrom has given way to jihad, a seemingly indifferent exchange of assaults, Jews now have tanks and aircraft. As for the holocaust, it is already appropriated by others who see in it the potential for major statement. We have *Sophie's Choice*. The Bible? The God of Israel? To see these as uniquely Jewish themes is to make Jews out of those American Protestants for whom the Old Testament and the exactions of the Almighty have long been the mainstay of their Christian faith. And as for suffering and martyrdom, they don't distinguish Jews in America from others who've known hard times. The Psalms may have given us lamentation, but it was Black America, steeped in Biblical tonalities, that gave us the blues. (Israel may have crossed the Jordan, but it is the Baptists who sing about it.) Nor does sorrow as a distinctively "Jewish" note tell us much about Jewish resilience, ingenuity, and resourcefulness, which are at least as historically evident as Jewish martyrdom. It doesn't help us understand Israel.

If details or themes do not alone define a cultural imagination, what might suffice, or are we destined to shuttle back and forth between the universals of the human imagination (archetypes, deep structures, universal biological or developmental determinants) and the specifics of the individual – the sediments of personal experience and personal history? I want to propose, if only as a stopgap, that an alternative approach to the cultural dimensions of the imagination might be through its characteristic structures, the *forms* taken by experience, for it is by the mediation of cultural forms that universals are filtered into the workaday and the particulars of experience charged with the generic. Culture packs the mind with rules of meaning, and it is through those rules that the raw data of life become our experiences of it. I do not claim that these configurations of imagination are timeless, for they too are products of history, and as history changes so do they. But because they are embedded in lore and ritual and because family and culture pass them down, they are tenacious; they resist easy uprooting, and one may find in them anachronistic remnants of past times and conditions. The structures of imagination lag behind the times, sometimes by generations, and continue to order the priorities of mind long after the conditions of life that had formed them have passed into oblivion.

I have written elsewhere about a structure of perception that seems to me to sustain a particular sort of Jewish imagining, and I stress *particular sort*, since it should be evident that the Jewish mind is not and has never been a simple entity. I call that structure "ghetto cosmopolitanism"[4] and think of it as a conjunction of identities within the same individual: contrasting internal frames of reference whose abutment and interplay give form and inspiration to Jewish imagining. Ghetto cosmopolitanism arose out the striking conjunctions of oppression and spirituality in the ghettos and shtetls of Ashkenazic Jewry in Eastern Europe and Russia, and it persists among contemporary American Jews whose lives are no longer in thrall to Old World conditions. The ghetto cosmopolitan is at once an insular and a worldly individual. He combines a parochialism bred of poverty and confinement with a universal consciousness bred of study and intellectual ambition. In him, vulgarity and sensibility go hand in hand; his coarseness of manner is not inconsistent with high orders of intellectual and aesthetic discrimination. Socially rude, even coarse in his demeanor, he is attuned to world events and is at home discussing Hegel or Henry James.[5] His character is a puzzle to non Jews, for whom education implies refinement, decorum, *breeding*, but among Jews he is accepted as a standard intellectual type.

Other cultures may have analogous forms; Lévi-Strauss has taught us that such dualisms in myth, in value, in character, are universal properties of culture, and it stands to reason that a form akin to ghetto-cosmopolitanism may prevail elsewhere, though the special conjunction of learning, spirituality, and material deprivation that formed the Ashkenazi character was not common to Europe. It was more oriental. Backward, poor, living amid the most wretched circumstances, these pariahs were a God-intoxicated and studious people, the most literate of all Europe's peoples through the close of the nineteenth century, however unworldly their learning may have been.

The Ashkenazim of Eastern Europe dwelled in two worlds simultaneously. One was the world of labor and trade, money, politics, love, marriage, family, trouble, death. Its domain were the six days from Saturday night through Friday, and its language was commonly Yiddish, though the Jews also spoke Polish, Russian, Czech, Magyar, German, Ukrainian, and to some degree had their imaginations shaped by those languages as well. The other was the world of the Sabbath, the world of prayer and study, Torah and Talmud, faith and prophecy. It was exalted and transcendent, and it had its own language, Hebrew.

The Yiddish scholar Max Weinreich spoke, in a famous formulation, of the "internal bilingualism" of the Ashkenazi Jews,[6] which placed them, imaginatively, in sharply opposed worlds, the one reverential, austere, bound by duty, ritual, awe, the other ironic, playful, mischievous. In practice the languages tended to fuse, as Yiddish penetrated the language of prayer and Hebrew formed a sacred canopy over common speech, so that each language was flavored by the other. The literature of the Yiddish renaissance reflects vividly this contrast at the heart of Jewish life. Its typical figures were the *shlemiel* who was also a saint, the victim of misfortune who was a hero of endurance; the impecunious scholar or rabbi who was the exalted moral arbiter of his people; the peddler, the shopkeeper, or luftmensch down on his luck who was also a visionary. I. L. Peretz's Bontsche the Silent, Sholom Aleichem's Tevye the Milkman, Isaac Bashevis Singer's Gimpel the Fool are all expressions of this same doubleness. The macaronic language of that literature also reflected the interpenetration of realms. It was a literature in which, as Maurice Samuel once observed, "Well-worn quotations from sacred texts mingle easily with colloquialisms, and dignified passages jostle popular interjections without taking or giving offense."[7] What one finds in a mind nurtured upon a higher and a lower language is one that is rather accustomed to shuttling between the transcendent and the worldly and defining its relationship to reality in terms of the ironies generated by such travel.

Although American Jews are no longer bilingual and the startling contradictions of ghetto life have melted into the suburban continuities of the American middle-class, habits of mind that were fostered in the Old Country stubbornly remain as structures of consciousness. Just as certain primal hungers persist long after every Jew has filled his stomach and has even joined Weight-Watchers in order to be hungry again, so too the habit of self-irony remains long after the disparities of the ghetto have either faded or been transformed. The contradictions of Doughty's ancient Semite no longer apply, though the ironies of cultural change and generational succession have partially replaced them. There was scarcely a Jew born of immigrant parents in America who did not in his or her lifetime experience a change of station so drastic as to feel like a rise from the cloaca to the stars. Where the circumstances are not absolutely tragic, the attendant discrepancies become ironies, sources of the comic doubletake. We need only turn to the Jewish comics or the novelists who have taken lessons from them for vivid examples of the comic doubletake in operation. Thus Lippman to Einstein:

Perhaps I should have told you that my fee is ten percent. But truly and honestly I am not in this business for money. I want to help people. I have taken colored off the streets, shoeshine kit and all, and turned them into headline tap dancers at roadhouses and nightclubs overnight. And my satisfaction comes not from the money, which in all honesty is not so much, but in seeing those boys getting dressed up in dinner jackets and learning to face an audience of people out for a nice time. Dignity far more than money is my business.

Such comedy is hooked right into Jewish history: the people of the book were also the people of the deal. What Roth has done here is to draw out the comic ramifications of this encounter of learning and business in the same culture.

The comic doubletake is a standard technique of Jewish humor.

Here are some routines by one Jules Farber, the comedian hero of Wallace Markfield's novel, *You Could Live If They'd Let You,*[8] a book in praise of stand-up comedy and the desperation for which it stands.

And they shall beat their swords into plowshares – and then, then first they'll give it to you with those plowshares.

By the waters of Babylon I sat down and I wept that I have not bought a little property.

If your brother should weaken and fall, don't move him until you first have at least two witnesses.

"Then spake Rabbi Israel: And the sages do say that we shall weaken their vitals, yea, with fish sticks and red hots shall we pierce their bowels. For hath he not promised us, blessed be His Name of Names, that He will send us an angel, and the angel will put them in confusion and alarm, for He shall cause their shelves to be empty of Campbell's Soups, and we shall fall upon them, yea, we shall smite them with the slats from our venetian blinds . . . ."

Or this, which strikes me as one of the cleverest of Woody Allen's short routines:[9].

And it came to pass that a man who sold shirts was smitten by hard times. Neither did any of his merchandise move nor did he prosper. And he prayed and said, "Lord, why hast thou left me to suffer thus? All mine enemies sell their goods except I. And it's the height of the season. My shirts are good shirts. Take a look at this rayon. I got button-downs, flare collars, nothing sells. Yet I have kept thy commandments. Why can I not earn a living when mine younger brother cleans up in children's ready-to-wear?" And the Lord heard the man and said, "About thy shirts . . . ."
    "Yes, Lord," the man said, falling to his knees.
    "Put an alligator over the pocket."
    "Pardon me, Lord?"
    "Just do what I'm telling you. You won't be sorry."
    And the man sewed on to all his shirts a small alligator symbol and lo and behold, suddenly his merchandise moved like

gangbusters, and there was much rejoicing while amongst his enemies there was wailing and gnashing of teeth.

The fun here is of just the sort I have been talking about: a sudden thrusting downward from the exalted to the workaday, from the tragic to the trivial, from the Hebrew to the Yiddish, from the Biblical cadence to the commercial slogan. It is the Lord who comes up with the alligator. But the indispensable element in each, without which these jokes would be scarcely more than routine exercises in ironic juxtaposition, is the cultural flavoring. Something of the humiliations and fears of Jewish life itself has been captured in these juxtapositions: the Jewish fear of violence, the sense of shame that underlies the show of pride, the fetish of insurance for a people who were vulnerable for 2000 years, the failing line of goods, the fear of lawsuit in world of shysters, the skepticism of a people who know from experience that anything even a plowshare, can become a sword.

This acidic power of Yiddish makes it a powerful corrosive to the pieties of more genteel cultures. Its homely punch lines pack a potent wallop. Our comedian, Jules Farber, recalls once going with his Uncle Shermie to the movies to see a Western.[10]

I went one time to the movies with him – a western. With a scene – you know the scene? Morning, first thing in the morning. The gunslinger gets up. The gunslinger rubs his beard. The gunslinger takes out his razor. And he strops his razor, he gives himself a lovely shave and again he rubs his beard. He rubs his beard and he wipes his face and he wipes his razor. He finishes wiping the razor, he takes his coffee pot, he goes to the stream, he fills the coffee pot with water from the stream, he collects twigs, with the twigs he makes a fire, on the fire he makes coffee, he drinks a cup of coffee, he sloshes out the grinds, he finished sloshing out the grinds and he pours himself a second cup, he drinks the second cup –

And my Uncle Shermie yells out, *"Nu, und pishn darft m'nisht?"* (Nu? And he doesn't have to piss?)

That the cowboy in an American Western doesn't need to piss upon getting up is too much for this old-time Jew, for whom the willing suspension of disbelief, not to mention the willing suspension of

water, is unheard of. Farber's conclusion is that Uncle Shermie's
outburst is a victory for reality, and so it is.

Sometimes an entire story or poem may be the punch line to an
absent text. Take this parody of T. S. Eliot's "The Love Song of J.
Alfred Prufrock," composed as a lark some time in the 1940s by Saul
Bellow and Isaac Rosenfeld. It was a party gag, and one recollection
of it goes like this.[11]

> Nu-zhe, kum-zhe, ikh un du
> Ven der ovnt shteyt unter dem himl
> Vi a leymener goylem af tishebov.
> Lomir geyn gikh, durkh geselekh vos dreyen zikh
> Vi di bord bay dem rov.
>
> Oyf der vant
> fun dem kosheren restorant
> Hengt a shmutsiker betgevant
> Un vantsn tantsn karahod. Es geht a geroykh
> fun gefilte fish un nase zokn.
> Oy, Bashe, freg nit keyn kashe, a dayge dir!
> Lomir oyfenen di tir.
> In tsimer vu di vayber zenen
> Redt men fun Karl Marx un Lenin.
>
> Ikh ver alt, ikh ver alt
> Un der pupik vert mir kalt.
> Zol ikh oyskemen di hor,
> Meg ikh oyfesen a flom?
> Ikh vel onton vayse hoysn
> Un shpatsirn by dem yom.
> Ikh vel hern di yom-moyden zingen khad gadyo.
> Ikh vel zey entfern, Borekh-abo.

*   *   *

Roughly translated, the parody sounds something like this:

> Nu, let us go, you and I,
> When the evening stands beneath the sky
> Like a lame golem on Tisha b'av.
> Let us go, through streets that twist themselves

Like the rabbi's beard.

On the window
Of the kosher restaurant,
Hangs a dirty bedbug
And bedbugs dance in circles. There is a stink
Of gefilte fish and wet socks.
Oy, Bashe, don't ask questions, why bother?
Let me open the door.
In the room where the women walk
They speak of Karl Marx and Lenin.

I grow old, I grow old,
And my navel grows cold.
Shall I comb out my hair,
May I eat a prune?
I shall put on white pants
And walk by the sea.
I shall hear the sea-maidens sing Chad Gadya.
I shall answer them: "Baruch Abba."

        *   *   *

I can't imagine a transliteration of Eliot in French or German capable of this kind of comic domestication. French and German are elevating languages and are just not geared for the crisp deflation of "Ikh ver alt, ikh ver alt, un der pupik vert mir kalt." Yiddish evolved in the Old country without a pressing need for a vocabulary of idealization. Hebrew fairly monopolized the task of providing the Jews with idealizing and spiritualizing concepts and thereby of satisfying the portions of Jewish culture that traded in ennoblement – in *edelkeit*. The Yiddish Jew is the historical Jew; the Hebrew Jew the transhistorical, the transcendent Jew. Or, to borrow terms from the writer and historian Arthur Cohen, the one was the natural Jew, the other the supernatural Jew.[12] With the Hebrew hegemony over higher worlds established, Yiddish was free to evolve as a worldly and domestic language, remarkably free from high purpose and its attendant distortion, cant.

At his best, in his earlier films and routines, but especially in *Bananas, Play It Again Sam,* and *Love and Death,* Woody Allen was the master of comic techniques based upon these sudden collisions of perspective: the serious side of himself suddenly brought crashing to earth by the madman in him. The basic Allen joke is the lofty perspective laid low by the common desire. "My parents were very old world people. Their values were God and carpeting." "I have an intense desire to return to the womb. Anybody's." In *Play It Again Sam*, Allen (as Allen Felix) attempts to pick up a young woman in the Museum of Modern Art as both stand before a Jackson Pollack.[13]

> *Allen*:   What does it say to you?
> *Woman*:   It restates the negativeness of the universe. The hideous lonely emptiness of existence. Nothingness. The predicament of Man forced to live in a barren, Godless eternity like a tiny flame flickering in an immense void with nothing but waste, horror and degradation, forming a useless bleak straitjacket in a bleak absurd cosmos.
> *Allen*:   What're you doing Saturday night?
> *Woman*:   Committing suicide.
> *Allen*:   What about Friday night?

This is American comedy of a sort that Groucho Marx or S. J. Perelman did between snacks: the mayhem of madcap juxtapositions, one frame of reference – popular, modern, awestruck – bombarding the other – classical, philosophical, reverent – with matzoballs. She's suffering an existential crisis; he just wants a date. The Yiddish theatre abounded in humor of this kind, because the Yiddish language was tuned for ironic deflation and was a perfect medium for the homely punch-line, even if God himself should be the butt of the joke. The lowly Yid who gets in the last word with God or death is a familiar figure in Jewish humor, as in an Allen routine, "Death Knocks,"[14] in which Nat Ackerman, visited by the Angel of Death, challenges him to a game of gin rummy in the hope of gaining an extra day of life, *and wins*. This Angel of Death is no big shot; he is a klutz who trips headlong over the windowsill upon entering Ackerman's house and cries out, "Jesus Christ. I nearly broke my neck." And he is a dreadful gin player. Ackerman not only beats him for a day of life but takes death for twenty-eight dollars. Death has to leave empty-handed, but not before warning: "Look – I'll be back tomorrow, and you'll give me a chance to win the money back. Otherwise I'm in definite trouble." Nat: "Anything you want. Double or nothing we'll play. I'm liable to win an extra week or a month. The way you play, maybe years." The *moloch ha-movitz* takes a beating here along with Ingmar Bergman's *The Seventh Seal*.

Allen gives us some of the most baldly diagrammatic examples of this formula for comedy in his "Hasidic Tales"[15] in which Rabbi Baumel of Vitebsk embarks on a fast "to protest the unfair law prohibiting Russian Jews from wearing loafers outside the ghetto" or Rabbi Yitzchok Ben Levi, the great Jewish mystic, applies cabalistic numerology to horse racing and hits the daily double at Aqueduct fifty-two days running. These inventions are naked formula: submit the exalted to the rule of the common and and you've got a joke. But it is precisely in such cases where the humor is nothing more than the routine application of method that its machinery is most clearly exposed.

This dialectic at the heart of Jewish comedy recalls Van Wyck Brooks's conception of American culture as a divided realm: spiritual and practical, incorporeal and commercial, highbrow and lowbrow.[16] But where Brooks, in "America's Coming of Age," was describing a collisions of values in American social life, the Jewish version of it exists *within the individual Jew*, who is highbrow and lowbrow unto himself. Maybe a more serviceable pair of metaphors for this cultural dualism is Philip Rahv's "redskin" and "paleface,"[17] in part because they suggest forms of reconciliation that are unavailable in Brooks' terms. Like Brooks' highbrow, the paleface in American culture is a product of "the thin, solemn, semi-clerical culture of Boston and Concord," and Henry James and T. S. Eliot its apostles in American literature. The redskin, on the other hand, is a product of "the lowlife world of the frontier and the big cities," for which Whitman and Twain were the classic spokesmen. However, though Brooks' and Rahv's terms describe the same cultural terrain, they suggest different forms of mediation, for if the synthesis of high and lowbrow is middlebrow, a term fixed for us by common usage, that of redskin and paleface is "redface," a term defined for us by Philip Roth.[18] The middlebrow, by common definition, is the commercial sublime, in which the trappings of high culture are thrown over the vacuities of popular taste like a Persian carpet over a trap door. A parody of high culture, the middlebrow novel or film takes world historical themes and straps them onto a romantic grid. The historical epic, or, nowadays, the space epic, are classic middlebrow productions: martial music, pseudo elevated speech, the grandeur of history or outer space serving as props for adolescent fantasies. Middlebrow art is a commodity; the middlebrow individual is its purveyor and consumer.[19]

The redface, however, as Philip Roth has defined him in an essay on himself, is the character in whom high and low are locked in powerful debate and who must define his own values by negotiating an uneasy detente between the two. He is a product of both cultures, and yet *"fundamentally ill-at-ease in, and at odds with, both worlds* although . . . alert to the inexhaustible number of intriguing postures that the awkward may assume in public, and the strange means that the uneasy come upon to express themselves." Unlike the middlebrow, the redface never confuses high and popular. He has no interest in ennobling the ordinary or making tragic claims for the merely heart-rending. He never uses words like "profound." He savors, rather, his own absurdity and relishes the idea of himself as a creature of unstable habits and volatile tastes. Middlebrowism strikes me as a uniquely American and commercial phenomenon, redfacism a Jewish-American and psychological one.

A line of humor that runs through comedians as diverse as Jack Benny, Henny Youngman, Morey Amsterdam, Harpo Marx, Victor Borge, and Allen himself is built upon the premise of redface-ism, the self-conscious byplay of *Kunst* and candy store. Each of these comedians carries or carried a musical instrument as a prop, though Allen's clarinet is a hidden prop that has never been introduced into his comedy, and Harpo didn't always drag out the harp. But we know about them in any case; the instruments are their credentials as serious artists, the signs of their higher faculties. In all cases, the musical props are indications of a prior, and abandoned, vocation that bears specific cultural weight. These violins, cellos, and clarinets are the remnants of the European high culture that Jews sought to adopt as an avenue of escape from the ghetto. Such aspiration produced in our own day the great Jewish virtuosi of German and Russian music: David Oistrakh, Yasha Heifetz, Yehudi Menuhin, Isaac Stern, Itzhak Perlman, Vladimir Horowitz, Pinchas Zuckerman, Vladimir Ashkenazi, *et al.*, and the comedy that alludes to them is the token of how successfully, and with how much guilt, their example has been evaded. In carrying his instrument on stage with him, the comedian carries his past as a sight-gag, a mechanical straight man that testifies to the stringencies of the ghetto and the dreams of Jewish parents. The Jewish comedian and his violin are not unlike the ventriloquist and his dummy, though roles are reversed. Whereas the ventriloquist plays straight man to his dummy, it is the comic who plays dummy to his violin, which is also his muse, his past, he superego, his parent, his better half. He brings it on stage in order to defy its sole command: *play me.*

Obviously, this strategy of splitting oneself up for comic purposes, when dressed in the colors of a particular history and tradition in which such inner divisions are validated by a cultural duality, can give rise to a humor in which the tradition itself is interrogated and its own tensions brought into clearer focus. The Jewish comedian is himself a one-man comedy team, an Abbott and Costello, Smith and Dale, Burns and Allen, Bergen and McCarthy, Caesar and Coca, Cheech and Chong all in one. That is because at heart, and by historical design, he really is two men, equally alive to God or the claims of high culture, our secular substitute for God, and to carpeting or baseball or sex. The comedian is one who is learning to negotiate the disparity between facets of himself and of the traditions in which he is immersed for the purposes of amusement. From conflicts that produce symptoms in others, he produces laughter. What others suffer from, he exploits, which is not to say that he too doesn't suffer from his material or isn't longing to be cured of it, but only that by his routines he holds his afflictions at bay. Failing to relieve himself by laughter, he may turn to psychoanalysis, and may even, turning the screw another notch, treat psychoanalysis to a dose of comic salts, as Roth did in *Portnoy's Complaint* and Allen did in *Zelig*.

The larger point to be drawn from all this is that *culture is comedy*, a perception shared by every man on the margin and every shrewd comedian. It is the experience of the modern Jew, an experience greatly attenuated of late, to be neither wholly or comfortably Jewish nor cozily American, a predicament that renders the hyphen in his identity the cutting edge of his wit. Everything is alien to him; even the commonplace is incongruous, and he tends to approach the world with a tourist's sense of wonderment. *The more familiar, the more strange.* If he is an intellectual he may turn that wonderment into a formal treatise or some other form of high-level scowling (an intellectual should always be alienated); he may become a walker in the city like Alfred Kazin or a sociologist of the ordinary, like Bellow, or the Margaret Mead of his own life, like Roth, for whom coming of age in Newark bears comparison to coming of age in Samoa or the Fiji Islands. It is not for nothing that Saul Bellow, our most acclaimed chronicler of middle-class social rites, has a Master's degree in Anthropology to lend formal credentials, as if they were needed, to his native instinct for seeing the common in the light of the strange. For what the great novelist tells us, like the great comedian, is that the familiar really *is* strange, and if only for an instant the scales would fall from our eyes we would see with the clarity of naked vision how outrageous is the world around us.

In a comedy of culture, then, the joke does not create the humor; it formulates a humor that is already there, defamiliarizing the familiar to make it seem suddenly alien. Cultural comedy is the disclosure of ironic conjunctions, not their invention. Where such a comedy is at its richest, the technique is the content; a heightening and distillation of common anomalies. Technique, to reapply an old formula for fiction, is discovery.

The relation of Jewish comedy to the Jewish religion, then, is apparent. It is its inversion, its negative, its shadow. The reversal of figure and ground. Where both comedy and religion acknowledge the interdependence of two worlds, a higher and a lower, each gives primacy to a different world. Religion subordinates this world to another; it translates upwards, while comedy undercuts the transcendent, criticizes it, subordinates it to the common. The one, in effect, Hebraizes, the other Yiddishizes. Which may tell us something about why that other great European comic tradition, the Irish, also arose in a culture in which religious authority has been central to cultural formation, and why in both cases the comedy should be to be so aggressive and so rude and should strike with such antinomian force at the heart of the exalted. Here again is Milton Lippman to Albert Einstein:

> I think sometimes that the Bible stories of God talking from above to the people down below is just what they had in those days instead of radio. People, whether then or now, like to hear "the real thing." Hearing is believing! . . . Today we don't *hear* God as they did in the Bible – and what is the result? It is impossible for some people to believe He is there. The same holds true with you, Doctor Einstein. I'm sorry to say. To the general public, who is Einstein? A name who doesn't comb his hair (not that I have any objection) and is *supposed* to be the smartest person alive. A lot of good that does the Jews, if you understand what I'm saying. At this stage of the game, I'm afraid that if an election were held tonight between you and The Answer Man, more people would vote for him than for you. I have to be honest with you.

There it is in a nutshell: God and Albert Einstein brought low by radio and The Answer Man. And we recognize right away that the world is full of Milton Lippmans, who would put the Lord himself on a quiz show if they could find sponsors to put up the money.

(And who would sponsor God? Who wouldn't?) Lippman speaks with a distinctly human and familiar voice. There are people who talk this way – they are our parents; they are embedded within ourselves – and though Lippman's entreaties are fantastic, Roth need not have invented a word of them. This is stone-cold realism and a program brought to you not by Philip Roth or Proctor and Gamble or Goodyear Tires but by the Jewish people.

NOTES

1. Harold Rosenberg, "Community, Values, Comedy," in *Discovering the Present: Three Decades in Art, Culture, and Politics* (Chicago and London: University of Chicago Press, 1973), p. 151.
2. Philip Roth, "On the Air," *New American Review*, 10 (1970).
3. "Jewish Writers," *Harvard Guide to Contemporary American Writing*, edited by Daniel Hoffman (Cambridge and London: The Belknap Press, 1979), pp. 191–239.
4. "Saul Bellow and Ghetto Cosmopolitanism," in *Modern Jewish Studies Annual II* (1978), pp. 33–44.
5. Portraits of the ghetto cosmopolitan as a social type abound in fiction, but I might suggest a reading of Norman Podhoretz's autobiography, *Making It*, for a particularly rich distillation of the type.
6. Max Weinreich, "Internal Bilingualism in Ashkenaz," in Irving Howe and Eliezer Greenberg (eds), *Voices from the Yiddish: Essays, Memoirs, Diaries* (Ann Arbor: University of Michigan Press, 1972), pp. 279–88.
7. Quoted in Irving Howe and Eliezer Greenberg, *A Treasury of Yiddish Stories* (New York: Schocken, 1973) p. 47.
8. Wallace Markfield, *You Could Live If They'd Let You* (New York: Alfred A. Knopf). The novel is a compendium of borscht belt routines and repartee, and though not a particularly good novel it faithfully reproduces the flavor and vibration, the timbre and pace, of Catskill comedy.
9. Woody Allen, "The Scrolls," *Without Feathers* (New York: Warner Books, 1976), p. 27.
10. Markfield, *You Could Live*, p. 128.
11. Rosenfeld and Bellow's parody of "Prufrock" appeared anonymously in David Neal Miller (ed.), *Yiddish Studies and MJS Newsletter* (Winter, 1978), p. 1. It has been cited as an example of the warmth and effervescence of the Yiddish language by Chaim Raphael, in *Jewish Chronicle Literary Supplement* (London), 6 June 1980.
12. Arthur A. Cohen, *The Natural and the Supernatural Jew* (New York: Behrman House, 1962).
13. See *Woody Allen's "Play It Again Sam,"* edited by Richard J. Anobile (New York: Grosset & Dunlap, 1977), pp. 88–89.
14. Woody Allen, "Death Knocks," *Getting Even* (New York: Warner Books, 1972), pp. 37–46.

15. The "Hasidic Tales" are in *Getting Even* (New York: Warner Books, 1972), pp. 52–56.

16. Van Wyck Brooks, "America's Coming of Age" (1915), in *Van Wyck Brooks: The Early Years. A Selection from His Works, 1908–1921*, edited by Claire Sprague (New York: Harper Torchbooks, 1968), pp. 79–158.

17. Philip Rahv, "Paleface and Redskin" (1939), *Literature and the Sixth Sense* (New York: Houghton Mifflin, 1969), pp. 1–6

18. Philip Roth, "On *The Great American Novel*," *Reading Myself and Others* (New York: Farrar, Straus & Giroux, 1975), pp. 82–84. This self conception of being a cultural hybrid, half raw, half cooked, runs through the interviews with Roth in this book and one can find there many formulations of the same idea.

19. It would take us far afield to discuss middlebrow taste at length here, but the reader might want to consult two of the classic formulations of it: Dwight Macdonald's definition of midcult in "Masscult and Midcult," *Against the American Grain* (New York: Random House, 1965) pp. 3–78, and Clement Greenberg's "Avant-Garde and Kitsch," in *Art and Culture* (Boston: Beacon Press, 1961), pp. 3–21.

5

The Survival of
Allen Ginsberg

We have three new books from Allen Ginsberg: a selection of recent poems, a second transcription of entries from his vast archive of journals, and an exchange of letters with Neal Cassady, who was once the elusive object of his tumultuous affections. But there is little to catch the eye here; two of the books – the journals and the correspondence – are sentimental journeys to familiar terrain – the mind of Allen Ginsberg. For years, Ginsberg been the most accessible of our writers, conducting his affairs very much in the open, if remarkably beyond the reach of talk shows, bookchat, and general literary blather. Nor do the poems break any new ground, thematically or technically. They serve up the standard brew of homosexuality, metaphysics, pacifism, stirrring declamation, muddled prophecy, and home-cooked Buddhism that is as familiar now as the morning coffee and about as shocking.

Ginsberg has long since graduated from being a subterranean and "know-nothing Bohemian" (Norman Podhoretz's tactful phrase) to being everyone's favorite prophet. He is our anarchist-in-residence, queer and avuncular, whose open passion for young boys and tirades against empire, oppression, and, lately, heroin are disarmed and domesticated by his irony. He reads poems about shit to packed houses in the prep schools. Even Diana Trilling, ever watchful for bad influences on the young, glowingly remembers him, in *We Must March My Darlings*, as a warm and comforting presence in the 1960s. Ginsberg is also that rarest of figures among American poets, a survivor, working vigorously into his fifties, despite the script he was handed early in life which called for a spectacular crack-up or a slow descent into alcohol or madness in the grand American tradition. He was cut out to be a *poète maudit*: a Poe, a Berryman, a Delmore Schwartz, a Plath, a Kerouac, and much of his initial impact in the 1950s derived from the impression he gave that he had privileged insight into the tragic fate of the imagination in America: "I saw the best minds of my generation destroyed by madness." But his own was not among them. Unlike Kerouac, he eventually recoiled from the allure of martyrdom, sparing us another tiresome lesson in how America abuses her poets and yet another case-history in poetry as a by-product of terminal euphoria. He was finally too ironic and willful for martyrdom, and, despite his rages against America and her wars, too enamored of the *idea* of America, which he confused with the idea of Walt Whitman, to renege on his initial promise: "America I'm putting my queer shoulder to the wheel."

Credit for Ginsberg's survival goes to his Buddhism, which has taught him how to marshal and conserve his energies and to suspend his urban, Jewish agitation in passive, Eastern repose. The aroma of wise passiveness that wafts through his public appearances these days is a studied calm, a calculated vigilance over seething emotions which he has learned to hold in check and sublimate into a keening, sonorous delivery. In a recent poem on the subject of being mugged in his own neighborhood ("Mugging" in *Mind Breaths*), Ginsberg tells of surrendering to a troop of young thugs while frantically intoning a mantra to keep his terror and rage under control: "I went down shouting Om Ah Hum to gangs of lovers on the stoop watching." But whatever such methodologies of self-discipline have contributed to his durability and his public figure – that is, to the pedagogic example – they have brought little to the poetry save heavy breathing and a treasury of lambent phrases to be sprinkled lightly over a poem like curry over lamb, for oriental pungency. Sanskrit scans marvelously in English meters, while spreading little wavelets of mystical illumination. Thus several of the poems in *Mind Breaths* are graced with such sweet cadences as "Bom Bom! Shivaye! Ram Nam Satyahey! Om Ganipatti, Om Saraswatti Hrih Sowha!" which mean something, we may be assured, in the original, but which, for most of us, might just as well be "Hey nonny nonny no." Yet, despite airs of Tagore or Lao-Tze that drift like incense through his poetry, Ginsberg had kept faith with his earliest mentors, Williams, Whitman, and Blake, and nothing he has done since the poems in *Kaddish* in 1961 shows any advance in vision or technique.

In *Mind Breaths*, except for a strange bit of romantic allegory, "Contest of Bards," which Ginsberg himself has hailed as a gift from the muse, but whose studied Blakeisms ("Icy intellect fir'y beauty wreck") sound false to an ear trained on his more vernacular,

American, line, most of the poems seem like refrains from earlier books, and far less inspired ones at that. This is Ginsberg's coolest book; its dithyrambic surges, at any rate, aim no higher than the foothills of the Adirondacks. The spontaneous composition that was a boon to earlier poetry, summoning up the long, rabbinic chords of "Howl," "Kaddish," and "Wichita Vortex Sutra," looks more and more like a recipe for instant altitudo: a shortcut to the poetic high. The paraphernalia of inspiration that serve Ginsberg so well in performance – what with the harmonium and the receptivity of audiences just dying for enchantment – are no promise of poetry that works in print, especially now that Ginsberg devotes so much of his attention to pure voice and pure breath, biomusic, if you like, that does not translate easily into words.

> Zalmon Schacter Lubovitcher Rebbe what you say
>> Stone Commandments broken on the ground
> Sufi Sam Whaddya say
>> Shall Prophet's companions dance circled
>>> round Synagogue while Jews doven bearded
>>>> electric?
> Both Gods Terrible! Awful Jaweh Allah!
>> Both hook-nosed gods, circumcised.
> Jaweh Allah which unreal?
>> Which stronger Illusion?
>>> Which stronger Army?
>>>> (from "Jaweh and Allah Battle")

One turns almost in relief from anti-war dovenning such as this to poems like "Sweet Boy, Gimme Yr Ass," and "Under the World There's a Lot of Ass, a Lot of Cunt," where, at least, the old sexual frankness shows signs of life, largely because Ginsberg's sexual imagination is so aggressive, so downright violent. "Under the world there's a lot/of ass, a lot of cunt/a lot of mouths and cocks,/under the world there's a lot of come, and a lot of saliva dripping into brooks" makes its raunchy statement with the same peevish assertion that Ginsberg could always summon up when aggravated, though now that these sentiments are tolerated in the prep schools, even his gnashing of teeth begins to sound like good cheer, which is not entirely his fault.

At this stage of the game, rather than try to push ahead poetically, Ginsberg has taken to doubling back upon himself, and the journals, correspondence, memoirs, and *obiter dicta* (see, for example, Gordon Ball's *Allen Verbatim*) that now tumble onto the market suggest that what we can henceforth look forward are neither breakthroughs nor refinements in poetry, but Ginsberg's efforts to clarify his image and carve out a place in American cultural history. One suspects that Ginsberg understands these days that he matters less as a poet than as a figure, an exemplary life. Certainly he has grown influential without being consistently great, or even consistently engaging as a writer, and most of us can count on one hand the poems that survive rereading, let alone study. As an exemplary figure, however, Ginsberg is something else again, and it is to the clarification of the example that the journals and letters are devoted.

But in what sense is such a life admirable? Are we compelled to admire the conspicuous alienation and rootlessness that has made of Ginsberg America's foremost wandering Buddhist-Jew? Are we *really* that comfortable with the aggressive homosexuality? Neither of those qualities is unambiguous. If his alienation has afforded him a critical distance from American society and institutions and given him a place to stand in opposition to it, has it not also separated him from poetry as well? Has not his writing been flawed over the years by his reluctance to study his craft, to brighten his language, to learn from others? As for the public homosexuality, even granting that as a campaigner for sexual pluralism Ginsberg has been instrumental in creating the current social climate in which coming out is encouraged and gaybaiting is on the defensive, except perhaps in the deep south or at *Commentary* magazine, doesn't the studied *epatism* grow tedious after a while? What surely *is* exemplary on Ginsberg's part is the risk he has taken in placing his own sexual nature out in the open; proclaiming it, writing about it, worrying over it, and insisting on its right to gratification, thus keeping himself clear of the enervating compromises of closet homosexuality. Ginsberg's acceptance of his own constitution as the very condition of his life and his poetry is certainly one of the sources of his strength and durability. Blakean that he is, he has not let himself be undermined by his own repressed desires. Admiration for the *idea* of sexual openness, however, does not make it any easier to read a poem like "Sweet Boy, Gimme Yr Ass." Even as an honored senior poet and a quasi-saint, Ginsberg can still make us squirm.

But Ginsberg's long involvement with mind-altering drugs is more problematic. His early exalted testimonials on behalf of his pharmacological experiments gave sanction, not only to the use of drugs in the 1960s, but to their glorification as the elixir of cosmic consciousness. Though Ginsberg has campaigned against heroin and now writes, "Nobody saves America by sniffing cocaine," his basic line on dope, as on everything else, has been the libertarian's *laissez faire*: let every man find out for himself. But hallucinogenic drugs once meant more to him than just another degree of American freedom; they occupied a place in his romance with madness, which, as Kerouac shrewdly saw, served his need to justify his mother. Though he eventually outgrew his illusions about redemptive insanity and took up spiritual self-discipline after the Indian trip in 1962–63, he had by then already made his contribution to the myth of the madman as antinomian saint "who drove cross-country seventy–two hours to find out if I had a vision or you had a vision or he had a vision to find out eternity." Some of those visions, we now know, were the mental vapors of neurons evaporating in the skull. Yet all this in Ginsberg: the aggressive homosexuality, the rootlessness, the anarchism, the celebrated expeditions in search of a better hallucinogen, cannot be seen apart from what is to be admired in him, for they are, however ambiguous, his efforts at salvation. The accumulating documentation of his life is slowly amounting to the authentication of a saint's life, a chronicle of beatitude whose theme, like that of all saints' lives, is crisis, conversion, and trial. The famous Blake vision, of which we have a half-dozen accounts, is like Paul's vision on the road to Damascus or Martin Luther's fit in the choir, a token of annointment, and the torments that follow are steps in the realization of a mission. The mother's madness had to be suffered and purged; the humiliating love for Neal Cassady had to be indulged and worked through; imprisonment and institutionalization had to be endured and made use of; shame and guilt had to be admitted and overcome. Allen Ginsberg's youth was an apprenticeship in failure, and in light of the dismal lessons he suffered his heroism would appear to lie not in his resistance to money or power or social convention but in his refusal of the original emotional ground rules of his life. He altered the deadly prognosis: by way of Blake and Buddhism he became that mythic American, the self-made man, the anarchist Horatio Alger. More bookish, more resolutely literary than any of the other Beats, he transformed and rescued himself through the medium of books. What else shall we make of the Blake vision that set into motion his career as a poet but this – that here was a man on his way down who was rescued by poetry? Little wonder that he is honored these days in the academy, to whose basic values – dispassionate toil, restraint, objectivity – he is seemingly so anathema, for he is a living defense of the literary vocation.

These journals and letters, by and large, have little to tell us about Ginsberg's survival, but much to show us about his early desperation. The *Journals* cover two periods, 1952 to 1956, and 1959 to February, 1962, the eve of his departure for India. The *Indian Journals*, previously published (1970), take up where these leave off. The correspondence with Neal Cassady extends farther back, to 1947 and the tender years at Columbia, and plots the vicissitudes of that difficult relationship into 1963. The Ginsberg who emerges from these pages is the lost and driven young poet seeking respite from his pains through determined reading, mysticism, and sex.

The letters to Neal, especially the very earliest, are the most readable and touching of these documents because they are the most thoroughly grounded in common humanity. Ginsberg's mysticism would later cast a veil of metaphysics over the emotions, making portions of the journals tough sledding for the reader in search of more ordinary revelations. But the letters are direct and ardent, full of passionate declarations of emotional dependency and pleas for punishment and love. Writing in 1947, a year after first meeting Cassady in New York, Ginsberg declared, "I am lonely, Neal, alone, and always I am frightened. I need someone to love me and kiss me & sleep with me; I am only a child and have the mind of a child. I have been miserable without you because I had depended on you to take care of me for love of me, and now that you have altogether rejected me, what can I do, what can I do?" I scarcely know of more abject appeals anywhere in literature or published correspondence. Yet even at his most desolate, Ginsberg would turn his sexual dependency into intellectual advantage, urging Neal, in a postscript to one letter, to read *Nightwood*, *Wings of the Dove*, and *The Idiot*. Cassady, who had received his education on Denver's skid row, where he earned advanced degrees in deprivation and drift, was vulnerable to learning, and Ginsberg knew how to gain leverage over him with exhibitions of Columbia erudition. The letters reveal the emotional quid pro quo of homosexuality, the give and take of power that became for Ginsberg the basic rule of psychic accounting. As applied to his relationships it took the form of the strategic dependency, the manipulative weakness. As applied to himself, it was the conversion factor in reconstructing paranoia as enlightenment, persecution as hypostatic union. His later messianism sprang full grown from his early masochism, his transcendence from his lessons in abasement. It is easy to understand the appeal of Cassady for someone like Ginsberg, though Cassady's magic does not come through in the letters. He was not an intellectual or even much of a reader; he tried to write and, for the most part, failed,[1] and even his letters are garbled. "I hate words," he complained to Ginsberg. "They are too much." What captivated Ginsberg and Kerouac was the rough and ready masculinity, the suggestion of complete male competence. They were Reichians, and he was a vessel of molten libido, blissfully pansexual and yet carelessly masculine. Moreover, he was almost a dead ringer for Kerouac, which surely played into the latter's exalted conception of him. Kerouac mythicized him in his books as Dean Moriarty and Cody Pomeroy; Gary Snyder saw him as the last cowboy, a Jedediah Smith hemmed in by the modern world; Ginsberg just loved him. He was their link to frontier manhood, their own urban cowboy, though they understood too that his skid row disorientation was an alienation not unlike their own. He was born to lose. After marrying his second wife, Carolyn, in 1949, he wrote to Ginsberg, "From what I can unerstand of them your doldrums are fine. All I can see is the long, continuous doldrum I'm in." Seeking release from the doldrums in spontaneous flights from one end of the continent to the other in search of the ease that always eluded him, he served Kerouac and Ginsberg as a tour guide to the American heartland and introduced them to an authentic American high, the high of the fast car and the open road. The rolling cadenzas of *On the Road* owe everything to Cassady and his cars, as do the lilt and flux of Ginsberg's highway poems, which are among his best: "The Green Automobile" (*Reality Sandwiches*), a poem about Cassady, "Wichita Vortex Sutra" (*Planet News*), and the cross-country "vortex" poems in *The Fall of America*.

But the open road is only a high while one remains in motion, savoring the illusion that trouble is back down the road somewhere. Cassady's fretful activity was only a scheme for buying a moment away from his panic and his incredible bad luck. Indeed, while William Burroughs and Lucien Carr could get away, literally, with murder, Cassady would eventually get caught for possession and sale of marijuana and wind up doing two years at San Quentin, from 1958 to 1960. Imagine that today. After his release he was reduced to doing his routine in miniature, driving the bus for Ken Kesey and his

Merry Pranksters, hitting the road as a parody of himself. He died in Mexico in February, 1968, under mysterious circumstances, though probably of alcohol fatally spiked with barbiturates.

Ginsberg and Cassady had already begun to drift apart after their reunion in 1954. Ginsberg met Peter Orlovsky, while Cassady attended fitfully to his family and his job as a railroad brakeman for the Southern Pacific. In the mid-fifties, Ginsberg was also discovering his own strength and his calling, spiritualizing his emotions and consigning his torments to his poetry. He was discovering *the heights*. The movement of the journals is away from the lucid, personal, and tortured writing of the early letters toward an elliptical and mystagogic style that is difficult to penetrate. Relationships surrender to casual impressions and dreams; almost half the contents of these journals are Ginsberg's transcriptions of his own dreams, though without the associations that might make them accessible. Indeed, there is a refractory quality to these journals, and the *Indian Journals* are the most resistant of them all. Despite their painstaking documentation of the inner life, they obscure personal qualities in a blizzard of fragmentary notations, alternately banal and dharmic, and shuttle back and forth between runaway empiricism and runaway mysticism.

Oct. 22.
Read at Gaslight, rainy nite, 3 a.m. Mist walking along Avenue D to E. 2 St. and up E. 2 St. in the blue haze of rain, overbright street lamps screaming down their mechano radiance onto the street, a violent-red damp sky above, walking in the Dream, remembering Shelley's insight, I repeated in my mind

The One remains

and glimpsed the One behind the transient clouds in the haze – The Many change and pass, as I was walking down the street, I passing this life toward my ever-menacing present Death – Inevitable –

Here, as practically everywhere else in these journals, the odd empirical/metaphysical impasto crowds out all more mundane preoccupations, making the most intimate revelations sound impersonal, oddly dreamlike. The journals, indeed, document the triumph of the religious imagination over the social, and only constant infusions of Ginsberg's irrepressible irony save the whole venture from collapsing into worship and trance.

> Bullshit Artist of Reality,
>   Ginsberg,
> Give up,
>   Forever
> To your Truth,
>   and Lose thy shoe on
> the Great Step.
>
>   *   *   *   *
>
> Allen – Does the Capitol
>   Believe yet
>   in the Imagination?
> Jack – Yes – they do – but it isn't official yet.

The appeal of Ginsberg in the sixties lay in the appearance he gave of seeing through or beyond the veils and blinders of ordinary social thought. I remember vividly a moment in the mid-sixties when Ginsberg, operating as only he could, through the medium of power poetry, affected a truce between anti-War marchers in the Bay Area and the Hell's Angels, who, egged on by local officials and police, were poised to assault the demonstrators. Appealing to the bikers that, more or less, "we're all social outlaws together," not only did Ginsberg pacify them, but apparently mollified the surly Oakland police as well. Moreover, the truce was sealed by the reading of a poem, "To the Angels," at a rally in the East Bay. Who could help at such moments but believe that here was a truly transcendent figure, someone who just, by his presence alone, dissolved the ordinary social categories. Strange it is, then, to find so little social reflection in his journals, as if the social and political self were to be treated as a stepchild and of relative unimportance compared to the prophet. We expect poetry that is sufficiently inspired to leap from one plane of meaning to the next, to zoom upwards from sensory data to the higher realms, but what seems like thrilling prophecy when spoken in Biblical accents does not satisfy in the form of a journal entry. Which is another way of saying that the journals and most of the letters to Neal are disappointing except for the light they shed on other things that may matter to us: Ginsberg's poetry, or American social history in the postwar decades. And that light is dim.

There is no reason for Ginsberg *not* to have published such journals and letters, nor to withhold the additional materials which will soon be forthcoming. Public self-examination of this sort is a rare and valuable gesture, even when as in this case, what is actually disclosed will interest few. Understandably, a confession, even to oneself, is a bargain struck with the superego to permit some more difficult and compromising knowledge to be withheld, though it is odd to find such a case in which primal fears and sexual anxieties are laid bare and social relations suppressed. But that reversal is in the antinomian manner of Ginsberg's life. And that is where the power lies too, in his difference, his strangeness, and his refusal to be one of us while insisting that we come to terms, as best we can, with him.

NOTES

1. Cassady's writings are not without their interest, however, for the life they depict. See Neal Cassady, *The First Third and Other Writings* (San Francisco: City Lights, 1971.) The reader might also want to have a look at Carolyn Cassady's memoir – letters strung together by a thin narrative, actually – of Cassady and Kerouac together, in *Heartbeat: My Life with Jack and Neal* (Berkeley: Creative Arts, 1976).

6

Bernard Malamud, or the Return of the Repressed

Our image of Bernard Malamud is so bound up with certain familiar sentiments concerning conscience and moral accountability that scarcely anyone writes about him without paying tribute to them. Malamud's books we are repeatedly told, speak for "the possibility of man's redemption through purgative suffering and selfless love," or betray a concern with "Love, Mercy (*Rachmones*), *Menschlechkeit*" or "probe the animal nature of man, reveal a fearful mistrust of instinctual behavior, and struggle toward an answer in discipline and love." With the prevailing consensus thus in favor of Malamud's mission of moral improvement, readers might well wonder whether it would not be more direct to bypass him altogether and proceed directly to the synagogue for the original teachings. Not everyone would rush off to the library for a writer's books after being told that, as one critic has put it, he "follows in the ancient tradition of the prophets, Amos, Jeremiah, the Second Isaiah who announce suffering to be the Jew's special destiny, evidence of his unique covenant with God . . . ." Some might sensibly conclude from such praise that the writer in question was altogether too morally accomplished for them, or too gloomy, and turn instead to Dr. Brothers, who at least is cheerful and reassures us that we can get what we want out of life.

This state of affairs has not exactly been imposed upon Malamud. If anything, he has encouraged this view of himself as a champion of humanism and spokesman for the special moral insight of the Jews by announcing on various occasions that "the purpose of the writer . . . is to keep civilization from destroying itself" and that "what has made the Jewish writers conspicuous in American literature is their sensitivity to the value of man." The books themselves, with their parables of affliction and endurance and their quasi-symbolic Jews, standing for all mankind in their existential

70

angst while remaining Jews in their historical particularity, give body to such intentions. In all of contemporary literature, there is scarcely a covenant between an author and critics more binding than that between Malamud and his. The latter have agreed in the main not to ask questions about Malamud's writing that fall outside the domain of humanist morality and Jewish suffering that he has staked out as his territory.

What has gone unnoticed in the rush to sanctify Malamud is that the very system of values for which he is acclaimed has been, from the start, marked by discrepancies – contradictions between his celebrated pleas for restraint and certain powerful emotional promptings – and that those contradictions have steadily been growing sharper. In early books they appeared as mere matters of dramatic conflict, so that in *The Assistant* Frank Alpine's "redemption" and his education in Jewish sexual taboos and rites, culminating in his circumcision, could be made to seem dimensions of the same moral development. But more recently those discrepancies between the emotional tenor of his books and their instructional premises have become too extreme for patching up and have threatened to fracture the Malamudian universe altogether. We seem not to have been noticing that Malamud has been changing on us, becoming more extravagant, and that in abandoning his early manner, with its special ethical coloration – its balance of longing and caution, irony and Talmudic strictness, Yiddish folklore and Depression realism – he has not merely been losing touch with his original talent but trying strenuously to get around its limitations. It now appears that Malamud, like many another Jewish writer who has grown weary of ethical or literary circumspection, has been trying to cut through to something else. How else are we to account for the heightened sexuality of recent books or the frightening bursts of mayhem that appear when his meticulously applied irony wears thin? What can the conventional formulas about Malamud tell us about the end of *The Tenants* where Willie Spearmint slices off Harry Lesser's balls with a razor, just as Lesser is sinking an axe into Spearmint's head, while the hapless landlord, Levenspiel, looks on in horror and cries out the ostensible moral of the book: "Mercy, mercy, mercy . . . ." as if that could dampen any of the accumulated rage? And how might it account for the raunchy conclusion to *Pictures of Fidelman*, in which Fidelman submits to the advances of Beppo, the Venetian glassblower, who knows the ins and outs of love and assures his neophyte Jewish lover that they don't hurt a bit: "It'll be a cool job, I'm wearing mentholated vaseline. You'll be surprised at the pleasure." Is this *our* Malamud, with a heart full of homoerotic love and a jar of vaseline? Is this just a new twist on redemption through purgative suffering and selfless love or on Morris Bober's "I suffer for you, you suffer for me"?

Dubin's Lives would appear to be the last nail in the coffin of the old Malamud, since this novel of middle-aged yearning and marital infidelity is certainly his most thoroughgoing venture into the erotic. William Dubin, biographer, who has written a life of Thoreau and is currently, and painfully, at work on a life of D. H. Lawrence, begins, at age fifty-six, to feel the itch of Lawrentian blood consciousness when his wife, Kitty, hires the nubile Fanny Bick as housekeeper, and Fanny, whose nipples are usually on show beneath her blouse, begins to hang around the biographer's study. Like many another Malamud hero, Dubin is teased to distraction by this peep show, which culminates at the stunning moment when Fanny, bent on calling Dubin's bluff – he has been lecturing her on the morality of living life "to the hilt" – barges into his study and removes her clothes. "Fanny tossed her yellow underpants at him. He caught them and tossed them back. They struck her breasts and fell to the floor." "'Whatever you're offering,'" he apologizes, "'I regret I can't accept.'"

But such resolve is only whistling in the dark. Dubin has taken the bait – those fatal yellow underpants – and he's hooked. Thus begins a furtive chase that takes him to New York, where he is miserably stood up in a hotel bar, and then to Venice with Fanny (telling his wife he needs to do research) in order to redeem at last the promise of those undies.

But readers who are familiar with the ground rules of the Malamudian erotic will anticipate what comes next – THE PUT-DOWN – though they may not be ready for the way it is done here. Malamud is a specialist in disappointment, the contemporary master of blueballs, and ever since Roy Hobbs in *The Natural* was shot down in that hotel room by the woman who had lured him there, and Frank Alpine in *The Assistant* was spurned by Helen Bober for being "an uncircumcised dog," Malamud has been contriving newer and more spectacular ways to liven up the scenario of male shame. After drinks, wine, a sumptuous dinner (Fanny orders brains), and hours of slow teasing ("She had removed her shoe and was caressing him under the table"), they retire to the hotel room where Fanny is suddenly beset by the effects of those brains. Losing control of her bowels she rushes to the bathroom, and when Dubin checks in on her after several minutes of impatient waiting, he is greeted by this Swiftian vision of the nymph: "She was standing at the toilet bowl, retching, a blob of diarrhea dribbling down her leg." Purgative suffering indeed. That Fanny remains ill and indisposed for the remainder of their stay, and then betrays Dubin with a gondolier and a motorboat operator, are strictly literary afterplay. That blob of diarrhea is the touch of a master and the irrepressible comedy of the unconscious. Dubin tries to salvage some dignity from his predicament by recalling Yeats's line: "Love has pitched its mansion in the place of excrement," but is neither comforted nor enlightened by the exalted point of view.

That scene might mark the climax of a Malamud short story or point the moral of an early novel on the rewards of appetite, but Malamud is no longer content with comic catastrophes and moral epiphanies, no matter what psychic depths they may divulge. What makes *Dubin's Lives* different is that Malamud rejects the customary conservative moral – that Dubin should act his age and patch up his marriage – in favor of something more problematic and more interesting. Like any Malamud character, Dubin is being educated by experience, but unlike the others he gains no wisdom and earns no "redemption," which is perhaps why this book, ostensibly the least Jewish of all Malamud's novels, may well be the most Jewish by interior design. For it is the most thoroughly devoted to the actualities of common experience, rather than to the mythic or moral patterns that might be extracted from it.

Malamud allows Dubin and Fanny to have an affair and to enjoy their share of sensual delight. Dubin has been taking instruction in sexual freedom from Lawrence, and though the choice of Lawrence – sexologue, primitivist, anti-Semite – may seem paradoxical for so cautious a man of modest appetites, it conforms to a deeper logic. Lawrence is the shadow self and a voice for the secret life that has been clamoring for release. He is mid-wife to this parasite Dubin, whose emergence into the host Dubin's life produces the sort of difficulties that come of mixing two literatures or two moral systems. Dubin tries to become a Lawrentian hero in a Malamudian world, a phallic narcissist in a life of modesty, conscience, and consequences. But then, as Dubin knows, Lawrence himself was not exactly *Lawrence*; his sexual manifestoes were not affirmations easily come by but protests against his own ruthless superego and unpredictable body. He was impotent at forty-two. If there is a touch of Lawrence in Dubin, there was apparently a touch of Dubin in Lawrence.

The second and more interesting half of *Dubin's Lives* begins when Dubin and Fanny consummate the long flirtation and embark on a hazardous affair, thereby raising the level of complication. On the one hand, the affair represents a genuine release into the erotic. Dubin and Fanny (what's in a name?) take full pleasure in each other, and Malamud indulges himself, by indulging them in blissful sensuality. But not too much of it. Even in this relationship, sensuality takes a back seat to the familiar commotions of conscience. Fanny may garland Dubin's penis with flowers, but she also wreathes his life with difficulties. It is symptomatic of Malamud's version of the bower of bliss that Fanny's apartment on New York's West Eighty-third Street should overlook an orthodox synagogue in which Dubin can see "a small candlelit room where a black-bearded black-hatted Jew, his white shawl glowing on his shoulders, bent back and forth in prayer." As a reminder that all is not lost to blood consciousness – or *traif* – here are the fathers perched at the very window like so many Jewbirds of disapproval, reminding Dubin of the old ethics and forsaken duties. Such reminders can lead him in only one direction: home.

Just as nothing succeeds like failure in earlier Malamud books, nothing fails like success in this one. Dubin's marriage, difficult enough before Fanny, becomes increasingly dismal as he withdraws from Kitty. Indeed, it is not in the affair with Fanny that we find the heart of this book, but in the portrait of a marriage, which, for all its gloom, its bitter asperities, its bleak climate of empty habit and desiccated affection, is a vivid depiction of a real relationship, a marriage in progress.

Against temptations to resolve Dubin's impasse and heal the split between his lives, Malamud holds fast until the very last page, where he violates the logic of the entire book by having Dubin leap out of Fanny's bed with a erection (she now owns a house up the road from the Dubins) and rush home to make love to his wife before the erection droops. The reader is advised to skip that page. Like Levenspiel's appeal for mercy in *The Tenants*, this ending simply contradicts everything that has come before and tries to rescue the book by magic from its own implacable conclusion: that the marriage is over. Up until that point, though, Malamud is fairly steadfast and pursues the desperate situation relentlessly and imaginatively through page after bleak page, through recrimination and withdrawal, as both Dubin and Kitty slowly retreat from each other into private enclaves of fantasy. Dubin armors himself against his wife, and she responds with bewilderment, then rage, then analysis, and finally the inevitable affair of her own, in this case with her analyst. Ethically contra-indicated or not, he seems to have made the right diagnosis.

That Dubin's crisis is no simple outcome of his secret life may be guessed from the alienation of the two children: Gerald and Maud. The former has deserted from the Army to Sweden (this is about 1974), where he remains incommunicado, and will not even speak with his father when the latter tracks him down at his Swedish rooming house. At the end he defects to the Soviet Union, so deep is his alienation. Maud has gone away to college at Berkeley, but has quit school after an unhappy love affair and joined a Zen Buddhist monastery, only to abandon it and return home for a few dismal days to announce that she is pregnant. (*Of course*, the father is black.) Neither Gerald nor Maud shares any particular warmth with Dad, who has never given much and is now totally encased in his own troubles. The affair with Fanny, rather than open him up, has shut him down entirely, and when he is not with Fanny, he is holed up in his study in the barn with his manuscript and his miseries. A man so vulnerable, Dubin appears to his family to be impregnably self-sufficient.

So, *Dubin's Lives* is the old Malamud after all, to the extent that Dubin's pleasure does not add up to satisfaction. Quite the opposite; it is just another road to disaster. Through the gradual dissolution of his marriage, the alienation of his children, impotence with his wife, writer's block, and a failing memory, Dubin pays richly for his victories over middle age, as his misery increases in geometric ratio to his pleasures. (The improbability of some of these punishments preceding his crime is not to the point, since it is Malamud's mind we're talking about.) Sexual liberation means no less trial than renunciation; the Malamud hero suffers either way.

Where this novel succeeds and is, in my estimation, the richest of all Malamud's novels, is not in the conclusion, which is false, nor in Malamud's judgments, which are more ambivalent than ever, nor in the tortuous vision of transgression and retribution, which by now is old hat and hardly in need of restatement. It lies in Malamud's command of the idiom of domestic warfare, the day to day details of a marriage in decline. Here as nowhere else Malamud pursues his favorite myth of moral exigency without resort to folklore or to the easy affirmations of packaged morality and the equally easy negations of psychic disarray. Malamud has been more considerate of his turmoil this time around, and produced a novel whose crises of conscience, erotic remissions, and ultimate vote for sanity are worked out with patience and therefore with credibility.

After *Dubin's Lives* it will be hard to treat Malamud as either a placid moralist or an ethnic *hors d'oeuvre*: as either an expert in timeless wisdom and contemporary ethics or an exotic miniature to be savored before the main course of American literature. Either view makes him sound like the kind of writer adults impose upon adolescents in high school English classes. For once, he has joined his private sexual obsessions to plausible contemporary circumstances in a convincing manner, and in the process secured a place for himself in the front ranks of contemporary writers. That does not mean, finally, that the Jewish element in Malamud's work is any less important, but only that it is more problematic and, I would say, more authentic than we used to imagine it was.

7
Malamud: The Still, Sad Music

Any doubts we may have had about Bernard Malamud's stature as a modern master should be dispelled by this collection of his stories. This personal selection of twenty-five stories presents Malamud at his best: as a writer of eloquent and poignant vignettes. Though Malamud has published seven novels, each one touched with his distinctive melancholy grace, the short story remains the purest distillation of his abiding *Leitmotif*: the still, sad music of humanity. Typically, the Malamud story is an epiphany of disappointment and failure, a document of the half-life – the shabby region of mediocre existence just a notch above pure disaster – bathed in the melodies of despair, the taut, concise adagios of woe. By and large, however, Malamud's range of characters and situations has been too narrow to sustain longer constructions. Lacking variety and any feel for the architecture of sustained fiction, his novels hold the note of sorrow too long, until what had begun as a lamentation ends as a *kvetch*. But in the short story, Malamud achieves an almost psalm-like compression. He has been called the Jewish Hawthorne, but he might also be thought a Jewish Chopin, a composer of preludes and nocturnes in prose.

The Malamud character is one we've long since come to recognize: the underground man transposed into a small merchant or retiree or pensioner. He is commonly alone or beset by family, creditors or customers: he seldom has friends. He runs a grocery, a deli, or a candy store where the cash register is always empty and the accounts receivable book full. His sons avoid him; his daughters, like Lear's, are ungrateful, and there is no Cordelia to love him in spite of himself. He may have a heart condition, like Mendel in "Idiot's First" or Marcus the tailor in "The Death of Me," or Mr. Panessa in "The Loan," or he may take his own life, like Rosen the ex-coffee salesman in "Take Pity," or Oskar Gassner in "The Jewish Refugee." At his most wretched he is a Jewbird, black as a caftan, fishy as a herring, and cursed/blessed with the powers of flight, though he longs only for the comforts of a home. With few exceptions, he is miserable, without hope, and waiting for death. Indeed, not only does the typical Malamud story end with death, but the keynote story in this collection, "Take Pity," begins with death, one that releases the character into a chamber of heaven that looks depressingly like a furnished room. Even death, it seems, brings no glory.

These are anything but glad tidings, and we might well ask why anyone would bother with a writer so insistently depressive, who peoples his stories with characters who exist for most of us only in memory and nightmare. That is not a simple question to answer, but we might begin with Malamud's own words. In one of the stories in this collection, "Man in the Drawer," an American journalist, Howard Harvitz, while touring Russia, is enticed by Levitansky, a Russian-Jewish writer whose work cannot be published in the Soviet Union, to read some of his stories. Harvitz, after much shilly-shallying, reads them and renders an approving judgment: "I like the primary, close-to-the-bone quality of the writing. The stories impress me as strong if simply wrought; I appreciate your feeling for the people and at the same time the objectivity with which you render them. It's sort of Chekhovian in quality, but more compressed, sinewy, direct, if you know what I mean." Levitansky, it appears, is a portrait of what Malamud himself might have been and suffered had fate sent his grandparents east to Russia rather than west to America, and these terms of praise are Malamud's own terms for what is strong in his art.

Sinewy, direct, simply wrought, close to the bone – Malamud's writing is all that, but an appreciation of his simplicity takes us only so far toward a definition of his appeal, which has, I think, two other sources: his music and his terror, the latter of which touches some core of panic in all of us. "Man in the Drawer" exhibits a dimension of the Malamud world that draws us in powerfully. Levitansky is the nightmare Jew, but he is also Harvitz's semblable, his alter ego, the victim who, but for an accident of fortune, might be himself. Plainly, he is *our* other self. Malamud's tenement Jews, his Russian-Jewish writers, his lonely pensioners, his forsaken fathers and embittered children are all stained by that tincture of possibility. Even in the midst of plenty, in this best of all possible diasporas, a portion of every Jew stands poised for flight. It is Malamud, more than any other Jewish writer, who retains that imagination of disaster and speaks the old dialects of loneliness, confinement, and exile.

The music of Malamud's writing is a curious one – dark and brooding but not overly abundant or reliably melodic. One comes repeatedly upon passages that are plainly clumsy, as though Malamud had forgotten the syntax of English or pieced together his own upon Yiddish syntactical patterns. He is no Bellow or Roth or Updike, primed with repartee and capable of a *mot* more *juste* on every page. His idiom is a limited one that has not noticeably grown in the thirty-four years he has been writing. He writes in basic English, now lyrical, now stumbling, reminding us more than a little of Isaac Babel in his regard for simple truths and his studied neglect of ornamentation.

Within that limited budget of words, however, Malamud achieves in his stories a *kleine Nachtmusik*, a simple melodic weariness that envelops his characters in sadness as dark as syrup and thick as oil.

> Davidov, the Census-taker, opened the door without knocking, limped into the room, and sat wearily down. Out came his notebook and he was on the job. Rosen, the ex-coffee salesman, wasted, eyes despairing, sat motionless, cross-legged, on his cot. The square, clean but cold room, lit by a dim globe, was sparsely furnished: the cot, a folding chair, small table, old unpainted chests – no closets but who needed them? – and a small sink with a rough piece of green, institutional soap on its holder – you could smell it across the room. The worn black shade over the single narrow window was drawn to the ledge, surprising Davidov ("Take Pity").

It takes us a while to comprehend that Rosen is dead and that death is no release, just a pane of one-way glass between himself and the living. The green institutional soap, the worn shade, the cot are the furniture of his life and of his heart, which has all the color and warmth of a cold-water flat. Alfred Kazin speaks of Malamud's poverty as "an aesthetic medium . . . coloring everything with its woebegone utensils, its stubborn immigrant English, its all-circulating despair." One might say that heartbreak, not just poverty, is the enveloping medium, but Kazin's point stands: some depletion of the spirit – call it poverty, call it defeat – not only commands the situation but choreographs every act, every speech, every word on the page. Through seas of sadness, Malamud's characters swim like fish.

The initial impression Malamud gave in the 1950s, with his early stories in *The Magic Barrel* and the novels *The Natural* and *The Assistant*, was that of being a purveyor of Jewish admonitions. The novels in particular cast long, didactic shadows and ask us to judge their characters as deserving of their trials. Moreover, *The Natural* and *The Assistant*, as well as stories like "The Lady of the Lake," "Girl of My Dreams," and "The Magic Barrel," broadcast suggestions of a sexual moralism as well, though its exact nature is never spelled out. The sexual moralist in Malamud has been largely excluded from this collection, and where sex turns up in a moral equation, as it does in "God's Wrath" and "The Magic Barrel," it posits mysteries rather than precepts.

And yet Malamud *is* a moralist and an insistent one, though the law to which he binds his characters has little in it of specifically Jewish content. It is the law of simple charity and compassion. Most of his characters either earn their misery through hard-heartedness or are the victims of others'. Kessler, the former egg candler of "The Mourners," is quarrelsome and a troublemaker and is self-isolated in his tenement apartment. Rosen, the ex-coffee salesman in "Take Pity," has been driven to the grave by a widow who, out of misplaced pride, rejects his charity. Glasser, the retired shamus in "God's Wrath," has had poor luck with his children, and we may guess that they'd had no better luck with him. In story after story coldness is returned for love, a warm heart is battered by a cold one. The word "no" is the most powerful and bitter word in all of Malamud.

Malamud is quintessentially a Jewish writer, though there is nothing of religious belief in his writing and only shards of ritual and *shmattas* of Jewish culture or history. Yet, for all that, his writing is so impregnated with Jewishness – as distinct from Judaism – that there can be no mistaking it. Sometimes it is the spectral Jewishness of Singer and Chagall, but more commonly it is the melancholy Jewishness of Roman Vishniac's photos of the Old Country in its last hours. In his modest and laconic style of narrative, Malamud has found the exact prose equivalent of the dull light and gray tones of Vishniac's world, a world exhausted by siege and conscious of its defeat. Perhaps Malamud's Jewishness is best understood in terms of Matthew Arnold's definition of Hebraism, "strictness of conscience." By such a definition, Malamud is our leading Hebraist of letters, for strictness of conscience is as much his abiding theme as sorrow is his abiding disposition. But though Malamud treats

it as a requirement of civilized existence, he often renders it as a
curse, a habit of withholding that interdicts the normal flow of
human feelings. Many of Malamud's characters treat others with
a rabbinical harshness, though one detached from a sacramental
life or a clear moral intention. They habitually ward off intimacy
and often give the appearance of performing archaic rites that they
have long since ceased to understand. A textbook approach to their
"problem" might call them compulsion-neurotics, for they are case
studies of conscience gone haywire.

In a Malamud story, conscience beyond an individual's need or
capacity or right to do good propels the argument. In "Take Pity,"
Rosen recites to a census-taker in heaven the tale of his failures at
charity toward the wife of a grocer. She would not heed his advice
to liquidate the store; she refused his offer of a place to stay when the
store went bankrupt; she recoiled at his proposal of marriage; she
returned money anonymously given, knowing it was from Rosen.
But, determined Rosen, "*I will give.*"

> "I went then to my lawyer and we made out a will that everything
> I had – all my investments, my two houses that I owned, also
> furniture, my car, the checking account – every cent would go to
> her, and when she died, the rest would be left for the two girls.
> The same with my insurance. They would be my beneficiaries.
> Then I signed and went home. In the kitchen I turned on the gas
> and put my head in the stove."
> "Let her say now no."

This is charity unto death. By what right does Rosen impose these
unwanted gifts upon the unwilling widow? And by what law of
self-reliance does she so obdurately decline what is offered her
solely out of love? Both Rosen and the Widow Kalish are stark
examples of a Hebraism so advanced, so unleavened by reflection or
sweetness and light as to be the literal death of one and the spiritual
death of the other.

> Davidov, scratching his stubbled cheek, nodded . . . .
> He got up and, before Rosen could cry no, idly raised the window
> shade.
> It was twilight in space but a woman stood before the win-
> dow.
> Rosen with a bound was off his cot to see.

It was Eva, staring at him with haunted beseeching eyes. She raised her arms to him.

Infuriated, the ex-salesman shook his fist.

"Whore, bastard, bitch," he shouted at her. "Go 'way from here. Go home to your children."

Davidov made no move to hinder him as Rosen rammed down the window shade.

Strictness of conscience has proven to be a moral cul-de-sac for both. Malamud's Jewish characters, one often feels, are automatons of conscience and fanatics. It is a commonplace of criticism that they are ruined by circumstance, but it is less often observed that those circumstances are helped along by their own narrowness and rigidity.

So deeply ingrained is this woe that it seems virtually biological, bound in helixes within every cell. But in the first postwar decade, it had the full sanction of the times and was well-nigh universal among Jewish writers and intellectuals. The sorrow that penetrates to the bone in Malamud was the mood of a generation of Jewish writers who had been raised on immigrant poverty and worldwide depression and brought abruptly to adulthood by the holocaust. Low spirits came as naturally to them as hunger or ambition or breath.

But for some of those writers sorrow was a transient mood and a burden, and they were glad to be relieved of it in the 1950s, when the prevailing conditions of life would no longer sustain their Dostoevskian migraines. As a character in an unfinished novel by Saul Bellow announced in 1950, "You heard me tell my old aunt a while back when she asked me what I wanted, that I didn't want to be sad any more." [Saul Bellow, "The Trip to Galena," *Partisan Review* 17 (November–December 1950), pp. 779–94.] Bellow, his stethoscope pressed to the bosom of the *Zeitgeist*, had uttered that sentence on behalf of a new mood which held that "being sad is being disfigured," and while in 1950 he was still tentative enough to put those sentiments in the mouth of a mental patient in a novel he could not complete, three years later he would confirm them in a full-blown festival of high spirits, *The Adventures of Augie March*.

Throughout the fifties and the sixties, Malamud stood aside from the cavalcade of cheerfulness and let it pass unapplauded. Though he *would* take detours into sunnier climes – Italy, in fact – and endeavor to compose in a more robust key, most notably in *Pictures of Fidelman,* he never strayed far from his sorrow. Throughout the 1950s, while other writers in the *Partisan Review* orbit were spreading the good news about "our country and our culture," Malamud was scouring the tenements of the imagination for vistas of misfortune, scenes of Old World pathos in New World ghettos. His major novel of that decade was *The Assistant,* his story of Jewish and Italian self-immolation in a failing grocery store. If the Kennedy era and the years of the counter-cultural revolution made any impression on his mood it is not visible in his stories of the sixties. One single note sounds long and uninterrupted through the stories of three decades: the note of mourning.

Collected Stories is a book of mourning, an anthology, one might say, of elegies. Even where there is no death, characters cloak themselves in talliths and recite Kaddishes for the living, as Salzman the matchmaker does for his client, Leo Finkle, in "The Magic Barrel" and Kessler the egg candler and Gruber the landlord do for themselves at the end of "The Mourners." Malamud has written stories of other kinds, but has selected these for reissue, as if to honor that region of his imagination that is most accustomed to grief. The singularity of this grieving marks the book as a testament, a memorial, we may suppose, to the world that disappeared into the crematoria of Auschwitz, the memory hole of Russia, the suburbs of America. This book, then, is an act of Yiskor, an admonition to remember.

But such a reading leaves certain things unexplained: the broken bonds between children and parents and the resounding "No" that frustrates every desire, every generous act. This sorrow, appended to history though it may be, is also unmistakably personal and was planted in the heart before it ever found its image in the world; we may be certain of that. But this heartache, whatever the source, has led Malamud to a deep identification with the tears of the Jewish past and an affection, to the point of love, for a world that his father's generation fled as best it could: the tenement, the candy store, the hand-to-mouth hardships of immigrant life. All Jewish writers respond in some degree to this undertow of ghetto misery, but only Malamud has made a monument to it.

This steady allegiance to a single grief, despite all the vicissitudes of personal fortune and historical change, calls to mind Isaac Rosenfeld's words about Abraham Cahan's David Levinsky, a man who, in *The Rise of David Levinsky,* courts a singular aridity of spirit that he himself does not comprehend.

Because hunger is strong in him, he must always strive to relieve it; but precisely because it is strong, it has to be preserved. It owes its strength to the fact that for so many years everything that influenced Levinsky most deeply – say, piety and mother love – was inseparable from it. For hunger, in this broader, rather metaphysical sense of the term that I have been using, is not only the state of tension out of which the desires for relief and betterment spring; precisely because the desires are formed under its sign, they become assimilated to it, and convert it into the prime source of all value, so that the man, in his pursuit of whatever he considers pleasurable and good, seeks to return to his yearning as much as he does to escape it.

Like Levinsky, Malamud's characters preserve the hunger and court the downside of life out of hidden motives that they mistake for principles. They clamor for their cup of sorrow.

I'm told by Japanese friends that Malamud translates better than other Jewish writers and has a larger audience in Japan than Bellow. I can't testify to the truth of that but it seems plausible. So much of Bellow's power springs from his linguistic virtuosity, whereas Malamud's is rather subterranean and prelinguistic, pressed into images rather than words, Jewbirds rather than Herzogs. These stories are, at their best, symbols of hidden things which have the power, much like myth, to spread wide ripples from very small disturbances. To paraphrase Gide, we should not understand them too quickly.

8

A Portrait of Delmore

It is possible to feel overwhelmed by Delmore Schwartz in death as it was in life. Twenty years after his death on 11 July 1966, the movement to resurrect Schwartz has taken a serious turn. The publication of Schwartz's journals is just a ripple in the tide of Schwartziana that has been swelling since 1975, when Saul Bellow's *Humboldt's Gift* brought Schwartz back into public consciousness as the kibitzer maudit and insomniac laureate of his age. That wave includes Robert Phillips' edition of Schwartz's *Letters*, published in 1984; Schwartz's *Last and Lost Poems* (1979); the collection of "bagatelles," *The Ego is Always at the Wheel* (1986); James Atlas's *Delmore Schwartz: The Life of an American Poet* (1977); the extended portrait of Schwartz in William Barrett's *The Truants* (1982), and Bruce Bawer's essay on Schwartz's poetry in *The Middle Generation: The Lives and Poetry of Delmore Schwartz, Randall Jarrell, John Berryman, and Robert Lowell* (1986). Virtually forgotten after his death, Schwartz has now been brought back to life as a symbol of Jewish intellectual life and a small but vigorous cottage industry.

Much of this industry is the work of Schwartz's literary executor Robert Phillips, who has been toiling in the ruins of Schwartz's career in the hopes, it seems, of making a shrine out of all that shattered masonry. The *Letters*, the *Last and Lost Poems* and the *The Ego is Always at the Wheel* are his labor, and he cautions us in the last book that other publications are likely to be forthcoming: verse plays, unpublished novels, stories, a book-length critical study of T. S. Eliot, and the autobiographical poem that Schwartz wrestled with for years, *Genesis, Book II*. "Much of this material," Phillips has been candid to admit in the preface to *The Ego is Always at the Wheel*, "is not Schwartz at his best," and it is doubtful that any reader of the most recent gleanings will take issue with him.

Phillips has not been alone. Working in tandem to edit, decipher, and publish Schwartz's gargantuan journals has been Schwartz's ex-wife, Elizabeth Pollett, who had been estranged from Schwartz for nine years at the time of his death. The journals, some 2400 pages of sulfur and ash, were among the papers rescued by Dwight Macdonald from a moving company after their whereabouts came to light during a chance encounter in a bar between Macdonald's son and the proprietor of the company. Those 2400 pages were eventually transcribed into 1400 pages of typescript then edited down to something like 900 pages. Entries after 1959, which Ms. Pollett found virtually indecipherable, are omitted.

Schwartz began the journal on his twenty-sixth birthday, 8 December, 1939, and kept at it for twenty-seven years until his death. It began as a diary of the most conventional kind: "In the evening I went to the movie . . . Yesterday we went to see the Fergussons . . . Jay called from Mt. Vernon." Except that literature is Schwartz's constant preoccupation, this is fairly indistinguishable from the diary of an ordinary teenager. It is self-conscious, gossipy, and bristling with resentment. Keeping track of social encounters and the social injuries he invariably provoked was Schwartz's chief preoccupation. But by 1942, the journal had become a catch-all for whatever impressions were percolating through his mind: poems, limericks, epigrams, puns, sendups, assaults, appeals, diatribes – the effluvia of his restless imagination. When Schwartz was in one of his manic moods, the journal took on the qualities of a Joycean *monologue interieur*, and Schwartz's lifelong fascination with Joyce, whom he transcribed into his notebooks as a discipline of style, may have inspired his erratic and spontaneous method of notation. But in Schwartz's hands the Joycean manner – fleeting impressions joined by threads of association – often dispensed with the associations. Early on, the journal suggests a basic disorganization. By 1942, when Schwartz was twenty-nine and at the height of his powers, the private writing was already showing signs of decomposition, as though the tide of impressions was no longer under control. Two years later, while keeping up a brave front as a poet and man of letters, he privately admitted defeat:

> This lifelong sickness which robs me of my self, which takes away my power, which made me a poor student, the author of unfinished works, or works which deceive me very much: at last I know it is a sickness, and that I am hardly to blame, to blame myself – at least that much is understood.

The sickness was never precisely pinpointed, though insomnia was Schwartz's chief torment, and the remedies he indulged to combat it had a shattering effect on every mental faculty: his concentration, his character, his work habits. The journal is a twenty-year-long pathogram, which shows us Schwartz sliding into a limbo of alcohol, amphetamines, and barbiturates until disorder has become his only order, scatter his only unity, everywhere his sole direction.

5 July [1945] I took Benzedrine at 3:30. St. Louis 7, Giants 5. I rejected ten mss. I took a haircut. I had breakfast with E.; lunch with [Milton] Klonsky; I dined with *The New Yorker* at the Sevilla. I wrote one painful page. I glanced through Auden's collected poems and was distressed by the titles. "Don't be Careful." Spoke to Edna [Phillips] on the phone.

Page after hopeless page, the journal proceeds in this fractured and banal fashion, the self-regard punctuated by jokes and epiphanies and, on good days, poems on the theme of his torment:

> I held a seashell to my year and heard
> My heart roar PANDEMONIUM which was to say
> Every demon from hell yells in your heart
> – Although you thought you heard the senseless sea,
> You only heard yourself.

Schwartz's poetry was all misery and form, and the misery being constant, his perennial quest was for a proper form. "Form is an endless effort," he writes, "and not only that, but perhaps the secret of life." Again, "Every success I knew was from the fecundative power of form." These are standard claims, and yet in the context of these journals they seem like pleas for redemption. Cut loose from any sustaining ideas, Schwartz took form alone for his grail, and even that grail could seem at times to be nothing larger than a shotglass: "All literature," he would declare nonchalantly, "is an effort at the formal character of the epigram" and he hoarded epigrams as a comedian hoards punch lines.

Schwartz's performance, as he turned the inner pandemonium into a theater of personality, had a hypnotic effect on others. "Mankind is stunned by the Exuberance and Beauty of certain individuals," observed Bellow in *Humboldt's Gift*. "When a Manic Depressive escapes from his Furies he's irresistible." In his book *New York Jew*, Alfred Kazin would remember "the headlong rush of words that seemed to engage every muscle in his face as he twisted and spat in the rage of his opinions." But Schwartz's improvisations are not so compelling in print as they were face to face. The command was in the delivery, which wedded the manic-depressive's intoxication to the tummler's sense of timing, without which the exuberant lines fade into narcissism and exaggeration; they seem merely gaudy without being particularly potent, and Ms. Pollett herself steps outside the glow of her own devotion long enough to express disappointment in "the lopsidedness of the entries and the impossibilities, finally, of language to render life." This book might be thought of as the script for a great tragicomic performance in which puns and one-liners take the place of heroic verse. Schwartz was a dynamo of quips, a machine for generating *bon mots* and a few *mauvais* ones as well. "What this country needs is a good five-cent psychiatrist"; "Philip Rahv has his good qualities, but he never lets them stand in his way"; "She was the wife of the party; he was engaged in holy wedlock"; "'How do you like Kipling?' 'I never drink it'"; "A horse divided against itself cannot stand"; "All gall is divided into three parts: arrogance, insensitivity, self-dramatization." Schwartz aspired, it seems, to be Milton Berle, but such a Berle as himself might yearn to be T.S. Eliot, taking the measure of modern life in iambs and singing to the mermaids while chewing on a cigar. Schwartz was a study in contradictions. On the one side lay a heaviness, immanence, a nervous, exasperated life, and a sluggish physicality, "the heavy bear who goes with me."

> When I go down to sleep
>   To sleep
> I am wood I am
>   Stone I am a slow
> River, hardly flowing
> & all is warm & all is animal
> – I am stone, I am river
> I am wood – a wood but not
>   A leaf . . .

Then again, in raptures of illumination, he was the bard of air and wind, music and light.

> Music is not water, but it moves like water
> It is not fire but it soars as warm as the sun
> It is not rock, it is not fountain,
> But rock and fountain, clock and mountain
> Abide within it, bound together
> In radiance pulsing, vibrating, and reverberating,

Dominating the domination of the weather.

This cadenza appears in 1959, when, gloomy and and dazed, Schwartz could still snatch a grace beyond the reach of amphetamines. Playing Ariel to his own Caliban, he could outflank his depression long enough to strike the silver note. It is remarkable. The journal, otherwise sodden and world weary, suddenly melts into air. Perhaps these were no more than the normal gyrations of the manic depressive, whose capricious moods can drag him from the condos of heaven to the ghettos of hell in minutes, but one is struck all the same by their extremity: how utterly black were the black moods and how dazzling the light ones.

I wish I could report that this volume was a joy to read or that it returned me to Schwartz's writing with renewed appreciation. Unfortunately, it is a trial that no one will pick up casually. The scatter is appalling, and if these journals in any way can be said to capture Schwartz's furious presence, it is only by documenting in brutal detail his confusion and grief and the venom that poisoned all his social relations. The brilliant range of reference that Bellow and others have recorded – "Yeats, Apollinaire, Lenin, Freud, Morris R. Cohen, Gertrude Stein, baseball statistics, and Hollywood gossip" – was no more than that, a range of reference and evidence of a mind that had mistaken gossip for thought and had gotten lost in the cosmopolitan wilderness somewhere between James Joyce and Hedda Hopper. Schwartz's mind was an encyclopedia from which everything had been scratched but the titles, and he had an inkling of his own depthlessness: "As with an onion," he wrote, "illusion after illusion is peeled off – what remains? Nothing at all – ".

What did Schwartz believe? These journals present us with a man without a gospel, who by that fact alone stood apart from his fellow *Partisan Review* editors, all of whom were virtuosi of gospel. One looks in vain for a significant politics: Roosevelt appears seven times in the index, Trotsky four times, Stalin only twice, and they are only names among names. One looks for an emotional agenda, a social doctrine, a code of human relations, a burning metaphysic – anything. Even a poetic. The terrible truth, alas, was that behind the poetry was a void that Schwartz sought desperately to fill with words, as if to hide from himself the absence of meaning. Instead of meaning we find personality, instead of thought, declamation. Schwartz performed the rare feat of baring his breast while hiding his heart, electing to complain, to joke, to dramatize himself, and above all to itemize with dull perseverance every drink, every pill, every slight, every grievance, every frivolity, every frisson, and every pang, until the tabula rasa was smudged with grief and clotted with verse.

It is not too strong to say that this is an appalling book and that Schwartz is diminished by these raids on his papers. The journals are 663 pages long, the letters 384, the "bagatelles" 143. By comparison, a fine little compendium of Schwartz's best poems published in England in 1976, *What is to be Given?* (Manchester: Carcanet New Press), is but 75 pages long and is simply overwhelmed by the ephemera. *Portrait of Delmore* shows us the poet at his most disheveled, stripped of his defenses and his dignity. Maybe what is lacking is only the ersatz dignity of literary form and verbal composure, but ersatz or real it is vital to the artist who digs deep into himself and mines the seams of his own shame for his art. At such times, one sympathizes with Kafka's plea to Max Brod to destroy all his papers after his death. We're all the richer for Brod's betrayal of his friend, but Schwartz left nothing like *The Trial* behind him when he died.

Delmore Schwartz in all his vanity and turmoil, his narcissism and pain, is growing uncommonly familiar to us these days, while the poetry is sliding out of focus. A generation of readers that knows nothing of Schwartz's great poem "Seurat's Sunday Afternoon along the Seine" is now expert in his insomnia, his drinking, his rages, and his crackup. There have got to be better forms of homage than these 648 pages of undigested journal. Surely there are shorter ones.

9

Zuckerman's Travels

Psychoanalysis may be passing from the scene of American intellectual life as a reliable index to human behavior, but not before making a permanent contribution to our common understanding of how fiction is to be read. Among the ideas to survive the demise of the system are *ambivalence, overdetermination* and the belief that all expressions of human desire save the most basic and biological express a collision, rather than a harmony, of motives. Certainly, without such concepts at hand we are disarmed before anything as complex as contemporary literature, and without doubt we are disarmed before a writer as nimble and as mercurial as Philip Roth, who has made of ambivalence not only an art but a theory of art, producing out of his arguments with himself a literature as richly conceived and intricately designed as any in America. No longer "case histories," however, as they once seemed to be, his books have lately evolved into theaters of uncertainty in which characters perform dramatic charades of ambivalence that in the past might have been interpreted as "acting out." *The Counterlife* (New York: Farrar, Straus & Giroux, 1987) is the most recent and most impressive of Roth's late theatrical novels, all the more impressive, I'd like to say, for possessing at once a theatrical lightness and a historical gravity. An elegant novel, it performs an elaborate counterpoint between the inertia of history and the agility of the imagination, and would appear to be evidence, if such were needed, that it is possible for a novel to contradict itself repeatedly and turn out all the more convincing for its contradictions.

The Counterlife is latest of the Zuckerman books, a series that now includes four novels, two stories – "useful fictions" embedded in *My Life as a Man* – and one novella, *The Prague Orgy*, an appendix to the collected Zuckerman tales, *Zuckerman Bound*. It is not, however, a unified story but a story cycle featuring Nathan Zuckerman, his brother Henry, Henry's wife Carol, and the usual troupe of delectable shiksas, all different and all named Maria. A tale told in five movements, *The Counterlife* more closely resembles *Gulliver's Travels* than a conventional novel, though the five acts rather than four voyages may be Roth's way of hinting that Shakespeare, not Swift, is its patron saint. (Or is it the five books of Moses that we are expected to recognize?) If the Zuckerman books up until now are the Zuckerman variations, this one by itself is the Zuckerman fugue: a Grosse Fugue to round out Roth's late quartets.

The movements are "Basel," "Judea," "Aloft," "Gloucestershire," and "Christendom," which form something of a circuit, insofar as the end of "Christendom" represents no particular resolution of the problems posed in "Basel." Each "voyage" (by plane, of course) is a restatement in different terms of the book's central problem: what is a Jew and how is he (and it is always *he*) to live? Setting the variations into motion is "Basel," the account of Nathan Zuckerman's brother Henry, a New Jersey dentist whose exhausted marriage has driven him into a couple of affairs, the first being with Maria from Basel. Though Henry and Maria are in love, their mutual marriages eventually win out, and in time Maria returns to husband, to Basel, and to oblivion. Ten years later, Henry develops an attachment to his dental assistant, Wendy, who treats him to regular after-hours fellatio, until Henry begins taking a medicine (a "beta blocker") for his heart condition, a side effect of which is the inhibition of potency. In despair over his inability to gratify Wendy's "oral hangup," he opts for by-pass surgery and dies on the operating table. The chapter ends after the funeral, with Nathan pondering his notes on his brother's affairs and his own guilt for failing to dissuade Henry from the operation.

The import of the book's title becomes at the start of "Judea," where Henry, fabricating a counter-life for himself, turns out to be alive and in flight from dentistry and domesticity for Israel and a militant Zionist kibbutz on the West Bank. This counter-Henry, now calling himself Hanoch, packs a revolver and sits at the feet of one Mordecai Lippman, an apocalyptic Zionist and pioneer of the settlement movement in Judea and Samaria. It is to this settlement, Agor, that Nathan goes to visit Henry, only to find himself under siege from Henry's colleagues for his "Diaspora abnormality" – four Gentile wives – and for his failure to make his own *aliyah*. Despite this, or maybe because of it, Nathan comes to appreciate, without ever falling under, the spell of Lippman, whose apocalyptic scenarios are charged with the elements of powerful, if primitive, art. Among his prophecies is one of a coming pogrom in America carried out by Blacks, whom the Gentiles are quietly grooming to wipe out the Jews. The Gentiles, it seems, will then fall upon the Blacks and wipe *them* out. The story is screwball enough to condemn Lippman as a paranoid and yet faithful enough to the racial tensions of American life to blur the line between paranoia and prophecy. And vivid enough to make it mesmerizing to the credulous. Lippman is a gifted story teller, like Roth himself, with a flair for making implausible dramatizations sound like imminent catastrophes, and Zuckerman, who has an appreciation for what the imagination does, has to be warned by an Israeli journalist friend not to mistake vividness for intellectual depth or moral stature. A lesson, one thinks, about art itself, not just apocalyptic messianism.

Previously, at the wailing wall, Nathan had been accosted by a young American pilgrim, Jimmy Ben-Joseph Lustig of West Orange New Jersey, who is a reader of Nathan's books and author of his own prophetic tractate, The Five Books of Jimmy. A baseball fan to boot, he laments, "That's the thing that's missing here. How can there be Jews without baseball? . . . Not until there is baseball in Israel will the Messiah come! Nathan, I want to play center field for the Jerusalem Giants!" Vivid, engaging, his eyes aglitter with prophecy, he finds himself in major league trouble in "Aloft," where he turns out to be a highjacker who sneaks a gun and a grenade aboard an El Al airliner in the name of abolishing the Jewish past. But he is jumped by Israeli security guards, stripped, searched, and beaten. Nathan, for sitting next to him, is forcibly undressed, given an anal search, and treated to a long, blithering, inspired lecture on Jews, Gentiles, Satan, Billy Budd, T. S. Eliot, and Eliot's Bleistein with a cigar by a security guard who coaches Nathan along the way: "If only we had T. S. Eliot on board today. I'd teach him about cigars. And you'd help, wouldn't you? Wouldn't you, a literary figure like yourself, help me educate the great poet about Jewish cigars?" Nathan, naked, handcuffed, and frightened out of his wits can only be agreeable: "If necessary."

This is vintage Roth, playing terror as vaudeville and devising fiendish new steps for the choreography of comedy and peril that has been his stock-in-trade from the start. I'll stop short of summarizing "Gloucestershire" and "Christendom," which, in any event, are rich and surprising and beyond paraphrase. Suffice it to say that in "Glouchestershire" it is Nathan who suffers the heart trouble, takes that Beta blocker, and dies on the operating table for the sake of *his* Maria, a young English woman. But death doesn't prevent Nathan from interviewing Maria from beyond the grave, nor Maria from answering him in the cool phraseology of the English midlands that makes her a dead ringer for something out of Jane Austen. Finally, in "Christendom," Nathan is brought back to life in England, as Henry had been in Israel, to settle down in London with his proper, ladylike Maria. However, a collision with English anti-Semitism sends him into a nasty tantrum that drives Maria not only out of his life, but out of his book as well. "I'm leaving the book," she announces when he refuses to be reasonable, and poof, out she goes.   This summary hardly does justice to a book so calibrated and nuanced and so attuned to the conundrums of Jewish identity that the reader has to attend it page by page to stay even with its maneuvers. And seldom have those maneuvers been more agile. Here as elsewhere, Roth shows us why it pays to read him closely; every line is packed with ore and nothing is thrown away. But beyond the deaths and resurrections, the sure-handed changes of pace, the swift and confident changes of costume and locale, and the brittle Tom Stoppard repartee, Roth is up to something major in *The Counterlife* that makes it seem a more auspicious novel than the three that preceded it: *The Ghost Writer, Zuckerman Unbound*, and *The Anatomy Lessons*? What is it?

The answer I think is two-fold, encompassing Roth's method on the one hand and his conception of himself on the other. Technically, Roth has put himself in unfamiliar territory, deconstructing Zuckerman in order to build a stage for his performances. Nathan Zuckerman is Roth's "decentered" character, not only lacking a firm and defined sense of self, which might describe any Roth character, but lacking here even a consistent story to give his life at least the unity of action. It is as if what was psychological in earlier books is finally structural here: neurosis, if you like, become technique. This lack of a firm profile has been Roth's compact with Zuckerman from the start, in *My Life as a Man*, and in one extreme moment, indeed, Zuckerman is emptied of virtually everything that had once constituted his identity. In a coda of despair at the end of *Zuckerman Unbound*, Zuckerman, having lost both father and mother, having alienated his brother and left his girlfriend, returns to the point of his origins to contemplate the ruins of Newark, and standing before his old house in what is now a Black neighborhood, he is confronted with a young Black man, his head shaved, with a German shepherd dog in tow. "'Who you supposed to be?'" the man asks.

"No one," replied Zuckerman, and that was the end of that. You are no longer any man's son, you are no longer some good woman's husband, you are no longer your brother's brother, and you don't come from anywhere anymore, either.

This is as despairing as any of Roth's bleak conclusions, yet it also holds out the promise, if only in the reader, for regeneration. "Now," says Alex Portnoy's Dr. Spielvogel, "vee may perhaps to begin," and at the end of *Zuckerman Unbound* we might perhaps to begin again. For to be no one is to be potentially anyone, and Zuckerman could be invented afresh, as in fact he is in each of the Zuckerman novels. In *The Counterlife*, indeed, Roth reinvents him fully five times, giving him a slightly different character profile and destiny in each chapter. Only their deep histories, their childhoods, seem to be identical. If that bears some resemblance to repertory theater, it is intentional, since Roth seems committed in his recent books to a theatrical view of the novel as inventive, playful, and improvisational, because, it seems, *life is that way*. The American myth of the self-made man is post-modernized: improvisational man takes his place in the novel as a stand-in for the self-improvising character of our time. "Look, I'm all for authenticity," announces Nathan Zuckerman during a squabble with Henry, "but it can't begin to hold a candle to the human gift for play-acting. That may be the only authentic thing that we *ever* do."

We know, because Roth has uttered such sentiments before, that we are being treated to a Wildean lesson about the authenticity of masks, and if we've been reading Roth right along we can even guess why: to deny, for the nth time, that his characters can be identified with their author, an error for which Roth has taken more than his fair share of abuse. One aim of the Nathan-Henry-Maria repertory theater in *The Counterlife* is to drive home the point once and for all about the separation of art and artist and to close the book on the question of whether Nathan Zuckerman or Peter Tarnopol or David Kepesh or Alex Portnoy is or is not Philip Roth.

But, then, read this way the book is not only discomfitingly defensive, it is also embarrassingly trendy: a work of fictive deconstruction in which Roth catches up at last with the Coovers, the Barths, the Hawkeses, the Gasses, the Federmans, and the whole international coterie of advanced writers who take their *Weltanschauung* from Jacques Derrida, their authority from Yale, and their style from the more extravagant chapters of Joyce's *Ulysses*.

Read as a theater of fashionable indeterminism, *The Counterlife* seems a bit of a shell game, one, moreover, without a pea. Under which Zuckerman do you find the Roth? But Roth is not a shell artist, and intuition tells us that he is after bigger game than an exegesis in *Diacritics* and that beneath the carousel of charades and improvisations there is a very substantial Roth, whose presence may be felt everywhere if located precisely nowhere.

It is a somewhat unfamiliar Roth, however, *Roth the Jew*. Of course, Roth's Jewishness has never been precisely under wraps, but it has been in the past largely a Jewishness of sensibility and self-consciousness – a bromide of panic and responsibility, to borrow a phrase from Richard Gilman. It was a psychological condition and a form of disablement, for which Kafka supplied the metaphor, impotence (or sometimes literature) the symptom, and psychoanalysis the treatment. In earlier books we had the vaudeville of *Portnoy's Complaint* and *The Breast* or the hijinx of *The Great American Novel*, in which the trials of a wandering baseball team stand for those of the Jewish people. The Jewishness of *The Counterlife* is, by contrast, a historical Jewishness and a source of meaning, if not precisely of strength. In *The Counterlife*, Roth begins to examine the collective identity and situation of the Jews, first through Henry/Hanoch and his aliyah and then, tentatively, carefully, inconclusively, through Nathan as well.

In "Judea," Roth plants in Henry's mouth a rejection of the very brand of selfhood that Roth's books, up until now, have been all about. Nathan has been pestering Henry to tell him more about himself, until Henry, provoked, responds: "The hell with *me*, forget *me*. *Me* is somebody *I* have forgotten. *Me* no longer exists out here. There isn't time for *me*, there isn't need of *me* – here Judea counts, not *me*!" Henry, as Hanoch, has submitted himself to a collective identity and turned against all that Nathan stands for: psychiatry, soul-searching, irony, self-dramatization, the purely personal – his diaspora abnormality. Nathan is not prepared to forswear that abnormality just yet; it remains the root and ground of his being, but he is not unmoved by sentiments of group solidarity, and for the first time in Roth's books, one senses that immersion in a collective, historically-determined culture is no longer entirely out of the question. It is not chosen, but neither is it rejected completely out of hand. All that is rejected is apocalyptic messianism, which is simply one of the forms that Jewish collective identity may take.

Where Roth remains steadfast is that the formation and understanding of the self is still very much his project, only now operating under new ground rules: the rules of *theater*, in which one exhibits oneself only in disguise, and the rules of *history*, in which the self appears as a resultant of forces: powers, cultures, traditions, movements, emigrations, wars, bloodlines, blood. Those ground rules are in direct conflict, however, since the theatrical view of the self denies authenticity while the historical demands it. The writer may play fast and loose with the *I*, doing anything with Zuckerman that suits his fancy or his vision of life, but he dare not tamper with the *we*. Jewish history is not something to be arbitrarily re-invented. And it is this collision of basic agendas, the theatrical agenda and the historical, that gives *The Counterlife* its weight and its tension and makes it the unsettling and absorbing book that it is.*

The plot lines of Roth's career are tangled, and it would be foolhardy to look for a simple story in the development of Roth's work since the onset of the Zuckerman series. It is not for nothing that the latest effort exfoliates into five distinct stories, featuring five Zuckermans in radically different situations. If repertory theater hadn't given us the model for understanding this, psychiatry would have, and there was a time in reading Roth when we'd have routinely reached for our Freud, if not our Havelock Ellis, to make sense of it all. I know I have. So, for that matter, has Roth; In the books from *Portnoy's Complaint* through *The Breast*, *My Life as a Man*, and *The Professor of Desire*, and including the comic capers, *The Great American Novel* and *Our Gang*, all that was problematic, mysterious, and beyond reason in human behavior was subject to understanding, when at all, in terms provided by the mental health professions, and Roth was quick to cite the analyst, Spielvogel in some books, Klinger in others, just in case we failed to grasp the point.

---

* As if to practice what Zuckerman preaches, Roth rounds out his latest book, the autobiographical *The Facts*, with a kibitzing Zuckerman who comes forward at the end to accuse Roth of eluding issues and begging questions and producing, under the guise of autobiography, just another novel whose relation to the "facts" of Roth's life is no less problematic than in any of the recent *roman-à-clef* novels. That book appeared too close to the completion of this essay to be taken fully into account, but it does nothing to disturb my basic conclusion that the fictional element, the "role playing," in Roth's books is neither interesting nor penetrating unless there is an authentic self – a self composed of heart and feeling and consciousness, *not* of facts – to make the theatrics worth caring about.

All that has long since been overthrown, and drama now is the new, and more capacious, metaphor and point of reference for the irrational self. Besides permitting more without the charge of pathology, it also just plain permits more, and what we used to see clinically we now see stylistically. Illness, we might say, has matured into dialectics. At the end of "Christendom," Roth, speaking *in propria persona*, addresses the Maria who has taken a voluntary leave from his book and explains to her as best he can what he has been up to in the performance of Zuckerman.

> I realize that what I am describing, people divided in themselves, is said to characterize mental illness and is the absolute opposite of our idea of emotional integration. The whole Western idea of mental health runs in precisely the opposite direction: what is desirable is congruity between your self-consciousness and your natural being. But there are those whose sanity flows from the conscious *separation* of those two things. If there even *is* a natural being, an irreducible self, it is rather small, I think, and may even be the root of all impersonation – the natural being may be the skill itself, the innate capacity to impersonate. I'm talking about recognizing that one is acutely a performer, rather than swallowing whole the guise of naturalness and pretending that it isn't a performance but you.

This is a step beyond a description of the Zuckerman tales as Roth's repertory theater; it is, rather, a statement of life itself as inherently theatrical, and the Zuckerman variations then being faithfully mimetic, true-to-life. That is all very postmodern of Roth, and I don't completely buy it except as a statement of method. It isn't as if the artist, anymore than the rest of us, recasts the ground of his being every time he sits down at the word processor to cut and paste another self. ˆKB, ˆKK, ˆKV, and voilà, a new person. The contemporary cybernetic self is notoriously mobile, but mobility has limits that define sanity in the individual and character in the novel. For a literary character to come to life it must have the consistency, the plausibility, and the limitedness of life itself. Zuckerman's roles all have that: the Zuckerman Follies is a determined and law-abiding theater. To cite a simple example: Zuckerman may marry a gentile – he may marry five of them – but he can never become one. Thinking in terms of music may make the point clearer. The variations have neither spirit nor charm without the theme.

The impulse behind Zuckerman's pronouncements, however, makes abundant sense. In the sixties, when Roth took up psycho-analysis, for whatever therapeutic reasons, it was also for reasons of expanding his sense of being: to find out what was in the unconscious and to enrich his characters, as well as himself, with a deeper and darker vocabulary of motives. But psychoanalysis was publicly overthrown when Peter Tarnopol in *My Life as a Man* walked out on his Dr. Spielvogel without looking back and used the book not only to chastise Spielvogel for sloppy ethics in publishing an article about him but also to register the claim that there were depths beyond the Freudian unconscious that a man had to explore on his own. In fits and starts, Roth's career since *My Life as a Man* has been an exercise in getting beyond the platitudes of the Freudian system and finding resonances and amplitudes that expand and enrich the character rather than, as psychoanalysis finally does, infantilize and deplete it. And that way points eventually away from analysis toward synthesis, toward putting the self back together through history and culture.

As he was working on the Zuckerman trilogy, Roth was also editing a series for Penguin books, *Writers From the Other Europe*, devoted to modern writers from Eastern Bloc nations: Tadeusz Borowski, Tadeusz Konwicki, Milan Kundera, Ludvik Vaculik, Bruno Schulz, Witold Gombrowicz, George Konrad, and others. What Roth discovered in his forays into Eastern Europe was a literature as paradoxical, as erotic, and as darkly comic as his own and a continuity between his own most florid imaginings and the main lines of modernist thought. But to discover himself as a European, Roth was obliged to invent his connection to that middle-European world, since for a boy from Newark to imagine himself a stepchild of Prague required a recycling of the self into a richer and more formidable creature than Weequahic High School commonly produced.

Franz Kafka was the catalyst for this recycling and was Roth's Virgil through the inferno of Eastern Europe. The Kafka influence first emerges in two lovely novellas of the mid-1960s, *The Breast*, an erotic reprise of Kafka's *Metamorphosis* in which the hero is turned not into an insect but a gigantic female breast, and Roth's most appealing piece of short fiction, "'I Always Wanted You to Admire My Fasting'; or, Looking at Kafka," in which Kafka, having cheated both tuberculosis and the Holocaust, turns up in Newark as the young Philip Roth's Hebrew School teacher and is maneuvered by Roth's parents into a courtship with Roth's Aunt Rhoda. Kafka being Kafka, something goes awry sexually, and Kafka disappears from Rhoda's, and the fictive Roth's, life, though not from the real Roth's imagination. Consider the story's underlying proposition: "Franz Kafka could have been my uncle." Kafka in Newark evolves into David Kepesh in Prague in *The Professor of Desire* and the dream vision of Kafka's whore inviting him to touch her genitals for the sake of literary history. Lately the Kafka line has given us "The Prague Orgy," the epilogue to *Zuckerman Bound* that finds Nathan Zuckerman in Prague on a mission to recover the manuscripts of a Yiddish writer who died in the Holocaust, but whose stories remain in the hands of a woman, and a state, that will neither honor them nor publish them nor give them up.

With Newark, marriage, therapy, and the bruises of the literary vocation seemingly exhausted, Prague has become a major element of Roth's usable past and a substitute for Spielvogel's couch as a center of myth. The old myths, of infancy, of libido, of a mother's love and tyranny, have given way to myths of Jewishness in torment, in which Franz Kafka stands as an exalted, and *echt* Jewish, symbol. Prague does double duty, as a new model unconscious and a more capacious, more mysterious, and more theatrical version of Jewishness than the one Roth experienced as a boy in Newark, which he symbolized rather bitterly in *The Ghost Writer* in the figure of Judge Leopold Wapter. This is something of a heterodox aliyah, not as Israel or Mordecai Lippman might welcome it but as a man make it in his own soul, its orthodox feature being the written word, the book, that presides over it, as *The Trial*, "The Metamorphosis," and "The Hunger Artist" are raised to the status of midrash, if not Torah itself. Prague, for all its straitness and repressiveness, has appeared to offer new possibilities for the self: involuted, ironic, neurotic, but also stoutly committed to Jewish identity.

Prague, however, is only a halfway house on the road to Judea, and *The Counterlife* comes into focus as the next station on the journey of self-integration, the port of call where the rootless cosmopolitan fits himself out with historical roots, not by surrendering himself to militant Zionism, but by listening, questioning, and absorbing the sense of the problematic in contemporary Jewish life. *The Counterlife* is steeped in perplexity *and* in Jewish history; it grafts the theatrical upon the historical, quite as if Roth has extrapolated his own ambiguities onto the Jewish nation and discovered in the world without as actual what was in his world within as possible. In a shrewd review of *The Counterlife* in *Commentary*, Robert Alter notes that the book's uncertainties reflect the condition of contemporary Jewish existence.

> It may sound puzzling that all this intense engagement with what deserves to be called, without apology, reality should occur in a novel constructed out of the playing of one fictional hypothesis against another. In point of fact, the self-conscious fictionality of *The Counterlife* proves to be the perfect vehicle for confronting the questions of what it means to be a Jew, given the ambiguous burdens of Jewish history at this particular moment of the late 20th century. Roth has no answers but he recognizes that the dimensions of the question can be seen only by following out a collision course of opposing ideas.

Exactly. The Jewish experience is a maze, a series of open questions that can be posed without being answered, and there is no guide to the perplexed handy for quick reference. We may even say that what Roth has done in *The Counterlife* is to attach himself to Jewish history as a particular instance of the problematic: finding in the troubled "we" a reflection of the turbulent "I." Nathan's brother Henry, casting off the merely personal for the collective, is trading in one unidimensional Jewish life – suburban dentist and after hours hedonist – for another – latter-day pioneer and gun-toting Zionist. One set of blinders is exchanged for another, while Nathan, who is too mercurial a person, can no more become a settler in Agor than he can be a squire in Christendom. Nor can Roth, who will take his own route to Judea, by way of England and Prague.

What saves Zuckerman's hegira from being just tourism is the constant testing of the new world against the self and the self against the world. It is a laboratory approach to life and is not without its problems. In "Christendom," Nathan, now married to his Maria and trying to settle in England, comes under fire from Maria's sister Sarah for playing the "moral guinea pig." It is an interesting charge, which Nathan doesn't really deny; he simply parries it.

> "I think you like to play the moral guinea pig . . . ."
> "How does a moral guinea pig play?"
> "He experiments with himself. Puts himself, if he's a Jew, into church at Christmas time, to see how it feels and what it's like."
> "Oh, everybody does that . . . not just Jews."

"It's easier if one's a success like you."

"What is easier? . . ."

"Everything, without question. But I meant the moral guinea pig bit. You've achieved the freedom to knock around a lot, to go from one estate to the other and see what it's all about. Tell me about success. Do you enjoy it, all that strutting?

"Not enough – I'm not a sufficiently shameless exhibitionist . . . . I can only exhibit myself in disguise. All my audacity derives from masks."

Roth often puts the truth in the mouths of peripheral characters, and Sarah has hit upon a portion of it, though she doesn't know what to make of it, seeing Nathan's rootlessness as merely an irresponsible deployment of freedom – the freedom of fame and money – rather than as a search for meaning in a life whose meaning has always to be constructed. Zuckerman himself seems to mistake his restless and exploratory impulse for nothing more than a propensity for role-playing, as he testifies in his last letter to Maria after she has absconded from the book.

All I can tell you with certainty is that I, for one, have no self, and that I am unwilling and unable to perpetrate upon myself the joke of self. It certainly does strike me as a joke about *my* self. What I have instead is a variety of impersonations I can do, and not only of myself – a troupe of players that I have internalized, a permanent company of actors that I can call upon when a self is required, an ever-evolving stock of pieces and parts that forms my repertoire. But I certainly have no self independent of my imposturing, artistic efforts to have one. Nor would I want one. I am a theater and nothing more than a theater.

If this is Roth speaking *in propria persona* – and there is no test for this except intuition – it is foxhole talk, situational ethics, and while it may have some marginal utility in keeping the New York critics at bay or entertaining the professors with those feints and tropes that academic criticism thrives on, it also keeps readers from consciously grasping what subliminally they must surely sense: that Roth's Jewishness (as opposed to his Judaism) is growing deeper roots and becoming more certain of itself. Despite all the fancy footwork, the book possesses a logic, a weight, and a center of gravity that no amount of theatrics will conceal. That center of gravity may be roughly defined as a movement eastward: elsewhere to Prague or to Anne Frank's Amsterdam (in *The Ghost Writer*), here to Jerusalem, London, Gloucestershire. Along the way, certain goods are acquired: a different slant – many different slants – on his Jewish identity, which he now is rather fierce to defend, and a richer personal culture. The writer from Newark whom Irving Howe once charged with possessing a "thin personal culture" is no longer vulnerable to such accusations, if in fact he ever was. Roth has not settled with Jewishness just yet, and it is quite likely that he never will, but his compass needle points east and the personal culture he has picked up along the way is thicker than ever.

10
Where's Papa

Not long before he died, Ernest Hemingway wrote to one of his literary executors, "It is my wish that none of the letters written by me during my lifetime shall be published. Accordingly, I hereby request and direct you not to publish or consent to the publication by others, of any such letters." That should have been enough to stay the hand of those biographers and publishers avid, like fight promoters, to get one last payday out of the ex-champ, no matter what the cost. Mary Hemingway, to her credit, held out against Carlos Baker and the Scribner Hemingway industry for eighteen years after her husband's death in 1961, only to cave in at last and authorize publication of a book that is both dishonorable and damaging. The dishonor lies in the violation of Hemingway's wishes in the name of some higher claim, some fanciful version of the advancement of learning that Baker calls "the continuing investigation of the life and achievements of one of the giants of twentieth-century literature." Yet to read these letters is to appreciate why Hemingway wanted them kept out of the marketplace, for they place on view in the most vivid fashion all that was most unsavory in the man's private character. The damage done here is not to the man or to the "legend" – which can only matter to those who insist that exemplary writers be also exemplary human beings – but to those books that we once read in confidence as documents of life "in our time." Such raw encounters with the man as these letters afford undermine the authority of the books and put the "continuing investigation" of them on a more treacherous footing, one informed by suspicion and distaste. It is an advance of sorts, but in the direction of substituting an author's life for his books and confusing a biography for a career. It is one of the unsettling side-effects of bringing a writer's life into sharper focus that our confidence in his writing may well be undermined. That appears to be the case with Hemingway.

Ernest Hemingway was a barbarian. That has never been precisely a secret, and yet we've always found chasers to help us swallow the bitter facts: Hemingway's precise, Spartan prose, his athlete's physique and actor's good looks, his independence, his Paul Bunyan feats of courage and endurance. These attributes, admirable in themselves, have made it easy for us in the past to mistake him for something familiar and reassuring: an engaging rough-neck, a devil-may-care adventurer, an American sportsman. Students of literature, who have been trained to take fine writing as sufficient proof of grace, have been most susceptible to Papalotry, the adoration beyond reason of Papa Hemingway. They – we – bridle at the suggestion that someone who writes like an angel may be beyond redemption as a man, which is why the Modern Language Association, with its doctrine of salvation through good words, sometimes strikes us as a Protestant sect – and up until about 1950 it was just that. That art ennobles the artist and redeems his trespasses is an axiom of our literary culture, turning biographers into disciples and giving us such kid-glove treatments of our writers as Carlos Baker's *Ernest Hemingway: A Life Story* and, now, his introduction to these letters:

> It is probable that his shortcomings, which were real, undeniable, and in fact not denied even by himself, were balanced by qualities that more than tipped the scales in his favor. Among his virtues must be named his lifelong perseverance and determination in the use and development of his gifts, his integrity as an artist, his unremitting reverence for the craft he practiced, and his persistent love of excellence, whether in his own work or that of others.

Consider the proposition: that Hemingway the man had his "shortcomings," but that a "reverence for the craft he practiced" counterbalanced them, tipping the scales in his favor. Indeed, if you lose sight of the critic's thumb as the scales tip over toward "innocent," you've missed the first trick of Papalotry – of all literary sanctification for that matter – the confusion of realms that allows skill and perseverance in writing to be evidence of personal moral standing.

The letters, however, are strong medicine for all but the most practiced Papalotrist, and the balances and mitigations customarily called forth in Hemingway's behalf will not sweeten them. They portray him as a tiresome braggart, a malicious adversary who heaped scorn on nearly everyone, a racist, an anti-Semite, and a shallow and boring correspondent who wrote many of his letters –

maybe most of them – when too drunk to write fiction. But first and last they show him as a killer who would catch or drop anything that ventured into the crosshairs of his scope or came within scent of his fishing lures: deer, bear, elk, antelope, tarpon, marlin, lion, pheasant, magpie, you name it. If it had fur, feathers, or scales, Hemingway killed it. The final body count must certainly have run into the tens of thousands, including by his estimate 122 men, 122 "sures" as he called them, taken in battle some time during the three wars he took part in as an ambulance driver and correspondent, without question a world's record for unarmed non-combatants. Ernest Hemingway was the exterminating angel himself, and in taking his own life with a shotgun in 1961 he was obeying the fundamental premise of his being: *life is there to be taken.*

If we have not been overly disturbed by this before, we needn't blame Hemingway. He did everything he could to let us know what sort of man he was, and could not have been more blunt about it than in his book about bullfighting, *Death in the Afternoon.*

> Killing cleanly and in a way which gives you esthetic pride and pleasure has always been one of the greatest enjoyments of a part of the human race . . . . . One of its greatest pleasures . . . is the feeling of rebellion against death which comes from its administering. Once you accept the rule of death, thou shalt not kill is an easily and a naturally obeyed commandment. But when a man is still in rebellion against death he has pleasure in taking to himself one of the godlike attributes: that of giving it. This is one of the most profound feelings in those men who enjoy killing.

Hemingway lived to kill, and the techniques he found aesthetically satisfying, those demonstrations of courage and grace under pressure that stir the heart of the aficionado, were, his protestations aside, strictly luxuries. He'd as soon blast prairie dogs from a car or machine gun sharks from his boat as run with the bulls in Pamplona or practice uppercuts on some hapless writer in a bar. On the subject of his profoundest expertise, the world took him at his word, that he was a quality man, an authority on the finer points of killing. But in his private correspondence he comes across unambiguously as a quantity man, who took exceptional delight in toting up the score.

> Charles shot a bull elk, we shot one together, and I killed one alone. He killed 2 damned fine bucks and a bear and I killed an eagle (flying), trapped a coyote and killed a hell of a big bear.

In April went to Cuba for 10 days and stayed 65 – caught 32 swordfish – learned a lot about Cuba.

Last month caught 18 good dolphin, 5 good wahoos, 6 kingfish (one 54 lbs), a 48–pound snapper, and 7 marlin.

Hemingway's famed precision was never more punctilious than in tabulating the day's slaughter, and there is scarcely anything more repellent in these letters than his repeated self-congratulation over his 122 "sures," who, presumably, were bagged during a brief few months of active combat in 1944. During the World War II, while attached as a correspondent to Colonel "Buck" Lanham's regiment of the 4th Infantry Division, Hemingway was usually armed to the teeth, for which the Army once nearly sent him packing for violating the Geneva Convention. His correspondent's quarters resembled a munitions dump, and he himself was often to be found in the thick of battle. At one point he even took command of a ragtag band of French resistance fighters, with whom he liberated a number of Paris bistros on August 25. Colonel Lanham held him in high esteem as a fighting man and paid him the compliment (or so he took it for a compliment) of calling him the most ruthless man he had ever known. It was some time around the liberation of Paris in 1944 that Hemingway killed his 122 "Krauts," among them, he boasted to Charles Scribner several years later, an SS officer who had been taken captive.

One time I killed a very snotty SS kraut who, when I told him I would kill him unless he revealed what his escape route signs were said: You will not kill me, the kraut stated. Because you are afraid to and because you are a race of mongrel degenerates. Besides it is against the Geneva Convention.

What a mistake you made, brother, I told him and shot him three times in the belly fast and then, when he went down on his knees, shot him on the topside so his brain came out of his mouth or I guess it was his nose.

The next SS I interrogated talked wonderfully.

The story is told with alarming violence. Hemingway was not just relating a grisly wartime experience; he was issuing a warning that Scribner was expected to pass on to others: don't fuck with Papa. The racial note here is unmistakable; his contempt for the snotty SS Kraut was one with his omnibus contempt for all lesser breeds without the law. The story may be fictitious – Hemingway was a notorious fabricator of exploits – but the rage was authentic, and the entire letter to which the murder story belongs is thick with fury. Goaded to anger by a reporter from McCall's who was seeking to interview members of his family, Hemingway threatened to cut off his mother's allowance should she consent to talk. "I hate her guts and she hates mine," he added, and as for the reporter, "Please give that woman such a throw out that she will think twice before she comes down to the whore's end of bar again." Wow.

One is constantly brought up short by Hemingway's anger and the callow social attitudes in which it commonly found expression. "Boid," he wrote to his old boyhood chum, William Smith, in the goony frathouse lingo he affected with his hunting and fishing buddies, "the number of genuwind all Caucasian white guys in the world is limited. I should say that maybe there were 5 or 6 at the most . . . . Ther'd probably be a number more if they didn't marry foecal matter in various forms." "You heard of course," he wrote to Pound, who could be counted upon to sympathize, "of Steffens marriage to a 19 year old Bloomsbury kike intellectual." Elsewhere, "Mason has kiked me so on money that I can't afford taxis . . . ." Michael Arlen, whose writing had been likened to Hemingway's, was "some little Armenian sucker after London names"; Samuel Roth's pirating of Joyce's *Ulysses* "does not make one love the Jews any better." In one letter he elaborated for the benefit of John Dos Passos a fantasy of seizing Key West for a private plantation to be called Southwestern Island Republic. "Am at work on a project to re-enslave the jigs overnight and am fixing up accommodations in the carferries to run chinamen."

> On the first night we massacre the catholics and the jews. The second the protestants who have been lulled into a false sense of security by the events of the first evening. The third night we butcher the free thinkers, the atheists, communists and members of the lighthouse service. The fourth day we fish the gulf and capture another ship to feed our faithful jigs.

To Maxwell Perkins, who complained of the portrait of Robert Cohn in *The Sun Also Rises*, he snorted, "And why not make a Jew a bounder in literature as well as in life? Do Jews always have to be so splendid in writing?"

All this sounds depressingly familiar. So many of Hemingway's contemporaries took the literary life for a sanctuary of the socially privileged that their art in certain tangents sounded like a school of racial contempt. Eliot's Jew, the landlord, squatted on the window sill in "Gerontian," while Pound's captains of usura ("Canto XLV") were off slaying the child in the womb, bringing palsy to bed, and generally playing havoc CONTRA NATURAM. Under the cloak of "making it new," there was much of such foolishness. Pound, of course, parlayed his generation's most bankrupt sentiments to their most desperate conclusions in his wartime radio broadcasts for Italian Fascism, though it is not Pound whom Hemingway most resembled in his social prejudices but Eliot. Pound's anti-Semitism was something of a harebrained radicalism heated by poetic fever. It was enriched with ideas about banking and credit, Jefferson and Confucius, and God-knows-what. It aspired to be a profound social idea. Hemingway's anti-Semitism, like Eliot's, was just old-fashioned midwestern old boy snobbery, the snobbery of proper birth, proper schooling, and proper know-how. The properly schooled white guy was one who knew how to bait a hook, tie a fly, slip a punch, load his own ammo, and mix a damn fine martini ("just enough vermouth to cover the bottom of the glass, ounce 3/4 of gin, and the spanish cocktail onions very crisp and also 15 degrees below zero when they go into the glass"). It was not without cause that Matthew Arnold called the English aristocracy "the barbarians" and described their fetishes as a passion for field sports, the care of the body, and the cultivation of manly exercises, good looks, and fine complexion. Hemingway's personal culture, it is plain, was bred in the bone by generations of barbarians who worshipped the twin gods of Manly Vigor and Savoir Faire.

It took the war and the example of Pound to finally purge Hemingway of his anti-Semitism, and after 1945 the more malignant of his bigotries slipped quietly away. He was being absolutely sincere when he wrote to Robert Frost in 1957 that he detested Pound's politics, his anti-Semitism, and his racism. He even struck up, late in life, a warm friendship with Bernard Berenson, whom he eventually addressed as "my brother, my father, my HERO." Make of that what you will. Hemingway was never to be free of his rage, but the war taught him to parcel it out in a more democratic fashion and to detest men for themselves alone.

It is generally conceded that Hemingway's career divides sharply in two: the first part comprising the two early novels, *The Sun Also Rises* and *A Farewell to Arms*, and two volumes of stories, *In Our Time* and *Men Without Women*, the second consisting of all subsequent writing, with exemptions granted to a few later stories ("The Snows of Kilimanjaro") and, with some reluctance, *The Old Man and the Sea*. In other words, by the 1930s and Hemingway's own thirties – he was born in 1899 – the freshness and vitality that had made him the bright star among the American expatriates in Paris had begun to deliquesce into the vanity and bluster of the later books, starting with *Death in the Afternoon* ("bull in the afternoon," said Max Eastman) and rising to intolerable crescendos in *Across the River and Into the Trees* and the posthumously-published *Islands in the Stream*.

The usual interpretation credits this deterioration to Hemingway's own befuddlement, his yielding up his gifts to his own heroic mythos of potency, courage, and action, until he lost entirely the ability to tell the difference between the sporting life and the life of the mind. There is truth in that: the later books are patently the work of a damaged and perplexed man, who had lost beyond retrieval the self-possession of his youth. But the letters also show us something quite unexpected: that the swaggering, vainglorious sportsman photographed with his marlin in Key West, his lion in the Serengeti, his elk in Wyoming – invariably beaming at the camera as if to say, "Here, I've just bagged the unconscious itself" – was there from the start, and that the early achievements of poise and grace in writing and the social ethic of *non serviam* were won against great personal odds. At the very height of his success in the mid-1920s, Hemingway could be as tedious, gauche, and maudlin as a college boy on a summer tour of the cafes and Bierstuben of Europe. "I guess this is a lousy snooty letter," he wrote to Sherwood Anderson, apologizing for his parody of Anderson in *The Torrents of Spring*. " and it will seem like a lousy snooty book. That wasn't the way I wanted this letter to be – nor the book."

> It looks, of course, as though I were lining up on the side of the smart jews like Ben Hecht and those other morning glories and that because you had always been swell to me and helped like the devil on the in our time I felt an irresistible need to push you in the face with true writer's gratitude. But what I would like you to know, and of course that sounds like bragging, is – oh hell, I can't say that either.

To Bill Smith:

> Sure I know how you felt when you indited that screed and I had made a more than offensive bludy ass of myself with Y.K.

but Doodles had my goat and a goatless male ain't renowned for sound and noble actions. To hell with all that.

To Harold Loeb, the model for Robert Cohn in *The Sun Also Rises*:

> I was terribly tight and nasty to you last night and I dont want you to go away with that nasty insulting lousiness as the last thing of the fiestas. I wish I could wipe out all the mean-ness and I suppose I cant but this is to let you know that I'm thoroly ashamed of the way I acted and the stinking, unjust uncalled for things I said.

Sure we know what some of those things were. To Pauline Pfeiffer, for whom he was about to leave his first wife, Hadley, he wrote a letter that took leave of grammar altogether:

> All I can think is that you that are all I have and that I love more than all that is and have given up everything for and betrayed everything for and killed off everything for are being destroyed and your nerves and your spirit broken all the time day and night and that I can't do anything about it because you won't let me /sic passim/.

> So I know this is a lousy terribly cheap self pitying letter just wallowing in bathos etc. etc. etc. and etc. and so it is. O Christ I feel terribly.

And to Scott Fitzgerald:

> If this is a dull shitty letter it is only because I felt so bad that you were feeling low – am so damned fond of you and whenever you try to tell anybody anything about working or "life" it is always bloody platitudes –

The dull shitty letters follow one after the other, without an idea, a fresh image, or an insight that is not a platitude. One looks in vain for the celebrated author of *The Sun Also Rises*, of "Big Two-Hearted River," of the Nick Adams who, propped against the church wall, a bullet in his spine, speaks to a dying Italian, "Senta Rinaldi. Senta. You and me we've made a separate peace." One finds instead just this tiresome young man practicing every day to become a legend and a bore and signing himself Papa at the age of twenty-eight.

What are we to make of this? Malcolm Cowley once proposed the mystical Jungian explanation of the "shadow side" of the personality to account for Hemingway's inconsistencies, and mystical explanations are as good as any when the subject is something as obscure as a man's relation to his art. What is apparent is that Hemingway was able at first to divide up his life in such a way as to exclude all that was soft in his nature from his writing, and permit only a wiser, more disciplined version of himself, Jake Barnes or Nick Adams, access to print. The writing matured separately from the man. And just as the callow, self-inflating side of Hemingway was prevented at first from spilling over into his work, so the sensibility that had taken the measure of modern warfare and the cruelties of life "in our time" with such keen assurance was not to be found in Hemingway's social relations. The young Hemingway in his letters consistently played the *faux naif*, and it is painful to observe this young man, the toast of the literary world and the inventor while yet in his twenties of an entire modern idiom for American writing, acting the fool for wives, lovers, fellow writers, and old fishing cronies.

The answer may be nothing more complicated than a case of Hemingway drunk and Hemingway sober, a distinction that would be most sharply drawn in the 1920s, before the long stupor of the banquet and safari years. Hemingway consumed prodigious amounts of alcohol, first as a discipline of manhood, later as a way of life. Yet nowhere in the many memoirs one reads of Hemingway is he spoken of as an alcoholic. Maybe that is because he always left the bar under his own power or had the constitution and temperament to cover the effects of his drinking with exploits rather than tears and recriminations in the manner of Scott Fitzgerald and Harold Stearns, the model for Harvey Stone in *The Sun Also Rises*. (Passers by in Paris, seeing Stearns sprawled in some doorway, were said to remark, "There lies civilization in the United States.") I find it heard to imagine that Hemingway drank less than they; he was simply built to drink as they were not and suffered the illusion that he was the better man for it. Here, at least, bravado and self-command served him badly. The manly art of holding your liquor is no favor to the shell-shocked brain that cares nothing for courage; it wants only oxygen.

I can think of no other American writer whose presence *as a writer* was so overwhelmingly physical. Norman Mailer has tried with moderate success to emulate Hemingway's compulsive masculinity, but he never produced a prose that was of itself symbolic of muscularity and power. Hemingway treated writing as an athletic event as, to a degree, it is for all writers. There are distinct writers' equivalents to being in shape, to warming up, to being up on your toes or back on your heels, at the peak of your game or over the hill. There were qualities in Hemingway's early writing suggestive of agility, foot speed, and economy of effort that were clearly symbolic of a young man's confidence in his reflexes and strength. Later, the prose grew fat and cruel like the man, lunging, stabbing, and making up in sheer force what it had lost in balance. Hemingway was not just aggrandizing an inflated ego in applying sports metaphors to writing (Eliot, we learn, couldn't hit the ball out of the infield; Faulkner overmatched himself in going up against Dostoevsky the first time out); he spoke from first-hand knowledge that writing well was no less a discipline of the body than boxing or bullfighting. His error lay in not taking those metaphors seriously enough and failing to keep himself in top condition. He dissipated, and every book after *Death in the Afternoon* was suffused with the pathos of the hopeless comeback attempt. The tragic side of this most successful of all American literary careers was Hemingway's failure to develop as a writer, beginning at the top of his game and going downhill with each succeeding effort. If alcohol was the key to this decline, then the increasing sogginess of the writing was wholly of a piece with the afflictions of the man: the debilitating headaches; the susceptibility to spills and accidents; the rushes of fury that came out of nowhere to possess him like dybbuks; the paranoid delusions and suicidal depressions that took hold of him toward the end and finally claimed him. All were the afflictions of a drinker.

Hemingway was a creature of contradictions from the very outset, and just about everyone who has dealt with him has been absorbed by the paradox of a man so vulgar, so boisterous, so eager for applause and so quick to applaud himself, being also a celebrant of grace and, for a brief portion of his career, the tragic poet of human vulnerability. "He inveighs with much scorn against the literary life and against the professional literary man of the cities," Edmund Wilson said of him in 1939, "and then manages to give the impression that he himself is a professional literary man of the touchiest and most self-conscious kind." These letters reinforce one's impression that Hemingway found writing a perilous adventure, and that the abuse he heaped upon other writers, usually in disparagement of their manhood – or womanhood, as the case happened to be – complemented his reverence for the literary life in a delicate system of balances designed to shore up his morale. So alien is the persona that dominates the letters from the deadpan heroes of the early fiction, and so utterly opposed, that one can't be blamed for seeing the mask of power and omnicompetence he wore in public as a talisman against all that was vulnerable in him and fearful.

From our arguments with others, said Yeats, we make rhetoric; from our arguments with ourselves, poetry, and the poetry of repression that sustains Hemingway's early writing glowed with a fine and cool light so long as the basic issues were unresolved and neither the tender nor the case-hardened ideas of himself held total sway. The splendid conception of Jake Barnes is a filament of energy hung in perfect equipoise between despair and courage. Though utterly without hope, Jake refuses to go to pieces, and nothing in his brand of self-composure strikes us as false. The wound and the bow. Later on, when Hemingway would deny the wound – excepting the shrapnel wounds he displayed like stigmata – and those apprehensions that had occasioned the stoicism and reserve to begin with, his exquisite syntheses went to pieces and with them whatever was lean and precise in his writing. Yet, true to the law of the return of the repressed, all the childish impulses he had strong-armed into submission: the hungers, the dependencies, the nightmares of impotence and dreams of omnipotence, came back to him as delusions which he mistook for realities. Hemingway's world, Isaac Rosenfeld once said shrewdly, is that which answers to a man's capacity for dealing a blow. The man who called himself Papa at twenty-eight and wanted to become the world's daddy was too preoccupied draining glasses and delivering knockout punches to notice how childish his idea of manhood was. The more grown up he strove to appear, the more infantile he actually became. No wonder Papa remains a source of such amazement to us: in our time he was the greatest infant of American letters.

11

The Truants

Thanks to Delmore Schwartz, everyone had a nickname. Meyer Schapiro was "a mouth in search of an ear;" Philip Rahv was "manic-impressive," Hannah Arendt "that Weimar Republic flapper," Lionel Trilling "the Matthew Arnold of Morningside Heights," later downgraded to "the Matthew Arnold of Grant's Tomb." Edmund Wilson, who called the magazine Partisansky Review and referred to its editors, Rahv and William Phillips, as Potash and Perlmutter (after Montague Glass's Broadway play about two Jewish tailors who quarrel incessantly but still manage to turn out a quality suit), when shown Rahv's anthology of Henry James, snorted, "The Henry James delicatessen." Rahv never forgave him. Rahv's own *mots* were seldom so *bon*. A tireless gossip, he had a line on everybody, and when cornered by other *Partisan* staff members demanding an explanation for his nastiness, he pled "analytic exuberance." That quickly became a bullet in Schwartz's verbal armory: "Analytic exuberance – Philip Rahv's euphemism for putting a knife in your back."

The Truants, William Barrett's memoir of his years at *Partisan Review*, is brimful of such anecdotes, which Barrett tells with gusto. Barrett was an attentive listener, and the charged atmosphere of intellectual mayhem and brittle repartee that marked the life of the inner circle is recalled with a clarity that brings it all alive. The freshness of Barrett's impressions, sometimes forty-five years after the fact, is startling; was he taking notes right along?

From 1945, when he was invited to join the *Partisan* staff, for no other apparent reason than that he was Delmore Schwartz's friend, until 1952, when he left the magazine to pursue his own professional interests as importer of European ideas for American consumers and professor of philosophy at NYU, Barrett was on intimate terms with the inner life of the magazine and a close observer of its editors. They could scarcely have wished for a more faithful or sympathetic witness. A Gentile among Jews and a retiring Existentialist among fractious ex-Marxists, he was a non-combatant in the struggles that regularly shook the office, struggles that, because they drew so deeply upon the national histories – Jewish, Russian – and personal afflictions of the combatants, were not his own. He was the outsider who was permitted a privileged view of the turmoil within, the Horatio who survived to tell the story. Schwartz poured out his troubled heart to Barrett, at first in his wonderful banter that sprinkled witticisms about like snowflakes, later in sodden and violent accusations that terrified Barrett and eventually drove him away. Rahv and Phillips used him as a buffer and a go-between, when they were not enlisting him in their plots against each other. "History does not record what Damon and Pythias became to each other in later life," he remarks. "but certainly their friendship would have been severely taxed if they had been on the staff of *Partisan Review* together." Barrett's capacity for being intimate with these men while standing apart from their tireless and sometimes hysterical sense of crisis gives his book its special balance of equanimity and warmth, and allows him to practice the etiquette of *nil nisi bonum* without surrendering his judgment of the disasters that Rahv and Schwartz drew down upon themselves.

Yet his detachment also draws him away from the fire that burned at the heart of the magazine. He did not always attend history with any great care, and was at times quite oblivious to politics. (You'd gather from *The Truants* that the importance of the War was the opportunity it gave French writers to invent existentialism.) His tenure at *Partisan* should have afforded him a special vantage point on the issues of the day: the Korean War; the Cold War; the other, cultural, Cold War, which involved *Partisan Review* directly through its affiliation with the American Committee for Cultural Freedom; the Hiss and Rosenberg trials, and the spectacular emergence of Richard Nixon and Joseph McCarthy at the center of American politics. Of these, only Hiss and McCarthy rate mention, and only in cameo. For a book that purports to be a closeup of political intellectuals, *The Truants* is remarkably thin on politics, suggesting either that Barrett was not so intimate with *Partisan's* secrets as he imagines, or that he was so bemused by the daily charades of gossip and intrigue that he took them for the whole truth.

If Barrett sometimes failed to take in the issues, however, he was alive to the personalities about him and shows a shrewd grasp of that portion of politics that belongs to character. He puts a skin on everything he says, and what politics there is here is refracted through his cast of characters. Typical of the book is the anecdote about Harold Rosenberg's complaining to Rahv that Lionel Trilling was making a case for "bourgeois values" in the pages of *Partisan*. Rahv, reports Barrett, was visibly shaken; the very word bourgeois set his teeth on edge, and it was not until Schwartz offered the interpretation that Trilling needed the magazine "to protect his left flank" that Rahv was mollified, for if it did not excuse Trilling's apostasy it did suggest that he was dependent upon him, Rahv, for cover. Not only are the characters of the four men brilliantly captured in this vignette, so is a moment in American thought when it suddenly became tolerable for stranded avant gardists to countenance the approval of bourgeois values in a magazine whose very covenant with modernity was to hold all things middle class as death to the spirit.

Barrett plainly endorses those bourgeois values now, and the lesson this book finally puts forth is one that has little to do with the litanies of anti-liberalism it recites in so casual a fashion. What has the ring of experience and reflection is Barrett's vote for common values, arrived at by a lifetime in the company of uncommon people. Citing Rahv in evidence, Barrett quotes Nietzsche's epigram about genius as a will to stupidity, an observation that might be applied across the board to the "homeless radicals" for whom Marxism and modernism, the first principles of *Partisan*'s charter, once supplied a home. If I read Barrett correctly, it was only in the repudiation of both that the Left avant garde of his generation at last came of age. Barrett chastises Jean-Paul Sartre as an ideologue who subordinated his sense of life to "the mania of an idee fixe" and could not bear to submit his ideas – his warm approval of Soviet communism; his esteem for Jean Genet – to the test of common experience. Albert Camus, by contrast, is admired for his defense of "those elementary feelings of decency without which the human race could not survive." Camus' final break with Sartre, records Barrett, was over Sartre's *Saint Genet*, in which Genet – "a pimp, a pederast, a homosexual prostitute, a thief, and a paid informer for the Nazis" – is cast into the role of existentialist hero, a man who seized upon his freedom to create himself as a writer. Barrett's example is well chosen, for the contrast between the two existentialists poses starkly the paradox of "the modern sensibility," which Sartre upheld to the end and Camus had finally to renounce. (Americans divided into similar camps over Ezra Pound's receipt of the Bollingen Award in 1949: those who were appalled at Pound's failures of humanity, and those who cheered his contributions to poetry.) Barrett takes his stand with Camus, lamenting of Sartre, "The intellectual spider spins his web and cannot come forth from it."

It is precisely with the decency of common sentiments in mind that Barrett wrestles with his memories of Rahv and Schwartz, and it is a wrestling in the case of Rahv, who was himself so wholly deficient in the virtues of kindliness and generosity. In reading *The Truants* one constantly wonders how Barrett is going to marshal the known facts about Rahv into anything resembling a tribute. That he manages to do so is a victory of character as well as of art, for the picture that emerges is recognizably that of a man, not a monster. Though he blackened the world around him, as Barrett's wife once observed, yet he is shown finally to be a man in battle with his own chaos, "which led him in advancing age to clutch his Marxist gods more fiercely and rigidly than ever," and who, yet, in a final burst of what Barrett reads as idealism, willed his money to the state of Israel. (A less charitable explanation that has been offered is that he wanted to be certain his wife didn't get a nickel.)

About Schwartz, Barrett is unashamedly elegiac. The friendship, while it was fresh, was the very richest portion of his life. "In his peculiar way," he recalls of Schwartz's buoyant youth, "he was the most magical human being I've known – the adjective does not seem to me excessive." The souring of all that magic into dread is by now an old story, to which Barrett adds little new besides the grace notes of personal tenderness. Their final farewell took place in a Village restaurant early in the 1960s, where Barrett encountered Schwartz in the company of an unknown young woman, one of the many who took him in toward the end. After a drink and some moments of normal conversation, Schwartz burst out into arpeggios of rant and filled the room with violent accusations, until the distressed woman managed to pull him away. Upon Schwartz's leaving, Barrett burst into tears. "'Don't take on so,'" urged his companion. "'There's nothing to be done. He's beyond salvaging.'" "I looked across the table at the straightforward and uncomplicated face that had spoken, and thought: Yes, that is why I weep, because he cannot be salvaged."

It will appear ungrateful to quarrel with so generous a book, but two caveats must be added. One is that Barrett's dates are unreliable. Too many of his anecdotes begin, "Around this time . . ." placing them roughly between 1945 and 1952, if that. He dates James Burnham's essay, "Lenin's Heir," in 1939, when in fact it appeared in the Winter, 1945 issue of *Partisan Review*. (That was the essay in which Burnham broke with the Trotskyist myth that Stalin had stolen the Russian Revolution and betrayed Lenin's dream of a worker's state, pointing out that Lenin himself installed the Soviet system of bureaucratic despotism under strict Party supervision and fashioned the instruments of the Soviet police state.) Barrett tells us also that he withdrew from the *Partisan Review* editorial board in Summer, 1952, as perhaps he did, and yet a check of the journal's masthead him listed as associate editor as late as Winter, 1956, three and one-half years later. This is a minor matter, and Barrett makes no claim to being a historian. But the discrepancy is one he might have anticipated and addressed in some way, if only to assure us of his fidelity to facts.

My other caveat is more substantial, having to do with Barrett's easy dismissal of the politics of the 1960s as "infantile leftism," which he finds even less palatable than the teenage revolutionism of his own generation, which was, at any rate, redeemed in middle age. Barrett shares with most of his generation a lack of serious interest in political thought after them and an intolerant conviction that their disenchantment was definitive for American politics and now forms a boundary marker for respectable political ideas. The agony and turbulence of an entire generation, then, appears to them as no more than, as one New York intellectual put it to me not long ago, "*your* failure to learn the lessons of *my* generation," a smugness and easy self-conceit that seals off all the questions that the 1960s so painfully posed and permits a decade of difficult politics to be dismissed by a fistful of banal slogans. Beyond the sixties, even, Barrett treats contemporary liberalism as little more than a revival of the old Popular Front *cum* Progressive love affair with Soviet Russia, quite as if Henry Wallace were still a candidate for President, *PM* were still agitating for the defense of the socialist heartland, and the Popular Front were still running world peace conferences out of the Waldorf. To read chastened revolutionists on liberalism, one would never suppose that the pressure for detente in the 1970s came largely from American business; that our failure to pull out all the stops with Russia over the Polish crackdown tells us more about the power of the agriculture and banking lobbies than about the illusions of the Left, or that it was Richard Nixon, not Owen Lattimore, who scuttled the Vietnam War and opened relations with China.

Here, inadvertently, Barrett reveals something of his generation that has long been its distinguishing feature: an intellectual self-conceit that gets along nicely without evidence and tends, when aroused, toward polemical recklessness, especially when the business at hand, now as in the thirties, is the savaging of liberalism. It may well be that when the histories of the *Partisan* legacy are written the single common thread uniting each decade with every other, through all the vicissitudes and realignments of politics and taste, will prove to be the contempt for liberalism that every revolutionary Marxist shares with every corporate board chairman, in virtue of which the revolutionist, as he sheds his beard to assume the board chairmanship, need never change his mind, just his slogans.

12

Gates of Eden

During the years roughly between 1960 and 1970 America experienced a radical insurgency of unprecedented intensity and strange, unconventional forms. It was a political movement that had all the trappings of a spiritual crusade, a blend of rebellion and revival, and though it eventually fell short of achieving anything like power or lasting institutional change it had deep and pervasive effects on the emotional tone of the country – the way people lived and felt about their lives. In our common language, that insurgency is the very definition of the era; it is what we mean when we say "the sixties," just as the depression, the onslaught of Fascism, and the fellow-traveling of Western intellectuals are what we mean when we invoke "the thirties". Though bound closely to the vicissitudes of American politics, the movement was by no means a uniquely domestic upheaval, for it drew upon international energies and had global reverberations: the Cuban revolution, the uprising of Parisian students in 1968, Czechoslovakia's canceled experiment in socialism with a human face, the Chinese cultural revolution, and above all, the Vietnamese struggle for independence, which spanned the decade and was, more than anything else, the galvanic force behind the movement.

Though the movement was political to the core, considerations of power and policy were obliged from the start to share the agenda with cultural and spiritual issues that spoke to the very style and purposes of American life: to the deeper, spiritual underpinnings of our politics. It is to some of these deeper politics of the decade that Morris Dickstein is drawn in *Gates of Eden: American Culture in the Sixties*. The revolt of the young in the sixties, Dickstein observes, was fundamentally a revival of the Edenic strain in the American psyche and an assault upon the climate of thought and emotion that dominated the previous decade: the thick, noxious ambience which emanated like a gas from the centers of power and had been internationalized by Americans, intellectuals especially, in the form of intellectual caution, a surplus of personal decorum, a conviction of the futility of social action, an emphasis on the "tragic sense of life," and a quasi-Calvinist vision of human imperfectability. The deeper politics of the sixties addressed this formidable culture of self-repression that marked the fifties; at the bottom of it was a politics of the life force, and it gave rise to a cultural struggle far more diverse and wide-ranging than the ideological and organizational wars of the thirties. Since the struggle was for hearts and minds rather than wages and hours or the means of production, the field of battle was the university rather than the factory, and its central challenges were issued to those elements of American life most vulnerable to the direct assault of revivalist enthusiasm: the school, the family, the individual psyche, the prevailing forms of the imagination. "What happened in the sixties," observes Dickstein, "was no one's deliberate choice, but one of those deep-seated shifts of sensibility that alters the whole moral terrain."

That shift was a Romantic revolution, which thrust into public life not only the aggrandized ego, the heroic figure of brooding, Byronic intensities that Norman Mailer would learn to exploit for its rhetorical cachet, but those quirky, recessed corners of the personality with which the self gains familiarity during Romantic eras. The sixties were an era of psychological rediscovery, in which aspects of the psyche that had been banished from the stage of public life returned front and center, speaking most unfamiliar lines. The universe was imbued with magic, and magical thought was released into politics: what prior generation in American history, this side of the seventeenth century, could have marched on the Pentagon for the purpose of exorcism and levitation? The elements of animistic thought and egotistical omnipotence (or "power tripping" as it came to be called) were not all delusional; they were only the extreme developments of a surge in imaginative self-definition that characterized the era. Above all else, the revolution of the sixties was a revolution of the imagination: urged on by unremitting moral pressure and abetted by fantasy-releasing drugs, the educated echelon of an entire generation set about confronting its own assumptions and re-imagining its relation to social and political life. "Call it Romantic socialism:" says Dickstein, "the Romantic vision of the redemption of the self, the libertarian socialist dream of a community of redeemed selves in the real world."

Among its effects was one of those rare reversals in the direction of cultural influence, as history suddenly gave the appearance of erupting from below rather than trickling down from the reservoirs of power and influence above. Though it may be said that the energies set loose corresponded to the hopeful mood brought to Washington by Jack Kennedy in 1961 and were therefore the shock waves of the Kennedy presidency, it is also evident that those waves, once set into motion, captured a momentum and logic entirely their own, independent of Kennedy's own small accomplishments, which in any event included making covert war upon Cuba and open war upon Vietnam. His assassination, if anything, only revved up the insurgency. What had been set into motion by Kennedy's high spirits became decidedly more virulent after his death, haunting Lyndon Johnson and finally driving him from office. Kennedy, whose eyes and voice seemed always pitched towards the horizon, symbolized those latent, visionary energies in the American psyche that had been held in check during the fifties, and as a symbolizing agent he proved to be more effective as a martyr than ever he had been as president.

As a revolution of the imagination, the movement in all its versions and phases implicated the arts, including literature which is, after all, the art of ideas. And in pointing out the crucial importance of literature to the movement, Dickstein does much to overthrow the facile, McLuhanite view that the aesthetics of youth in the sixties were overwhelmingly sensual: that film, rock, light shows, and "happenings" had wholly eclipsed the printed word in the short-circuited minds of a generation whose chief claim on art was the instant fix of the immediate experience. Dickstein observes that the generation was passionately literate and literary, hungry for meaning and meanings, and that such writers as Allen Ginsberg, Norman Mailer, Joseph Heller, Kurt Vonnegut, and Thomas Pynchon could be counted among its heroes, as could hectoring psychologists and social theorists like Paul Goodman, R. D. Laing, Norman O. Brown, and Herbert Marcuse, who were regularly consulted as trail guides to the liberated future. Indeed, for a brief time, these writers seemed to live out the Shelleyan dream of legislating for mankind, and if they were not the principal figures in Lionel Trilling's or F. R. Leavis's pantheons, their importance nevertheless served to point up the generation's eagerness for ideas, preferably radical ones. (This having been duly acknowledged, Dickstein is free to admit the obvious, in a chapter on rock music, that the prevailing aesthetics of the sixties in fact were kinetic – the dance, the concert, the mobile sculpture – whereas "the arts of the fifties tended mainly toward speech: their hallmarks were irony and control, the sublimation of energy into form.")

Dickstein's special point of departure is the nexus of politics and literature: *Gates of Eden* is the literary history of a moment in culture, and though such an exercise sounds precious and academic on the face of it, it becomes in Dickstein's hands both subtle and rich, capable of insights into the emotional weather of the age that are not generally available to more personal forms – memoirs – or the "objective" disciplines, like sociology. Following Lionel Trilling, his mentor in the arts of defining culture through fiction, Dickstein builds his case on the faith that "writers and artists . . . are the most sensitive reflectors of alternations of consciousness, both in themselves and in the world around them."

> I've operated on two premises, both of them loosely Hegelian – first, that each phase of culture is coherent and full of meaning, that it can be read like a text, and second, that it's precisely our texts – novels, poems, songs, polemics, autobiographies – that can shed light on the larger Text. In other words, the culture of the arts can illuminate the texture of feeling and opinion in the culture as a whole.

The ease with which such ideas are proposed reflects Dickstein's schooling at Columbia, where critical empiricism never made the inroads it did elsewhere in the forties and fifties, when the New Criticism forced a separation between literature and society. As Dickstein notes, New Criticism ruled out the human environment of literature and erected capitalized taboos around the text, like the Biographical and Affective Fallacies, which warned the critic against speaking of literature in terms of what it felt like or where it came from. Dickstein works within an intellectual tradition which combats the scientism of American criticism with strong doses of *Mitteleuropa*: Hegel, Marx, Freud, dialectics, and the historical imagination – Nietzsche's sixth sense – are all siphoned into a view of culture and experience for which the New York intellectuals on the one side and the Frankfurt school on the other are models and sources. It is no surprise that certain key English words in Dickstein's lexicon can scarcely conceal German overtones: that culture, art, and spirit should give off such potent whiffs of *Kultur*, *Kunst*, and *Geist*. The posture might well be called Popular Trilling, a sort of demotic Hegel, twice removed.

Dickstein supposes an historical dialectic which sees the sixties as an answer to the previous decade, and the insurgent forms of imagination as varieties of aesthetic rebellion. Put in its crudest form it is a dialectic of repression and liberation, which is the view of things the insurgent generation itself consistently promoted. But such a pendulum view of history is more Saint Simonian than Hegelian, and its wholesale adoption commits Dickstein to some reductively uniform views of both decades, fifties and sixties. It falsifies the tortured ambivalence of the best fifties writers, turning their heartbreak into mere routines of fussiness and forms of submission to the overwhelming situation. But though down-playing the inner life in Bellow's, Malamud's, and Ellison's fiction by seeing it as a mere by-product of political constraint and cultural paralysis, the method does tell us much about the permissible limits of discourse that marked each decade and about those emotions and ideas that each was willing to release into public life – the common pool of shared dreams and circumspections that so determines "what life felt like." For though the creative achievements of any era are far more idiosyncratic and disorganized than pendulum principles can allow, Dickstein is not wrong in telling us that the examination of what life feels like can turn up uniformities of emotional texture, and that such textures commonly seem to fluctuate according to crude dialectics. National depressions do give way to national moods of elation; group alienations do move toward group accommodations. There are measurable regularities to the rhythms of the spiritual stockmarket, these bulls and bears of the *Zeitgeist*. It is to this meteorology of the spirit that Dickstein refers in proposing that "the culture of an age is a unified thing, whatever its different strands and apparent contradictions. Touch it anywhere and it can reveal its secrets: the texture exposed, the part reveals the whole."

Fortunately for someone in search of internal consistencies, American intellectuals of the sort that interest Dickstein most – the New York intellectuals – have a weakness for symposia and other rites of tribal bonding which make the year by year fluctuations of the community *Geist* comparatively simple to track. By tracing the representative moods of those intellectuals from the 1944 *Contemporary Jewish Record* symposium, "Young in the Forties," through the 1952 *Partisan Review* symposium, "Our Country and Our Culture," to the 1967 *Commentary* version of the rite, "Liberal Anti-Communism Revisited," Dickstein plots the arc of their journey from the Socialist left in the thirties to the Kierkegaardian right in latter times, and remarks the air of growing self-assurance and declining social concern that they contributed to the general mood. They earn low marks for libertarian vigilance, high ones for metaphysical torment.

Fiction too, touched anywhere, reveals its whole structure to the dialectician's eye, and the course of American fiction for fifteen years is seen as having been set in 1944 by Saul Bellow's first novel, *Dangling Man*, which, "in its small and weightless way . . . foreshadows the metaphysics of the self, the elusive mysteries of personality, that would dominate the fiction of the fifties – the legion of small novels which would recoil from the Promethean extremes of modernism and naturalism to take refuge in craft, psychology, and moral allegory." That legion of small novels, which includes the work of Updike, Salinger, Jean Stafford, and Truman Capote, consists largely of what we have come to think of as the "Jewish novel," which, for a time in the forties and fifties, moved into the center of American fiction: the work of Saul Bellow, Delmore Schwartz, Isaac Rosenfeld, Arthur Miller, Bernard Malamud, and the young Philip Roth of *Goodbye Columbus*. In this revised estimate of the post-war climate of fiction, a literature whose adherence to the inner life had just recently seemed such an advance in articulateness, subtlety, and power over the social fiction of the thirties is declared to have been a retreat from public responsibility and political intelligence. A literature of quiet desperation whose high moments of neurotic intensity are not unworthy of Kafka and Dostoevsky now appears to be "metaphysical and hermetic, closed in upon itself: the Bomb evokes despair rather than anger or opposition. The Jewish novel reflects this spirit and ministers to it, for it is literally overwrought – anguished hemmed in by form – offering finally the uneasy absolution of art for a torment whose origin it cannot know and whose course it cannot alter."

The antidote for such withdrawal is a step-up in the rhythm of generational succession and a therapeutic return of the repressed. The new sensibility that would break loose in the sixties began to suggest itself clandestinely in the mid-fifties in the poetry of Ginsberg, Ferlinghetti, and Corso, the fiction of Burroughs and Kerouac, the incessant carping of Paul Goodman, the sociology of C. Wright Mills, and the violently antinomian essays of a transfigured Normal Mailer. Its politics was a faith in the potency of the individual and its ethic was not just a new politics but a new personal relation to psychic and political energy. Behind many of these voices stood the figure of Wilhelm Reich, whose optimistic energism – his faith in the orgasm as personal and social redemption – stood in contrast to the dour stoicism of Sigmund Freud, whose less hopeful views of human perfectibility and social progress had been called upon to justify some of the more civilized versions of fifties discontent. But the new generation, armed with Reich and seething with thwarted yearning, hurled itself against the deadly platitudes of the cold-war consensus. "Every age has a tendency (as Hegel and Plato long ago demonstrated) to cultivate its own principle of decay, to foster the spirit that will eventually overthrow it." The sixties was the sort of era to which the cold war might be expected to give rise: an oedipal rebel.

In chapters on black humor, the new journalism, Black writing and Black nationalism, the age of rock, and experimental or "post-modern" fiction, Dickstein does a penetrating, if selective, interpretation of the era's arts as they mirror its passions. He has a deftness of touch and a mastery of the rhetoric of criticism that makes his treatment of even the most unpromising themes, such as Tom Wolfe and the new journalism, lively and fresh. And an epilogue on his own experience of the era is handled with grace; he knows how to speak in his own voice without blunting the analytic edge of his thought or belaboring us with unwelcome intimacies. Dickstein responds to his own emotional promptings in terms of ideas; he has a penchant for turning his own mixed emotions into issues of ideology and value. Such a mind, which treats ideas as formulated emotions, has no need for the protective cover of critical fallacies any more than it does the language of uninstructed feeling that is for some of the sixties' chief contribution to public discourse.

What I want to question here is whether the shifts of mood and value that took place in the sixties can be successfully gauged through literature, and whether Dickstein's attempt to annex this revolution in sensibility to the canon of literary modernism does not shed a false curricular light on the counter-culture's revolt against curriculum. Dickstein's reading of the sixties is built upon two consistently reiterated premises. One is the central position of literature in the moral life of an age, especially the novel, Lawrence's bright book of life, which the main humanist lines of criticism hold to be the most sensitive vane of the social weather. The second is a definition of the movement itself, "modernism in the streets," initially put forward by Trilling and taken over by Dickstein as the key to the phenomenology of the sixties' rebellion. Both suggest an agenda of thought that is the book's special bias and the sign of its locale; they bring a program of education into the foreground and elevate the view from Columbia into a vision of history.

But what if the novel is not the bright book of life at all, or at least not any longer? What if it has ceased to have any privileged access to the tensions of the age and the movements of the *Geist*, and has become no more than the voice of a beleaguered and self-conscious corner of the culture, the record of something fragmentary and incomplete? That is, I think, just the case. We needn't invoke the overrated death of the novel to observe that the range of experience the novel currently seems able to entertain is severely constricted, and that its most celebrated line of development – the modernist – has radically closed in on itself and become precious and hermetic, leaving it to other forms of expression to take up the job of reporting the social weather. Even adding, as Dickstein does, observations about poetry and whole chapters on journalism and rock music does not substantially fill in the picture of the social experience of the sixties. It is telling about *Gates of Eden* that the messages of the different arts seem hardly to press against each other. As a matter of course, we should expect to find more of the pressure of contradictions and play of alternatives that was endemic to the spirit of the age. Behind the public moral certainties of the counter-culture was the alarm and ambivalence of people suspended between lives. But in Dickstein's view, everything appears to be cut from the same cloth; the post-modern novel and the lyrics of Bob Dylan and Mick Jagger conveniently confirm each other. As acute as Dickstein can be, his approach obscures extenuating and contradictory features of the age.

Dickstein begins by acknowledging that he has left out a portion of the history, the "blissed out" side, to concentrate on the political, but in practice far more than just the stoned life goes by the board. Much of the period's creativity and resourcefulness gets lost in the novel-cum-politics view of it. Dickstein's chapter on the new journalism, which might be expected to emphasize the rise of the alternative press and the explosion of public information at a time when anyone with a mimeograph could become a news agency, limits itself to recalling the more spectacular local manifestations of personalized reportage: the *Village Voice*; Norman Mailer, the quintessential New York writer of our time, and Tom Wolfe, a trendy self-promoter who is largely a creation of the attention lavished upon him by the New York press. We hear nothing about the structural dimensions of the new journalism – the essential democracy of the printed word that turned so many bookstores overnight into switchboards of ideas and dynamic universities of the streets. We hear little of important West Coast journals like *Rolling Stone*, or *Ramparts*, nothing whatever of professional journalists who had a direct effect on opinion about the War: Seymour Hersh, or the peripatetic Australian Communist, Wilfred Burchett, or, astoundingly, I. F. Stone, who conceivably had a greater effect on the public attitudes toward the War than anyone else in the sixties. And, compared with the attention lavished on Wolfe, surprisingly little space is given to Hunter Thompson, whose strange, chemically-enhanced campaign reports for *Rolling Stone* in 1972 were doctrinal to a portion of the American electorate, and who may even take some credit for the nomination and election of Jimmy Carter in 1976. It is hard not to observe, here and elsewhere, how much of the book is a view from Morningside Heights and a form of special pleading for Dickstein's own place and discipline.

To take another, more fundamental, example, Dickstein calls the years from 1968 through 1971 the "Weatherman" phase of the period, which is substantially in accord with what anyone might have concluded at the time, living in New York, learning about middle-class bomb factories on W 11th Street, observing the deterioration of radical leadership at Columbia, and following the expansion of the war and the exhaustion of the movement in the *New York Times* and *Village Voice*. And turning to the literary record, one would discover a fiction of corresponding futility, like the self-canceling fiction of Donald Barthelme, Robert Coover, John Barth, and Rudolph Wurlitzer, which looked so much like modernism at the end of its rope. Barth himself would designate it a literature of exhaustion.

But to restrict one's attention to such manifestations of the age is to take a fragment for a whole and turn a blind eye to those efforts at regeneration that were creative, far-flung, practical and, here and there, successful, but which gave rise to no important fiction or spectacular instances of journalism – alas for both. For it was roughly in 1968 that the movement split up for good and abandoned its visionary attempts to forge a cultural synthesis among its New Left, Marxist, therapeutic, and agrarian groups. Young people were forced to choose among alternatives; to remain in an increasingly futile and embattled movement on ever more militant terms, or to regroup around new ideas and habits that would put into practice the talk of community, authenticity, and self-reliance that had grown out of the general ferment. I'm thinking here of the experiments in communal living and rural self-sufficiency that sprang up in New Hampshire, West Virginia, Oregon, and New Mexico, where inexpensive land could be had and styles of life could evolve in isolation from the urban pressure cooker. The Weatherman phase was also the agrarian phase, which, in the long run, had greater importance and durability – it is still in progress. But there is no way to perceive it through modern literature – or rock or the new journalism. It found its voice elsewhere, largely in the abundant do-it-yourself manuals that began to pour out of small, local presses in the mid-sixties, teaching the arts of meditation, bread baking, butter churning, VW repair, composting, dome designing, and adobe making. These books did not reflect culture so much as they set about to create it; they were its very backbone. How does the novel in the sixties measure up to Eliot Wigginton's *Foxfire* books or Stuart Brand's *Whole Earth Catalogs* for sheer influence or usefulness, not to say sales? During the down years after 1968 the spiritual energies of the thwarted radicals who did not turn to terrorism – and how few they were – or towards transcendental or therapeutic pursuits, or back to their prior lives, were channeled into new forms of material organization: the commune, the farm, the co-op, the alternative economy. It even appears that the cultivation of the material life grew more urgent as the era's politics grew more desperate: as Democratic mendacity gave way to Republican plunder, the war moved disastrously into Cambodia, and the dead hand of the Nixon administration took hold. Though the new agrarian socialism took many forms, all put emphasis on work, self-reliance, discipline, participation, agriculture, and communal reconstruction of the fractured American family. What relation could modern fiction or poetry or even the modern anti-psychiatry of Brown, Laing, and David Cooper have to a radical culture that was suddenly geared to Hatha-yoga and *Popular Mechanics* and put a premium on cooperation and know-how? And why should the effort to measure the cultural pulse through literature, which seems to work so well for the fifties, now take us so far afield?

One answer is, again, locale; what we take to be the record of fiction is largely the view from New York City, whereas the regenerative aspects of the sixties counter-culture were rural and dispersed. Our fiction is urban whereas the efforts at community took place largely on the land, where they lacked access to or need of the forums of contemporary consciousness – the big city news media and book publishers. Moreover, the spirit of the age, as represented in the novel or implied in its experiments in form, is likely to sound modernist because the novel as an evolving genre is committed to views that modernism has laid out in advance; the novel confirms reality in its own historical image. In our time it has become adept at depicting consciousness in crisis: in portraying man's battles against culture, against himself, or against the void. The modern hero is not a man to manage his own feelings or cope with his marriage, let alone grow a zucchini or rebuild a carburetor. Faced with the pressures and obligations of modern life, we expect him to prove fragile and incompetent, even a bit insane. "In late-sixties writers like Barthelme or Wurlitzer," observes Dickstein, "the sense of disconnection is complete, as it is in the Weatherman phase of sixties radicalism, where futility and frustration spawn random violence. Barthelme and Wurlitzer write as if they were surrounded by the curious artifacts of an extinct culture which they plunder like collectors, or stroll past vacantly like sleepwalkers."

But the fictional record of the entire decade is not so different. If most novels fall short of the radical autism of Wurlitzer's *Nog* or *Flats* they do not lack for their own sorts of alienation, usually expressed in the condition of their heroes: dispossessed husbands, estranged sons, isolated drifters, rebels and madmen, losers of every description. Recall Bellow's *Herzog*, Roth's *Letting Go* and *Portnoy's Complaint*, Heller's *Catch-22*, Pynchon's *V* and *The Crying of Lot 49*, Malamud's *A New Life* and *The Fixer*, Nabokov's *Pale Fire*, the *ficciones* of Borges and Cortázar, the continuing episodes in Beckett's on-going comedy of entropy, and, in drama, the plays of Pinter and Albee. "If I'm out of my mind," boasts Moses Herzog on everyone's behalf, "its alright with me." To venture a Trillingism here, the modern self appears to be in process of going under. The forms of literary imagination that bear the imprimatur of high culture – fiction, drama, poetry – all support such a view; even the rock music of the sixties was at its best when promoting disintegration, unto the nineteenth nervous breakdown. The Rolling Stones were the poets laureate of modern *Schadenfreude*. Who can blame a sensitive reader like Dickstein for mistaking the end of the decade for a full scale *fin de siécle*? Has any time ever sounded more grim?

I find *Gates of Eden* most satisfying where New York is the locale or ultimate point of reference: in the discussion of Norman Mailer, or the Jewish novel, the late fifties' revolt against the cold-war ethos, or the political undulations of the New York intellectuals, topics well suited to the vista from Morningside Heights, that Belvedere of Manhattan. If Dickstein's contribution to our knowledge of the fifties sounds more authoritative than what he has to say about the sixties, it is partly because the narrower age fits more snugly into his field of vision. In the fifties the cultural exchange was more localized. Lionel Trilling, Columbia, Philip Rahv, *Partisan Review*, *Commentary*, *New Yorker* magazine, the *New York Times*, and the major New York book publishers were a hub of energy, even of power, which absorbed information about the world and processed it into *haute* New York's major export – judgment. But with the sixties came not only an explosion of new ideas about how life might be lived, but a migration of intelligence out of the cities and the universities, and the burgeoning of the rural communes and local presses. The inherent democracy of print asserted itself against the oligarchic tug of New York's publishing, which was becoming, in any case, the educational arm of ITT, Gulf and Western, and Columbia Broadcasting. The position held in the sixties by a periodical like the *New York Review of Books* is not comparable to that of *Partisan Review* in the previous two decades, never mind subscription figures, because the dispersal of energy and opinion undercut the ability of any New York publication to speak for contemporary opinion, let alone hope to marshal it. Imagine any journal in the sixties summoning up the self-assurance to elect itself a New Leader, when the known reality was that all efforts at leadership had been consistently outflanked by events. For the historian of culture, this means that he can no longer read all the signs by standing in one place.

All of which is why I take the real subject of *Gates of Eden* to be the reflection of the cultural upheaval within the academic and social enclave Dickstein inhabits, rather than the event itself. Dickstein begins his history with an account of Allen Ginsberg's 1959 and 1968 readings at Columbia and rounds off the experience with a reminiscence of Ginsberg's nostalgic return in 1974 as Columbia's rebel emeritus. Here are the three ages of Allen Ginsberg: harbinger, embodiment, and memory, all come to Columbia. The question posed by the very structure of such a book is less, "What did the experience mean?" than, "How do *we* receive it?" – no trivial question and possibly the best one to ask, for it is in the impact with a received tradition of ideas and values that a cultural revolution takes on meaning. *Gates of Eden* is first and foremost a chapter in the history of the New York intellectuals, and though Dickstein's sympathies are his own, shaded by those of his generation, the cultural geography he takes for granted has been mapped out for him in advance, as have his methods of interpretation. Behind this book stand others; this is so very much a book about other books, almost a bibliographic essay. On the same shelf are kept Diana Trilling's *Claremont Essays* (1964), which features *her* version of Ginsberg's first Columbia reading, Saul Bellow's *Mr. Sammler's Planet* (1970), Lionel Trilling's *Sincerity and Authenticity* (1972), and Midge Decter's *Liberal Parents, Radical Children* (1975), all judgments issued from New York on the youth of today. Housed over on the right is the whole mixed history of the New York intellectuals themselves.

With *Gates of Eden*, Dickstein, a young critic (b. 1940) and a contributing editor of *Partisan Review*, bids to establish himself in the dwindling line of succession to the generation that started out in the thirties, even while casting off the incubus of their liberal anti-Communism and the legacy of hardened doctrine and political collaboration that it entailed for many. But Dickstein disclaims such attitudes only to better embrace a larger perspective, the view of art and culture as an arm of politics and power, which is the New York intellectuals' special contribution to American critical thought. It is a quarrelsome book, but it is part of a family quarrel.

Gates of Eden is not consistent in its judgments, nor always fair to its targets. It is far from comprehensive in its review of the sixties, terribly repetitious, and, like the novel itself, a loose and baggy monster. But it is also brimming with erudition and a detailed knowledge of the literary terrain, reflecting a mind that has assimilated an entire tradition of critical thought and turned it into a private sensibility. In all, it is the best book we've had so far on the intellectual history of the sixties, much against the belief, widely held in New York, that the period had no intellectual history to speak of.

13

Elusive Trilling

When Lionel Trilling died in 1975 it was generally conceded that literature had lost the most influential critic of the post-war era and that, in effect, a literary office had fallen vacant. Trilling had long since become something more than just a critic; he was a *figure* and almost that rarest of creatures, an academic celebrity. Even when he spoke for no one but himself he was looked upon as a spokesman and even came, in time, to be something of a standard source, a coiner of commonplaces.

Among his special advantages was standing in both the academy and the cockpit of literary politics and polemic: New York. He was a pivotal figure among the New York intellectuals, and though he was a *primus inter pares*, a crude silhouette of his career would look like a shadow of what they all had experienced. He was a Jew and as a Jew had been schooled, if ever so briefly, in the left politics of the thirties, whose programmatic views he was quick to forsake for the sense of "variousness and possibility" represented by Arnold, James, Forster, Mill, Freud, and Hegel. Like most New York intellectuals he styled himself a modernist even though he distrusted modernism and was more at ease with the nineteenth century, whose complex ideas and thick textures were more congenial to his own brands of moral concern.

He shared with the others the view of literature as the expression of history, politics, class and the *Zeitgeist* (as a Hegelian, he maintained sufficient faith in the material life to invoke class as an *idea* of great power), and made a practice of keeping watch over the eddies and currents of what his circle called "the culture," which consisted largely of the opinions and social habits of the eastern, liberal intelligentsia. But he was also a scholar and a teacher, an historian of modern social thought whose early books on Matthew Arnold (1939) and E. M. Forster (1943) and later studies of Freud took him beyond the customary range of New York intellectual life and gave him credentials in the Modern Language Association and

International Psychoanalytic Association that served to heighten his stature in *Partisan* and *Kenyon Review* circles. In addition, as an editor of The Readers' Subscription, Trilling enjoyed a successful venture into the commercial side of letters – a rarity for an academic. As others have noted, Trilling felt no contradiction in any of this: rather, he took exception to the view that the life of the mind gained strength from its exclusions or profited from its streamlinings.

Though the advantages that attend such a marriage of scholarship to ideological *savoir faire* and commercial success have lately devolved upon Irving Howe, including the access to publicity and glamour that are special by-products of acclaim in New York, the differences that highlight Trilling's uniqueness are now all the more plain. Trilling's influence was bound up with a certain kind of reticence and irony. Howe's voice these days is unmistakably charged with the energy of his bluntness and the authority of his learning; it is a recognizably urban voice, pugnacious and smart, its assertiveness honed to a point by scholarship, whereas Trilling's more diffident notes needed the amplitude that was to be gained in the acoustical chamber of Morningside Heights. To read now critics as different as Steven Marcus, Quentin Anderson, and Morris Dickstein is to hear the lapidary phrases and subtle modulations of Trilling's own voice. The difference between Howe and Trilling is not only the difference between two drastically dissimilar styles of being Jewish, but between the City University and Columbia, that is, between New York in its immanent and its transcendent modes.

Though much of Trilling's stature was bound up with his position as a Jewish intellectual who had penetrated the protected and largely anti-Semitic enclave of Ivy League humanities, it is hard to think of him as Jewish at all. Only rarely did his thoughts come to rest on Jewish themes, and nothing in his personal elegance or the suave composure of his writing suggested the restlessness, vividness, and readiness for combat that we now regard as the special contributions of eastern European Jews to the style of American thought. He was no browbeater. The word that comes most readily to mind in trying to place Trilling "ethnically" is cosmopolitan, by which is meant a certain Jewish internationalism, a penchant for reading literature as a symptom of the cultural and political situation, an easy familiarity with European ideas, a working knowledge of Marx and Freud, and, not least, charm.

One of the more prominent aspects of Trilling's character was his refusal to honor limitations upon thought that seem to belong to race, moment, and milieu, or, as he called it, culture. Though he never failed to lend culture his grudging endorsement, Freudian that he was, he normally fretted over Freud's moral coerciveness, and it might be supposed that his adventures in Jewish literary circles in the twenties, no less than among the organized left in the thirties, were on his mind in later years when he spoke fearfully of "cultural omnipotence" and expressed concern over the growing homogeneity and seductiveness of American culture. Though Trilling was anything but a social rebel, his insistence on standing apart from the cultural *donnée* and his disposition to decline convenient and ready-made identities suited him well to becoming a Jewish exception at Columbia College in the thirties, where for many years, as he would recall, he was looked upon openly as an experiment.

Trilling began publishing in 1925 in Elliot Cohen's and Henry Hurwitz's *Menorah Journal*, the monthly publication of the Menorah Society, whose broad purpose was the formation of a non-sectarian, humanist, and progressive Jewish consciousness in America. But he readily deserted that magazine and its efforts at "cultivated" Jewishness in 1930 for the swifter tides of the intellectual mainstream, which meant largely *The Nation* and *The New Republic* but included a brief and gingerly debut as a leftist in V.F. Calverton's *Modern Quarterly/Modern Monthly*. In 1944, reflecting on the depth and import of his Jewishness, he declined to waste any nostalgia on his youthful torments over his Jewish identity, with which the better part of his *Menorah Journal* stories and essays concerned themselves, or to discover any redeeming grace in the parochialism of organized Jewish life. "As the Jewish community now exists," he harshly observed, "it can give no sustenance to the American artist or intellectual who is born a Jew. And so far as I am aware, it has not done so in the past. I know of writers who have used their Jewish experience as the subject of excellent work; I know of no writer in English who has added a micromillimetre to his stature by 'realizing his Jewishness', although I know of some who have curtailed their promise by trying to heighten their Jewish consciousness." Subsequently, amid much stir, he refused Elliot Cohen's invitation to take part in the founding and operation of *Commentary*.

But the brand of cosmopolitanism that Trilling adopted in place of the discarded Jewishness was anything but a dimensionless receptivity to ideas, for it featured a special proclivity for the literature and thought of England's Victorian age. Such a thoroughgoing

Anglophilia was both idiosyncratic and commonplace; though unique in its devotion, it followed certain lines of cultural force that were bound to affect a Jewish literary intellectual whose education had put him in touch with the expressive powers of the English language and the enormous vitality of English literature, and who could train himself, as most did, to look past the discomfiting presence of the Fagins, Shylocks, Bleisteins and Jews of Malta who are native to the Anglo-Saxon view of evil.

The strain of Anglophilia that was particularly intense in Trilling was latent in the very schooling of his generation; in more attenuated form it had an effect on Alfred Kazin, Saul Bellow, and Delmore Schwartz, and became particularly visible in the hundreds of Jewish academics who flocked into "English" after the War and quickly became leading authorities on Shakespeare, Joyce, James, *Paradise Lost*, and *The Fairie Queene*. Though the gap between British and traditional Jewish culture would seem to be enormous – and we have Maurice Samuel's *The Gentleman and the Jew* to spell out the differences – there are points of moral contact that make the transfer of loyalties relatively convenient. It is not difficult for a Jew who has been indoctrinated at home in habits of responsibility, prudence, thrift, achievement, and other moral austerities of the "Protestant ethic" to lend sympathy to a literature so saturated with a concern for individual conduct as the British, and especially the Victorian with its stress on faith, discipline, stoic forbearance, and self-improvement. It was the appeal of one culture grounded upon ethical precept for another. If Jewish literary intellectuals were to forsake the Torahs and Talmuds of their fathers for secular learning, they were not so far afield in finding spiritual brotherhood with a culture whose Hebraising tradition could be traced all the way back to *Piers Plowman* and whose moral tone was adopted from the very Bible of the Jews, and in the thrilling cadences of the King James translation at that. Taking on English manners and morals was not like choosing to become, say, a Hindu or a Navaho; no strenuous rites of conversion were demanded.

From the standpoint of professional survival in the world of high-WASP gentility, such a transformation was one way a Jew might soften the blow of his presence in those "exclusive" but troubled circles that could be persuaded to try out a Jew of the proper sort, and for self-conscious young Jews just a generation removed from the pushcart and the sweatshop being the proper sort of Jew was no small concern. By the end of the War, when so many of the institutional walls came tumbling down, the individual passion for correctness intensified in the face of real opportunities, and drawing the line between the Jew and the Yid within oneself was a major preoccupation of the academically minded sons of the garment district who chose books over book-keeping and took Trilling for the model of successful comportment.

In the forties, one heard no demands for kosher service in the faculty dining clubs. Though Delmore Schwartz, affecting a grudge against Jewish high-mindedness, would complain of those sons of the ghetto who cultivated a "fantastic precision of speech and an accent which is more English than the English accent," it is not to be thought that all was convenience and assimilation where Trilling was concerned, for that seriously underestimates the Jewish affection for the English language and English literature that Trilling and Schwartz shared in common, and overlooks the anxious search for an appropriate high style that engaged all Jewish writers and intellectuals in the forties.

Trilling, then, was a complex man: a principled antagonist of culture, including all of the more available versions of Jewishness, and an acculturated gentleman and master of persona, of protective coloration. Such an assumption of a new identity *in toto* was a very American gesture, even if the new self happened to be an English squire. If, in the wake of *Roots* and *World of Our Fathers* and *The Rise of the Unmeltable Ethnics*, there seems something priggish and fastidious in Trilling's adoption of such High Church accents, his great success at it might be offered in mitigation. His affectations were, if anything, absolutely sincere; as he avowed, so did he feel. Nor was this mere "passing"; it was going Protestant America one better by becoming a thoroughly accomplished British man of letters. Still, such achievements had to be paid for in self-consciousness, and if the rhetoric of personal authenticity that highlighted the sixties was to meet with Trilling's disapproval, it is not difficult to imagine why that should be so. In his last book, *Sincerity and Authenticity* (1972), he quoted approvingly Oscar Wilde's aphorism that "the truths of metaphysics are the truths of masks," as if Wilde had given his endorsement to the rich blend of masks and metaphysics in Trilling's own character and thought.

A review of some of the commentary on Trilling by his contemporaries leads one to conclude that Trilling's mind was one of those to which it is difficult to give assent without bouts of irritation and distrust. Yet from the tone of the eulogies and state orations that have followed his death it would be hard to know that his ideas encountered much opposition in his lifetime – and not just from New Critics or unrepentant Stalinists or unredeemed liberals – and that his voice was one of the more tormented, ambiguous, and elusive of the post-war period. Efforts by Steven Marcus (*New York Times Book Review*, 8 February 1976) and Quentin Anderson (*The New Republic*, 23 April 1977) to press the claim for Trilling's moral heroism give the impression that his greatest achievement was to embody a kind of clear-sighted resistance – to be a leading stoic, a spokesman for "moral realism" and the conditioned life, and an expert in admonition who was instrumental in setting a wayward literary culture to rights in the forties and fifties. "To my mind," says Marcus, "Trilling's spiritual heroism was in large part bound up with his exigency and his minimalism – his ability to affirm, without illusions, qualities and virtues that his own group, his own culture, his own audience had largely given up on as being at once excessive in their demands upon us and insufficient in the gratifications they return."

It does appear that Trilling is presently best remembered among the New York intellectuals largely for his resistances, his antagonism to the articles of progressive faith held dear by his own literary culture: Stalinism, liberalism, the fetish of "authenticity" in the counter culture of the 1960s. If there is meaning beyond the obvious to the witticism that cosmopolitanism is the Jewish parochialism, the remark has particular application to Trilling, whose brand of cosmopolitanism was resolutely parochial after its own fashion, not only in its exaggerated regard for Bloomsbury mannerisms but in Trilling's general preference for defining himself by negatives – against the grain of the avant garde ideas, positions, and identifications he had cast out and areas of modern thought he would not approve. Here, then, was a cosmopolitanism with a stringent sense of limits and a habit of being old-fashioned in the name of the higher Hegelian syntheses.

If Edmund Wilson is the model of the cosmopolitan intellectual for our time, it is plain how much broader was Wilson's range than Trilling's, and how much more vigorous and prehensile his grasp. To consider modernism, one of the few areas in which their overlap is significant, is to think of Wilson's pioneering *Axel's Castle* and Trilling's essay, "On the Teaching of Modern Literature," and to observe the difference between a catholic imagination and a scrupulous one, an imagination of enthusiasm and one of measure and concern. To place this penchant for disapproval in its best light, we might say that Trilling was a master of negation whose contribution to discourse in America was a brilliantly dialectical style of setting "the self" against the *Zeitgeist*, even while taking full advantage of its influence.

But, as Trilling was at pains to point out in his studies of writers divided against themselves, such oppositionism arises out of an inner need and reflects a mind in contest with itself, and it is as such an interior quarrel that his stands against the spirit of the age come most clearly into view. There is no outstanding virtue let alone moral heroism to devil's advocacy where nothing is risked or where the positions set forth are not attempts to resolve basic tensions by giving them words and forms. Trilling's case against the liberal imagination, which sustained him ideologically through three books: *E. M. Forster, The Middle of the Journey*, and *The Liberal Imagination*, was nothing if not the fallout of his efforts to unburden himself of the vestiges of his own beleaguered liberalism and to justify to himself his waning interest in the ruling passion of his generation: social justice. For if the organizational and ideological dimensions of liberalism could be quickly dispensed with in the 1940s, there were still the lingering claims of conscience, and it was largely for reasons of self-exhortation that Trilling's accounts of the 1930s portrayed it as so brutal, rigid, and soul-deadening an age.

Trilling held the liberal era to be not only the birthplace of the intellectual class as we now understand it but also the scene of its original sin. The liberal era in Trilling's view was a time of moral failure, and he adverted to it in his introduction to Tess Slesinger's *The Unpossessed* with loathing, remembering above all "the dryness and deadness that lay at the heart of [the liberals'] drama and that they had brought to the fore a peculiarly American desiccation of temperament." Such views not only lacked any hint of fondness for the moral conflicts of his own youth, but repressed all memories of the depression, the unemployment, the labor battles, the advances of Fascism in Europe, and the pervasive belief in the exhaustion of American, indeed, Western institutions. What remained was a movie of the thirties starring the self-deceived and self-destroying intellectuals themselves, and consequently dominated by its ideas of itself rather than the circumstances that made those ideas seem vital.

I think Marcus, Anderson, and other of Trilling's students and memoirists mistaken in viewing Trilling's efforts to redeem liberalism by infusing it with tragic views, stoic ethics, and complicating ironies as simply the expression of his running feud with Stalinism, since it is Trilling's feuds with himself that gave his arguments their intellectual vigor. Such influence as *The Liberal Imagination* retains depends little upon positions for which it is now difficult to muster any enthusiasm, so much as from the show of competing ideas in a mind that was learning how to draw strength from its own ambivalence and from a style of thought that successfully subordinated its tensions to an overarching grace of intellect. The book's importance in the fifties, I think, was similarly based. Against Anderson's belief that *The Liberal Imagination* was a salutary corrective to a liberalism that, in 1950, was strongly tinged with Stalinism, the fact was that Stalinism in America by then had been gutted politically, discredited rhetorically, and its organized ranks so thoroughly infiltrated by the FBI that it had ceased to be very interesting to anyone but those who were condemned to rehearse the old battles out of a continuing urge to admonish or atone, and to the professional anti-Communists who were tuning up the crusade for loyalty that was to mark the decade. As a force to be dealt with in American politics, liberalism had performed so miserably behind Henry Wallace in 1948 that it was hardly on the map at all except as a dim remembrance of things past.* It is hard to imagine how, in such an atmosphere, *The Liberal Imagination* could have become doctrinal to a generation of literary intellectuals as it did were there not something more to contend with than just the dying embers of Stalinism in politics and Socialist Realism in art.

In fact, the book's importance did not lie in its demonstration of how the last nail could be driven into the coffin of progressive ideas – others would do that with less torment and greater efficiency – but in how intellectual and political energies that could no longer be released through social thought or action could be channeled into higher regions. What made its call for the transcendence of socially-defined versions of reality attractive was the palpable urgency of the conflicts that smoldered beneath the repose of style and coolness

---

* I read somewhere not long ago that Wallace's final vote total ran somewhat behind that of Howdy Doody, the puppet who ran a write-in campaign for President that year. True or not, the story is symbolically true. The Progressive movement had less of a following than Howdy Doody in 1948.

of doctrine, the shadow of powerful emotions being held in check and turned magically into limpid phrases and fine ideas. It was the emotional alchemy that was gripping, the transmutation of the lead of inner contradiction into the gold of literary intelligence. The retreat from the boldness of social rhetoric toward "ideas in modulation" would scarcely have qualified as a serious appeal to left intellectuals were not the compensations of interpretive boldness offered in exchange, and did not Trilling's obvious vigor of mind seem to surpass that of those stymied intellectuals after whom Slesinger's *The Unpossessed* was named. It was they who seized upon *The Liberal Imagination* as a handbook of intellectual survival and took lessons on how to give ground on the political front while pretending to upgrade the terms of political discourse. Such a turn to politics *in the larger sense* announced, as it always does, that politics in the narrower had been defeated. The establishment of taste and sensibility in the place formerly held by justice and progress, coupled with a renewed interest in psychoanalysis as a key to art and a view of the novel as an elixir for weary emotions were new directions for liberal energies and constituted a program of interior revitalization that was supposed to enrich liberalism through infusions of complexity and depth.

The intellectual strength of such a plan for renovating "the modern will" was also its political weakness, since the effort to rejoin politics and the imagination was made at the expense of politics. As Morris Dickstein now points out, "Somehow Trilling's . . . insistence that the political and literary minds had much to teach each other turned into the notion that they were fundamentally inimical, perhaps because most of the lessons flowed in one direction." By finessing all talk of issues, power, and institutions except at the highest levels of abstraction, Trilling could attack the shallowness of liberalism without having to confront the world in which such shallowness seemed to have merit. As a critic of contemporary ideas, Trilling departed from the example of his mentors – Mill, Arnold, and Coleridge – in proffering no social ideas of his own, only social sentiments and tastes which did not and could not add up to an alternative liberalism, or, for that matter, an alternative conservatism. His revitalized versions of the liberal imagination could never be put to any political tests but only aesthetic ones, in which their validation was assured.

Such an improved liberalism was the elevation of an hypostasized *mind* over circumstances and a thrusting forward of *ideas* against the liberal, and American, conception of reality which is, as he put it, always material reality, "hard, resistant, unformed, impenetrable, and unpleasant." By renovation of the will, Trilling meant something like transcendence or grace, qualities of mind more spiritual than engaged and standing quite apart from ordinary political categories. Dickstein's observation that Trilling was a "Tory radical" is useful provided we understand the radical element to have been largely a genius for manipulating ideas and imagining ever more subtle essences rather than a program of uncovering roots. If radical thought in its customary modern forms is the paring away of "superstructures" in order to lay bare the brute facts of biological need or infantile experience or class interest behind an idea or ideology, then Trilling's brand of radicalism was just the opposite, an upward distillation of the vapors of thought into their rarest and most abstract expressions.

And yet, ever at odds with his own insistent spirituality, Trilling would enter frequent pleas for the conditioned nature of experience and even for biological determinism, especially in the essays that make up *The Opposing Self* (1955) and *A Gathering of Fugitives* (1956). By the mid-fifties, as music master in his own fast game of musical chairs, he was taking the liberals to task for too rare a spirituality, for failing to see "that spirit is not free, that it is conditioned, that it is limited by circumstance." However disorienting this may be to a neophyte in dialectics or the tactics of legal reasoning or ordinary ambivalence, it was a characteristic ploy of Trilling's to disavow liberalism in order to adopt and regenerate its categories: the reality principle, the durability of the world, the inexorability of conditions.

Having put aside the vulgar Marxist rhetoric of social determinism he was prepared to assume spokesmanship for the reality principle, conceived of modestly as "the familial commonplace . . . the materiality and concreteness by which it exists, the hardness of the cash and the hardness of getting it, the inelegance and intractability of family things." And though such views should have brought him into alliance with liberals in acknowledging the hardness of life, he continued to cast a cold eye upon monocausal theories of envirnomental conditioning and the blueprints for social engineering to which they gave rise, and indeed upon all organized hopes for social melioration. Here was a Hebraism with a passion for righteousness but little of the accompanying faith in social machinery. Bolstered by Freud's dubious conception of a biological death instinct as a fundamental property of life itself, the tragic view that was first expressed in *The Middle of the Journey* and *The Liberal Imagination,* seemingly in response to the War and the Holocaust, was refined into a metaphysic, taken out of history and made an autonomous property of the modern spirit.

But to go any further into this strange fondness for the conditioned and the circumstantial as it was wedded to a thoroughgoing idealism would take us far afield and get us into the perplexities of the later thought, including a surprising turn against art, which can't be treated in brief. Trilling's proclivity to take refuge in reified abstractions, like *mind, thought, the self,* and *the modern will,* which were often locutions for himself, and his continuing efforts to transcend culture while recommending those novels in which it was most diligently recorded, and his fondness for a Hegel who promised to lend order to such ambiguities, exfoliated into aviaries of thought in which his positions became more elusive, the dialectics more hermetic, and the abstractions more vaporous, and the elegance of his prose shades off into mere pageantry. *Beyond Culture* (1968) and *Sincerity and Authenticity* (1972) are troubled and troubling books whose difficulties reflect the perplexities of Trilling's own thought and the ambiguities of his own system of metaphysics and masks. The very title of his last publication in book form, the monograph *Mind in the Modern World* (1972), bespoke the sense of mental embattlement that in later years came to dominate his self-conception. These later books did not exert any influence comparable to that of *The Liberal Imagination,* though their prestige may grow at some later time when their exquisite ironies and superb balances can be better appreciated. Brilliant exercises in dialectical reasoning, their brilliance is abstract and cold, and their pose of cultural oppositionism seemingly assumed more from force of habit and a resolute will to be disengaged than from a reasoned assessment of conditions.

Despite all this, Trilling more than Wilson left behind a legacy of thought that it is not localized in New York or at Columbia but diffused through academia where it has accompanied his students and been passed on to their students in turn. It may even be thought that Trilling's career was the signal for that dispersal of Jewish energy into the literary profession which precipitated the decline of the New York intellectuals as focal points of intellectual influence, and saw the rise of the English departments and university presses as independent centers of thought after the war. But the radically altered demography of postwar English and Trilling's role in it is another subject for another essay, and will have to await in any case a fuller evaluation of his ideas and their cultural meaning in the 1940s and 1950s.

14
Criticism and Culture

"As Charles Peguy said," wrote Lionel Trilling in the preface to *The Liberal Imagination* in 1950, "'*Tout commence en mystique et finit en politique*' – everything begins in sentiment and assumption and finds its issue in political action and institutions. The converse is also true: just as sentiments become ideas, ideas eventually establish themselves as sentiments." In Trilling's case the converse became the rule: *Tout commence en politique et finit en mystique*. No intellectual of his generation was fonder of mystique than Trilling, none more guarded and elusive, cryptic and oracular. His prose was sinuous and elliptical, hinting at depths beyond words and while at the same time disclosing a mind ever attentive to the ballet of ideas, indeed, to its own pirouettes and pliés. As Mark Krupnick's *Lionel Trilling and the Fate of Cultural Criticism* shows in detail, the favored choreography was one of balances and antitheses, of exquisite tensions and unresolved dialectics. Long before deconstruction became a fashion in the academy, Trilling was practicing it on himself, defending positions from one essay to the next that seemed to stand in opposition to each other, suggesting a turn of mind Krupnick characterized by Krupnick as an "allergy to closure."

It should come as no surprise, then, that of all the New York intellectuals, Trilling thus far has gained the most solicitude from historians: Krupnick's book is the third such study since Trilling's death in 1975. (The other two are by William Chace and Robert Boyers.) The most productive of the New York intellectuals, the most scholarly, and the most elusive, he was unique among his generation in having a Ph.D. and being a teacher by design rather than by default. He was not a *Luftmensch* who had fallen on his feet in the Ivy League but a *bourgeois gentilhomme* and a literary scholar who kept fast company in his youth. Trilling was a man of parts, and the complexity of the picture is a portion of the mystique.

That mystique has exercised a fascination for younger intellectuals schooled in the aesthetics of the difficult and trained to appreciate a modern self that, like a modern text, is intricate, elusive, and demanding. Unlike most of his contemporaries, Trilling possessed the sinuousness and complication of a modernist novel; he refused to be understood too quickly. Of his life apart from the profession of letters we know little; he guarded his privacy with care, though in point of either adventure or scandal or political engagement there would appear to be little to know. After a flurry of radical activism in the early thirties, he seems to have led a cloistered life. The intricate self he set out to create was entirely a mental construction, a clockwork of nerves that needed little in the way of social stimulation to keep its delicate mechanisms in traction.

His sense of himself as a divided creature was there from the start in the double life he lived in the 1930s uptown and downtown, as an English instructor at Columbia College and as a restless young man of the left. "Inevitably that sense of his role [as a Columbia humanist] was at odds with his self-identification as a New York intellectual. As a *Partisan Review* writer, Trilling was committed to opposition to the established order; as a humanist at Columbia he participated in a project of acculturation." It was from these discrepancies as intellectual and professor, Village Marxist and denizen of Morningside Heights, lukewarm Jew and tepid Anglophile, that he formed his basic identity: the opposing self, the thinker at odds with his own thought, the Hegelian dialectician in search of a fresh synthesis. For all the richness and variety of his thought, Trilling was at bottom a bilateral thinker who saw life through its polarities: will and idea, energy and inertia, eros and death, culture and biology, sincerity and authenticity. "His shifts of position seemed only the present particular manifestations of a prior dualism of mind that remained essentially unchanged."

The dialectical habit seems to have arisen during his youthful apprenticeship in Marxism. *The Menorah Journal*, in which Trilling began his publishing career in 1925, was briefly a crucible of revolutionism, and many of its inner circle in the late 1920s – Herbert Solow, Felix Morrow, and George Novack in particular – would be drawn deeply into the Trotskyist orbit. Trilling himself drew back from revolutionary Marxism early; by 1935, his future as a scholar and professor in view, he broke ranks with his revolutionist comrades and set himself on a more traditional humanist path. Krupnick tells us that Trilling's dissertation on Matthew Arnold, published in 1939, was first conceived as a rigorously Marxist tract on Arnold's intellectual development, stressing "development by contradiction, triadic progression by phases, the necessarily progressive character of such change, and the centrality of class struggle." As the project took shape, however, the dialectics yielded to a more organic and humanistic conception of Arnold. But the habit of development by contradiction stayed with Trilling, and the practice of seeing the world in terms of thesis and antithesis survived the material bias of Marxism. No longer a dialectics of historical change, it became a fetish of oppositions, "a static doctrine of sustained tensions," which explains why even as a young critic, in the heat of political passion, Trilling was developing a "taste for stasis" and equilibrium. If that made for a certain dramatic tension and refreshing unpredictability in Trilling's writing, it also fostered routines of equivocation, the most notorious example of which is in Trilling's novel of post-Marxist recoil, *The Middle of the Journey*, where John Laskell can take a stand on nothing more substantial than "negative capability" and his own loving meditation on a rose. With all vitality and assertion distributed to the characters whose moral standing is in question – Emily Croom, Duck Caldwell, and Gifford Maxim – the book's moral center is vacant of anything more exciting than a refusal to act. The "tragic sense of life," for which Trilling would lobby in later decades, is latent in this strategic passivity, needing only the philosophical imprimatur of Freud's "death instinct" to be upgraded from a *Weltschmerz* to a *Weltanschaaung*.

Why, one is bound to ask, should anyone get excited about all this sackcloth? The profile Krupnick himself presents seems uninspiring enough. Harold Rosenberg once remarked that when he first encountered the style of Lionel Trilling he looked for the joke and discovered there wasn't any. The answer is that one doesn't get excited about Trilling. One is simply, slowly, inexorably drawn into his orbit, learning at one's own pace to appreciate his nuances, his vapors, his tics, his hesitant command. To struggle past the fastidious mannerisms of the late writing, in *Beyond Culture* and *Sincerity and Authenticity*, is to discover a mind cautiously incandescent and stealthily adventurous, and one learns to be patient with it. Krupnick himself had once been impatient with Trilling. In 1971 he reviewed Trilling's anthology of literary criticism, *Literary Criticism: An Introductory Reader*, in the pages of Philip Rahv's short-lived *Modern Occasions* and dealt harshly with Trilling's "reverence for the customary and the established" and his "increasingly priggish distaste for less elevated conditions of being."

That was an alarmed and politicized view of Trilling, fostered by the insurgent temper of the times, a temper that Trilling himself had greeted in the main with a shrug of weariness. Krupnick's book is in part a reconsideration of those words: "I missed Trilling's leadership at the time and wrote about him with some bitterness in 1971," Krupnick concedes. "I am not disposed to judge him as harshly now as I did fifteen years ago."

> Given the uncertainties Trilling had about nearly everything, it was right for him to turn to history for understanding rather than to trumpet opinions about which he was unsure simply because, in his intellectual milieu, everyone was supposed to have a ready opinion about everything.

Contrition is a great teacher. *Lionel Trilling and the Fate of Cultural Criticism* is a model of intellectual biography, scrupulous and precise, firmly grounded in Trilling's writing yet alive with speculation. Krupnick is also a first-rate writer, a quality that anyone who has slogged his way through clumsier books on contemporary culture is bound to appreciate. The book's most impressive quality is Krupnick's firm command of the cultural environment of New York intellectual life in which Trilling worked. That is more slippery terrain than one might suppose, for once the critic has exhausted the vein of anti-Stalinism that Trilling himself exhausted after *The Liberal Imagination*, he has to scale the higher regions of the cultural *Geist* that Trilling himself occupied in his later years: modernism, psychoanalysis, modern "weightlessness," the tragic sense of life, the rhetoric of authenticity, the adversary culture of the sixties. He has to do his homework. The chapter on "The Uses of Freud," which examines Trilling's strange turn toward biologism in the 1960s, when he wrote the essays that make up *Beyond Culture*, is a small triumph of insight and exactness. To be biological in the sixties suggests a turn toward Wilhelm Reich, but biology in Trilling's hands meant something far removed from Reich's world-transforming eroticism. It was, rather, an abstract principle of moral ballast, a counterforce to the tides of culture that were threatening to drown the modern ego. How one was to behave more biologically was never specified by Trilling, and one suspects that word in his lexicon to have been more a verbal icon than a social program, something remotely to do with instincts and genes. But as Krupnick argues convincingly, it was as provisions in the charter of modern selfhood that terms like "biology" and "beyond culture" (and "energy" and "inertia" and "conditions" and "weightlessness" and "sincerity" and "authenticity") came to life for Trilling.

As death gathers the New York intellectuals into a generation – Irving Howe's memorable phrase – they become fertile ground for critics and historians and, in due course, explicators and exegetes. A cavalcade of memoirs has appeared in elegiac commemoration of those writers and thinkers who had once drawn up the curricula of study and set the agendas of debate for American intellectuals, and the latest critical books are filling up RAM all over America, waiting to be printed out. With *Lionel Trilling and the Fate of Cultural Criticism* Mark Krupnick has set a standard for these studies; the discussion starts on high ground. The book may not make waves, but only because the figure of Trilling presently in eclipse. Our era cherishes other critical temperaments: the hermetic and the hermeneutic, and Trilling was neither. Krupnick's book is a strong argument for the middle ground of sensibility and a case in point of its continuing virtues.

15

In Defense of the Imagination

In the universities these days courses on Jewish literature. history and consciousness are proliferating as a result of student demand and a momentary relaxation of professorial embarrassment, and scholars who had previously devoted their researches to the literary monuments of British culture are being pressed into service as instant Jewishists or, as is commonly the case, Jewish-Americanists, experts in the lower East Side and its cultural legacy. This is step two of the academic naturalization of the Jews; step one was letting them in. So far this is largely back-door operation, relying heavily on Irving Howe for history, Abraham Cahan, Henry Roth, and Saul Bellow for canonical texts, and volunteer labor for instructional personnel. But the underlying shift in self perception, though fraught with confusion, is widespread and beginning to take curricular shape. Students of literature, for whom French and Latin were once *de rigueur*, are now turning to Yiddish and Hebrew as second languages and recognizing the YIVO Institute and New York Public Library for the great scholarly resources they are, where once they dreamed only of the Folger Library or British Museum.

But as anyone knows who has endeavored to reclaim his Jewishness and turn it to intellectual account, Jewish self-definition is no easy matter. One isn't born again as a Jew the way one is as a Baptist; salvation is less to the point than study, and one approaches Jewish culture only to encounter the variety of its traditions and histories and the necessity of making choices: for declaring a specialty. Like Irving Howe, one can pursue one's familial links to the culture of Yiddishkeit and its historical provenance in the cities and shtetls of Eastern Europe. That is a natural line of investigation, since the great majority of American Jews descend from Yiddish-speaking *Ostjuden*, and also because because the conventions and values of Yiddishkeit feed directly into Jewish-American literature, so that writers like Bellow, Roth, and Malamud can seem at times like America's contribution to the last flowering of Yiddish literature.

But there is also the rich and varied bourgeois and assimilated Jewish culture of *Mitteleuropa* that gave us Marx, Freud, and Kafka, and had far less affinity to Yiddishkeit than to the modern and secular culture of post-Enlightenment Europe. And there is Israel, with a literary and linguistic history quite its own.

And, of course, there is the religion: the beliefs, the strict and elaborate ethical codes, and the rituals, as defined in the Torah, the Talmud and its vast train of commentaries, and the Shulhan Arukh, without which the Jews are at best a far-flung and decomposed family of tribes – like the Celts – whose kinship is an illusion of nomenclature and of oppressors shared in common. To draw close to Jewish culture is to see its international, multilingual diversity, the variety of its beliefs and practices, and a religious history so schismatic and tumultuous that, if we are to believe the historian Gershom Scholem, the Jews have forgotten or repressed some of its most trying and spectacular moments.

To draw up an agenda of study, then, we need guides, and Robert Alter deserves to be one of them. Not because Alter presents a fully articulated picture of Jewish culture, but because he is at ease with, and even a partisan of, Jewish pluralism. He believes, with Scholem, "'There is no way of telling *a priori* what beliefs are possible or impossible within the framework of Judaism . . . . The Jewishness in the religiosity of any particular period is not measured by dogmatic criteria that are unrelated to actual historical circumstances, but solely by what sincere Jews do, in fact, believe, or – at least – consider to be legitimate possibilities.'" That makes him a pragmatist of culture as well as an enthusiast of permutation who writes of Jewishness as though it were an adventure that is still unfolding, rather than an achieved body of beliefs, practices, and legends.

That may explain his method of testing his views of Jewishness after the manner of Scholem himself, by seeking out its limiting cases and then arguing for their centrality. Scholem, of course, has done that brilliantly with Jewish mysticism, documenting how an apparently marginal and aberrant line of religious thought has in fact been at times from the twelfth through the nineteenth centuries the very mainstream of the Jewish religion. Alter's test cases in this book are Osip Mandelstam, the Russian-Jewish poet who was nominally Lutheran (it was a conversion of convenience) and began his career thinking of himself as a vestigial Jew; Walter Benjamin, the German critic whose Jewishness had no outstanding doctrinal components (though he was a Zionist) and thus seemed to Hannah Arendt largely a source of "an energy of disengagement," and Scholem himself, the scholar in revolt against traditional lore, whose studies have complicated Jewish historiography by demonstrating just how protean and schismatic the religious history of the Jews has really been. Though other writers figure prominently in these essays, including Hermann Broch, Israeli novelists S. Y. Agnon and Amos Oz, Israeli poets Uri Zvi Greenberg and H. N. Bialik, and the American poet Charles Reznikoff, it is Mandelstam, Benjamin, and Scholem who emerge as Alter's exemplary cases, who confirm a tradition by illustrating how supple and far-ranging "Jewish" thought may be.

Mandelstam and Benjamin were writers *in extremis*, literally under the gun, the one dying in a Soviet prison camp in 1938, the other a suicide in France in 1940, after having been stopped at the Spanish border in his flight from the Nazis. But it is not their victimization that Alter calls attention to, though that is what unites them with the fate of Europe's Jews and makes them symbolic of it, but the commitment to thought and imagination up to the very end. Nadezhda Mandelstam, her husband's memoirist and the person to whom we owe most of our knowledge of Osip Mandelstam, recounts a story told of her husband in a prison camp in Vladivostok, reciting his poems to a gang of non-political prisoners, that is, criminals. "'The criminals offered him bread and the canned stuff and he calmly helped himself and ate . . . . He was listened to in complete silence and sometimes asked to repeat a poem.'" Of Benjamin, we are informed by his friend Scholem, "'[He] could not bring himself to leave Europe for Palestine, even at the eleventh hour, [for] he could not abandon his work at the Bibliotheque Nationale on the book he would never complete, *Paris, Capital of the 19th Century.*'" Such stirring images suggest the core of Alter's concept of heroism: a vital attachment to thought and imagination, conceived as a realm apart from politics and even from impending disaster. Faced with his own imminent extinction the intellectual hero presses on with the business of thinking, writing, and communicating.

Alter writes in defense of the imagination because he holds the imagination to be the last line of defense against the dehumanizing trends of modern history, and writers are heroes because they conserve their humanity in extreme situations: Mandelstam recites poetry to the very end; Benjamin is glued to his desk at the Bibliotheque Nationale; Hermann Broch completes *the Sleepwalkers* in Austria on the eve of Hitler's ascent to power, and , after a brief imprisonment, begins work on *The Death of Virgil*, a novel of pure ideas whose apparent relevance to contemporary politics is tangential at best. But not so, insists Alter, for the vivid inner life is itself subversive and therefore relevant because it challenges totalitarianism at the very source of its power, the power to enter the mind and compel assent from within.

There is nothing uniquely Jewish about the inner life, and Alter cites the example of Vladimir Nabokov, especially in such books as *Invitation to a Beheading* and *Bend Sinister*, as promoting the idea of a rich interiority as the individual's response to the forces that are poised to crush him. "I would contend that . . . his art-centered literary enterprise must finally be seen as a rescue operation on behalf of human consciousness in a world variously contrived to obliterate such consciousness." But it is because Jews have faced history *in extremis* so often that the principle of imaginative resistance becomes a focal point of Jewish identity. The proposition that Mandelstam "did not believe in Judaism or Christianity: he believed in poetry" describes an imaginatively integrated Jewishness deeply interfused with the personality beneath the level of formulated, or even formulable, belief. However marginal his connection to the community of Jews, or to doctrinal Judaism, his faith in the book as a defense of dignity identifies him. Like Benjamin and Broch, Mandelstam holds the book to be sacramental, even though its articles of faith are of his own devising. Doctrinally uncommitted, these writers are deeply religious men. In praising Benjamin, Alter invokes the Talmudic injunction, "Even in the hour of death you should devote yourself to the study of the Law," and observes that "the statement could serve as an apt image of Benjamin in his last years."

> His writing . . . implicitly affirms the ultimate importance of the kind of "study" he had set as his lifework, and its radiant serenity derives in part from that affirmation, made as it is by an extraordinarily supple and original mind confidently aware of its own powers even when delineating the dimensions of chaos.

By making books in general the heart of one's conception of Jewishness in place of the doctrinal books which, until Scholem, we *thought* were the first principles of Jewish identity, Alter allows for Jewish identities more various, extreme, and even heterodox than received notions will allow. He even appears to surpass Scholem in admitting secular Jewishness as a fully integrated portion of the tradition, and saves us the usual lament about the secular Jew as a deteriorated remnant who prefigures the imminent death of the entire culture. Benjamin and Mandelstam are precisely the sorts of intellectuals that Jewishness as secular culture is likely to produce: men in whom traditional practices and beliefs are vestigial and the appeal of ritual non-existent, but for whom the influence of Judaism as intellectual and moral culture is deep and pervasive. Alter appears then to argue that the vitality of Jewish culture and thought may even depend upon ambivalence, biculturalism, and heterodoxy, and that upheavals in consciousness, like the eruptions of mysticism Scholem has unearthed, are authentic efforts at revival, rather than terminal spasms. We may guess that such attitudes toward Judaism imply a politics, and those who are unfamiliar with Alter's work but observe that he is a contributing editor of *Commentary* where most of these essays were first published may suppose that the politics of *Commentary* are latent in his literary attitudes. But that happens not to be so, since the explicit politics of this book is that of the imagination, not of power or social organization, and hence does not observe the tedious polarities of left and right. If it is a conservative politics at all, it is conservative after the example of Lionel Trilling in that it commends intellectual "variousness and possibility," plenitude and depth, which cannot be comprehended by a vocabulary of liberalism and conservatism.

Alter's politics of variousness, which is a cosmopolitan politics, does point to an inevitable conclusion, which he draws in his own calm and lucid fashion: that cultural disarray can be looked upon as an advantage, a respite from tradition that gives us room to re-imagine and revitalize the tradition and to examine tendencies at the farthest reaches of the culture that may prove to be instructive about values at the center.

16

The Partisan

The name of Philip Rahv calls to mind a canonical chapter in the history of the American Left: the romance of American Communism in the early years of the depression, its traumatic end in the wake of the Moscow Trials and the Hitler-Stalin pact, and the recoil from radicalism in the 1940s and 1950s, when anti-Communism made a home for the homeless radicals whom revolutionism had cast adrift. It is a history known, celebrated, and occasionally brandished as a club by its survivors.

Rahv played a pivotal role in this history. Together with William Phillips he founded *Partisan Review* in 1934 under the sponsorship of th New York John Reed Club, a cultural arm of the CPUSA, and three years later stole the magazine away from the Party to re-establish it as a voice of an independent, literary Left, which was nominally Trotskyist but given mainly to the ventilating of radical perspectives by bringing avant-garde art into the claustral arena of Marxist politics. *Partisan Review* quickly became a rallying point for anti-Stalinist radicals and a clearing house for new ideas in a time of political and intellectual confusion. Its rise to prominence in the 1940s, when it was instrumental in weaning the prevailing progressive culture away from what Lionel Trilling called its "liberal imagination," was due largely to Rahv and Phillips' skill in marshaling a restless coalition of radical and avant-garde elements and in knowing, at any particular moment, where to throw their weight and when to pull their punches.

Appraisals of Philip Rahv lead automatically to appraisals of *Partisan Review* because the meaning of his career is synonymous with the historical role of the magazine. If anything, its achievements overshadow his own, at least insofar as his reputation as a writer has been eclipsed by those figures for whom he provided a forum including Lionel Trilling, Saul Bellow, Meyer Schapiro, George Orwell, Sidney Hook, Leslie Fiedler, Harold Rosenberg, and Robert Lowell. To a considerable extent he sacrificed his own career as a writer in order to promote theirs; discovering and promoting talent *was* his career. More than any selection of Rahv's essays, *Partisan Review* itself for the thirty-five years of Rahv's editorship is his authentic collected works, and it is not to slight the contributions of William Phillips or the others who labored with Rahv, or sometimes fretfully under him, to say that the character of the magazine in its heyday, with its adventurous juxtaposition of mandarin aesthetics and socialist politics, its zest for withering polemics, and its trans-Atlantic center of gravity, bore the stamp of Rahv's personality.

Rahv himself was fairly unproductive as a critic: his collected writing would scarcely total up to more than a thick volume of occasional essays and book reviews, a scattering of uncollected editorials and manifestoes, and an unfinished book on Dostoevsky which he labored at in desultory fashion for more than thirty years. Yet the editors of this new volume of his essays [*Essays on Literature and Politics 1932–1972*] are entirely justified in claiming that he was, in his own right, one of the finest literary critics of his generation. I am certainly not the only reader, weary of contemporary academic prose, with its post-modernist vanities and ponderous simulations of scientific rigor, to come happily back to Rahv in admiration of his economy of means, his passion for social ideas, his dialectical dexterity, and his sensitivity to the social and cultural environment of the individual mind. Though he wrote slowly and with considerable pains, he was a formidable rhetorician who drove home his points with a pungency and directness – some would call it ruthlessness – that suggested not only a certain grasp of situations but of the resources of English and the tactics of argument. One thing about Rahv that has been too little understood, perhaps because in conversation his Russian accent could be so overbearing, is his immigrant's love of the English language and his skillful deployment of its riches. Yet his style was no isolated achievement of technique but a quality rooted in the very cast of his mind: of his rationalism and his historicism. Mark Krupnick, who worked with Rahv on his last editorial venture, *Modern Occasions*, which ran for six issues in 1971–72, has observed that Rahv's most important contribution to critical thought was "his insistence on the importance of historical consciousness, Nietzsche's 'sixth sense,' at a time when it was unfashionable."

Rahv was saturated in history, though his involvement with historical ideas had scarcely any resemblance to the placid historicism commonly known as "literary history," which is essentially an abstract assemblage of major "texts" silhouetted against the glow of distant events. Never mind that that glow was sometimes a fire. Nor did he draw Marxist lessons about history as the ineluctable press of "objective conditions," though he had been indoctrinated in the Marxist canons of analysis with their insistence on objective and ineluctable material powers. He was a Jew, a Russian, and an immigrant (he had come over at the age of nine) for whom history was bred in the bone; it was the medium in which a man *had* to live, just as he had to walk on the earth and breathe the air. (The Jews are to history, says Philip Roth in a recent book, what the Eskimos are to snow.) And as a modern Jew and expatriate Russian he took history to be a tragic medium whose keynote was brutality and whose anthem was mass destruction. Yet as a writer and intellectual in search of what Van Wyck Brooks had called a "usable past," he also saw history as the zone of opportunity, the element in which a writer could define his being, which is why literary modernism and revolutionary Marxism did not strike him as fatal opposites, for both were radical efforts to grasp hold of the same desperate experience, the crisis of the European social order, and extract from it principles for conducting one's life. Thus he could honor such writers of reactionary tendency as Eliot and Dostoevsky with the same passion with which, in the early thirties, he did homage to Lenin and Trotsky. It never dawned on him to regard criticism as a refuge above the fray, and even in the post-war decades, when the New Criticism ascended in the academy and battle-scarred ex-communists made their peace with Kierkegaard or Freud or Bishop Sheen, with the mysteries of universal alienation, or the analgesic benefits of psychoanalysis and religion, Rahv remained engaged and loyal to his historicism, even if his ardor had become firmly anti-Communist, like everyone else's.

No one among his contemporaries was more adept at distilling from literature the play of forces impinging upon the artist's imagination, and the writers whom he embraced, Tolstoy, Dostoevsky, Hawthorne, and James, were men whose passions and contradictions implied the historical currents in which they were awash. Dialectician that he was, he always sought the general in the particular, the prevailing tensions of the age reflected, and responded to, in literature. Thus his judgment of the Transcendentalists is stated in that distinctive idiom that gave timbre and weight to his voice:

The Transcendentalist movement is peculiar in that it expresses the native tradition of inexperience in its particulars and the revolutionary urge to experience in its generalities. On a purely theoretical plane, in ways curiously inverted and idealistic, the cult of experience is patently prefigured in Emerson's doctrine of the uniqueness and infinitude, as well as Thoreau's equally steep estimate, of the private man. American culture was then unprepared for anything more drastic than an affirmation of experience in theory alone, and even the theory was modulated in a semi-clerical fashion so as not to set it in too open an opposition to the dogmatic faith that, despite the decay of its theology, still prevailed in the ethical sphere.

This is from Rahv's much-anthologized essay, "The Cult of Experience in American Writing," written in 1940, by which time Rahv had turned away from Marx and Society to something that sounded like Hegel and culture. Even as the centrality of class struggle receded, Rahv continued to imagine the historical process, and the creative process as well, as dialectical, and was confirmed in his view of the latter by Freud, whose Byzantine dramatics of the mind reinforced Rahv's native feel for the drama of self-deception and self-discovery that he found everywhere in fiction. In an earlier essay he had praised Dostoevsky in terms that sounded like a veiled self-appraisal: "The fact is that it is not in the construction of harmonies but in the uncovering of antinomies that his genius found its deeper expression." Yet this turn of mind was no simple methodology or a strategy of interpretation: it was a donnée of experience; a man of contradictions, Rahv just happened to see the world after the manner of Hegel.

In "The Cult of Experience," Rahv struck a note that he would strike time and again: that America's social and intellectual life was marked by a poverty of experience and a thin social and political intelligence. (In this he was essentially following Henry James and echoing Lionel Trilling.) The legacy of Puritanism, which had set stringent limits upon feeling and behavior, and of a primitive capitalism of accumulation that had little use for ideas, let alone for an intelligentsia, had brought into being a national literature of inexperience which overvalued internal energies, underestimated social realities, and ignored entirely social ideas. Rahv's summary dismissal of the proletarian novel, which was ostensibly geared to the exposure of social conditions and which Rahv had once striven to promote on that score, was that it hadn't the vaguest conception of the true inner workings of politics and was devoid of political ideas and of characters who could entertain or act upon them. Cut off from knowledge and experience, it fell back upon pure romance. The problem in Hawthorne, he felt, was that of inexperience, registered in the perplexity with which Hawthorne dealt with, or failed to deal with, the appetites. "He was haunted not only by the guilt of his desires but also by the guilt of his denial of them." Of the romantic symbolists of the nineteenth century: Poe, Hawthorne, and Melville, he charged, "The dilemma that confronted them chiefly manifests itself in their frequent failure to integrate the inner and outer elements of their world so that they might stand witness for each other by way of the organic linkage of object and symbol, act and meaning." Even Henry James's clear realization that life in America was hostage to narrow convention was the sign of his disadvantaged relation to European novelists: "The idea that one should 'live' one's life came to James as a revelation, to the contemporary European writers this idea had long been a thoroughly assimilated and natural assumption."

Upon such a criticism of the American mind Rahv founded the mission of *Partisan Review*: to import Europe into the American consciousness. Before 1938, that meant to expose America to Marx, Lenin, and Trotsky – afterwards, to the likes of Dostoevsky, Orwell, Koestler, Malraux, Berdyaev, and Sartre. In literature, modernity always boiled down to Dostoevsky, his chief example of the writer at one with the modern crisis. Dostoevsky's characters, like the Russian intelligentsia itself, are possessed by ideas and suffer for them. "To his characters," Rahv pointed out, "ideas are a source of suffering. Such people are unknown in countries like America where social tension is at a relatively low point and where, in consequence, the idea counts for very little and is usually dismissed as 'theory.'" Of all modern novelists, Dostoevsky stood in closest relation to the modern experience, which meant for Rahv, as often as not, the Russian example. The peculiar timeliness of *The Possessed*, he would argue in 1938, "flows from the fact that the motives, actions and ideas of the revolutionaries in it are so ambiguous: so imbedded in equivocation, as to suggest those astonishing negations of the socialist ideal which have come into existence in Soviet Russia." By that year the Moscow Trials had confirmed Rahv's earlier break with the Communist Party and set him resolutely on the course of anti-Stalinism that would grow into a full-blown anti-Communism in the 1940s, when, like so many others, he reassessed his earlier revolutionism, embraced America, an uttered two cheers for democracy and capitalism. The Trials also sent Rahv back to Dostoevsky in search of the historical factors that had galvanized revolutionaries with such ardor and then dealt them such a crushing defeat.

Rahv's lifelong engagement with Dostoevsky began at just the moment when his break with Communism was confirmed, as though he had taken the novelist on as a Russian antidote to his particular brand of Russian fever: Bolschevism. He cherished Dostoevsky's suspicion of "the compulsory organization of human happiness," his skepticism about reason and progress, and his instinctive conservatism that is shot through with rebelliousness as bracing alternatives to the chiliastic pep-talks of infantile revolutionism and the authorized camaraderie of the Popular Front. Yet Rahv held Dostoevsky to be, for all his skepticism, at bottom (or *au fond* as he liked to say it) a revolutionist of a uniquely Russian type: a religious revolutionist. "Whatever Dostoevsky's manifest intention," Rahv wrote of the Grand Inquisitor section of *The Brothers Karamazov*, "actually it is one of the most revolutionary critiques of power and authority ever produced." Of *Crime and Punishment* he would add that whatever its manifest theme its latent one was "the right to violent rebellion." It was the violence that Dostoevsky condemned, even as he was secretly drawn toward it, fearing that "if let loose it would tear down the authority of both heaven and earth, and Raskolnikov goes down to defeat to prove his creator right."

Initially it was to draw out the lessons of the Russian revolution and its terrible aftermath that he attended to Dostoevsky, but his focus shifted over the years to become both more literary and more self-regarding. Dostoevsky eventually appealed to Rahv as something of a double in whom he could catch a glimpse of his own contradictory nature. He praised Dostoevsky's ambiguous handling of Raskolnikov's motives in *Crime and Punishment*, observing that "Dostoevsky's capacity to combine his contradictions in a single brain and a single psyche, while staving off the danger of incoherence at the one end and of specious reconciliation at the other, is the victory scored in this novel by the imaginative artist over the ruthless polemicist."

These essays on Dostoevsky's enigmas merit special attention because in them Rahv came close to, if not defining himself through the novelist, at least announcing an intellectual agenda by examining what a life of ideas, pressed to its limits, might sound like. It is not hard to recognize how self-consciously his praise of Dostoevsky is rendered in the passage quoted above, or to see that Rahv was enlisting Dostoevsky in his own struggle with the part of himself that Mary McCarthy had once called an "intransigent . . . pontificating young Marxist." Little wonder that the contradictory Dostoevsky appealed to that element in Rahv that was torn between Bolschevist declamation and Jamesean fastidiousness, between playing exile, rebel, and stranger and settling in with his own exquisite tastes in food, clothing, and women.

The many disarming accounts of Rahv's grand manner at home, his imposing imitations of the bourgeois *gentilhomme*, give us pause to wonder to what extent that manner was a studied incongruity, a dressing up of what Lionel Trilling called an "opposing self," to be played off against his grim, Dostoevskian persona as an assertion that he was no man to be pinned down. Of course, expatriate or not, he was really neither an underground man nor a Raskolnikov, however he may have been beguiled by the dismal charm of life in St. Petersburg. But then, as he took pains to point out, neither of those figures was Dostoevsky, though both enacted various parts of their author's potentials and played them out as if in study of their consequences

A good part of the rationale for this new volume on the part of its editors, Arabel Porter and Andrew Dvosin, was to bring together Rahv's Dostoevsky essays for the first time and present them as a book-in-progress. Yet brought together they explain why Rahv could not finish the book, for they were written by two, maybe three, men with widely divergent points of view. No manner of tinkering could have drawn together the strands of thought or endowed these essays, written as much as thirty-four years apart, with a book's uniformity of design. The earliest essay, on "Dostoevsky and *The Possessed*," written originally in 1938 in reaction against the Moscow Trials and later revised for inclusion in Rahv's first anthology, *Image and Idea* (1949), was conceived in outrage and desperation and is both intensely personal and thoroughly political. In 1938, Rahv was reasoning his way out of his allegiance to the Russian Revolution, and even in the 1940s, when he revised the essay, he was still busy extricating himself from doctrinal Marxism. The revision, which is published here, reflects, in its agitation, the depths of Rahv's revulsion and uncertainty. As late as 1954, in writing about "The Legend of the Grand Inquisitor," Stalinism and Fascism were still very much on his mind, and Rahv was impelled to return to the relevance of that parable to the "modern historical experience." "The figure of the Grand Inquisitor is dramatically compelling enough to stay permanently on our minds as a symbolic character-image of the dialectic of power." It may be too simple to call this particular essay a Cold War piece, though the Cold War was certainly the context and occasion for it, but it spoke for the lingering outrage of the betrayed revolutionists for whom the question of Russia and the collapse of "their" revolution had not yet been laid to rest.

By the sixties, in an essay on *Crime and Punishment*, Rahv seems at least to have abandoned his obsession with Russia's politics and traded in his historicism for an *ad hoc* psychologism. Taking up the question of Raskolnikov's crime, Rahv praised Dostoevsky's handling of motives in rendering Raskolnikov's behavior indeterminate. He congratulated Dostoevsky for his insight that "in the last analysis . . . human consciousness is inexhaustible and incalculable. It cannot be condensed into something so limited and specific as a motive." Two later essays, on "Notes from Underground" and "The Other Dostoevsky," both dated 1972 by the editors of this volume, one year before Rahv's death, take leave of both psychology and history and veer off toward something that sounds like conventional literary study, with their diffuse surveys of literary "themes" and Dostoevsky's ideas. They are disheartening. Set alongside of Rahv's vigorous writing of earlier years they sound donnish and impersonal; the mastery of idiom has grown slack and the prose turned fussy and verbose, as Rahv's classic muscularity of phrase has faded into dreamy expositions punctuated by cranky tirades against other critics. In sum, there was no book in the offing, and eleventh-hour efforts to produce one revealed just how stalled the project had become, probably, I would guess, at the point where the fuel of anti-Stalinism had run out. Without it, or a suitable replacement, Rahv had simply lost the thread.

A second rationale of the editors for bringing out this new selection of essays was to include some of the purely political writings that Rahv himself had kept out of his own authorized anthologies: *Image and Idea, The Myth and the Powerhouse,* and *Literature and the Sixth Sense.* "For unexplained reasons," puzzles Dvosin in his introduction, "Rahv omitted from his three collections of criticism most of the . . . essays which dealt directly with politics." It is a welcome addition to our picture of Rahv to have some of these essays and editorials made accessible, though it is plain to see why Rahv had endeavored to put them out of sight. Most are occasional pieces, hectoring, strident, and perishable pronouncements that reveal Rahv to have been far more rigid in his political judgments than in his literary ones and embarrassingly submissive in his youth to Party dogma and Marxist assault tactics. In a 1934 review of Fitzgerald's *Tender is the Night* (in the *Daily Worker*), he bravely admonished the author that no amount of good taste nor "the standards of the *Satuday Evening Post*" would protect him from the coming revolution. "Dear Mr. Fitzgerald, you can't hide from a hurricane under a beach umbrella." Rahv knew well enough that no lasting reputation could be founded on such stuff, nor upon later anti-Stalinist manifestoes (such as "Trials of the Mind," included here) which are both overbearing and confused, and couched in rhetoric that hardens in the throat just as it does in the heart. In giving us a taste of Rahv as a propagandist, Porter and Dvosin have inadvertently vindicated Rahv's apparent judgment on the matter: that he was not a political thinker of the first rank. He was a *literary* intellectual first and foremost.

Moreover, Rahv's politics were just too unstable to be fairly represented in a trade-press anthology of such scope, and what we get as a result is an unduly linear view of his ascent from Communism, uncomplicated by the intricate maneuvers and delicate mid-course corrections – including a brief return to revolutionism in the 1960s – that his politics really entailed. Briefly presented like this without a more ample introduction to put them in perspective, these essays make Rahv sound like a more simple-minded representative of his generation than he was.

It is good to have Rahv back in print, though for my money I'd prefer to see Houghton Mifflin reissue his 1969 collection, *Literature and the Sixth Sense*, possibly augmented by some of the Dostoevsky chapters and a few essays from *Modern Occasions*. *Literature and the Sixth Sense* is the fuller collection of the two, forty-four essays to thirty-five, and the richer in its selection of Rahv's best criticism. Porter and Dvosin have come up with less by attempting to do more and have given us in consequence a Rahv sampler rather than the definitive edition we sorely need.

17

Ambition and the American Scholar

It was not so long ago that Jewish intellectuals in America carried on in public like exiled Russians, one minute exhorting the masses to revolt, the next issuing moody notes from the Dostoevskian underground. In those feverish days, revolutionism and alienation seemed like two sides of the same romantic coin. Now in the age of the Superbowl, Jewish intellectuals come on more like football coaches: upbeat, All-American, and avid for victory. There is still that quaver of fear in their exhortations; this is halftime and America is 24 points down. But in lieu of fiery denunciations of the dying order we now get pep talks. As if to rally our fallen spirits, they write books with decidedly boosterish titles: *Making It, Breaking Ranks, Two Cheers for Capitalism, We Must March My Darlings, Free to Choose,* and now, *Ambition.* They belabor us with positive thinking. One is a little astounded at how smooth the journey was from Trotskyism to Rockneism. There are even Jewish intellectuals today who will not rest easy until there is a quarterback in the White House. [Author's note, 1988. That campaign has recently fall flat once again, but in politics as in sports, the Quarterback Club keeps its nose in there.]

On the evidence of *Ambition,* Joseph Epstein would appear to be one of them. Certainly had Jack Kemp been this year's Republican nominee for President, *Ambition* could have been passed out at prayer meetings and homecoming rallies across the country as campaign literature. Though Kemp is nowhere present by name, he is there in spirit, hovering with ah, bright wings above the book's heroes of luck and pluck: Ben Franklin, John D. Rockefeller, Meyer Guggenheim, Henry Ford, E. I. (Eleuthere Irenée) du Pont, and Joseph Kennedy. A rags-to-riches kid, who parlayed a simple gift for throwing a football great distances into a professional career and, afterwards, a major political one as well, Jack Kemp should be Epstein's kind of American: an example to youth of how opportunities should be exploited in a free-market economy.

Why this detour through Jack Kemp when the subject is Joseph Epstein? Because to read Epstein here in Buffalo, where sports is a Jacob's Ladder into politics, is to think of Kemp, currently our most notable case in point. Epstein is a sports fan, who trusts in the adage that competition builds character (and, as a corollary, that taxation saps the will), extols those virtues of business that apply equally to the gridiron, and is steeped in the ethic of the lately defunct United States Football League: that the best defense is a good offense.

Ambition is a book about the national character. Unlike its predecessor in celebrating the successful life, Norman Podhoretz's *Making It*, *Ambition* is not an exercise in self-aggrandizement. The side of Epstein's public persona that is inclined to preen itself, which is no small portion of it, appears to have had its say in his collection of *American Scholar* essays, published in 1979 under the title, *Familiar Territory*. *Ambition* is a more impersonal book, a rambling dissertation on the passion for self-improvement as the cornerstone of contemporary life and, lest that sound insufficiently ambitious, as the *sine qua non* of a high civilization. "Whatever its excesses," Epstein assures us, taking the long view of Western Civilization, "ambition has at all times been the passion that best releases the energies that make civilization possible." While that word blankets a world of attitudes, Epstein leaves no doubt as to what he means by it. It is a desire for the world's acclaim and its goods, a coveting of what the world recognizes as success.

That, precisely, is the book's fatal flaw, from which it never escapes. No matter how Epstein manipulates his definitions to wring broader conclusions from his narrow sympathies – to claim, as he does toward the end, that his book is really a praise of the will and the *vita activa* – his overwhelming message is that ambition's only rewards lie up the greasy pole of capitalist success. The *vita activa* is fine if you happen to be a captain of industry, and as for the will, so much the better if your employees can exert it for you. Epstein's brands of ambition and will leave no room for the modest or the private: the pride of craft extolled by Veblen or such non acquisitive ambitions as the desire to live well, to gain pleasure from life, to brighten the corner where you are. What can he make of something like Malcolm Cowley's recent recollection that as a young man "he had few worldly ambitions; that is, he didn't want to be rich or famous too soon, or occupy a place of influence, or be a leader; he simply wanted to write better than others." Is that not an ambition to be reckoned with, or was the young Cowley just kidding himself, hiding behind his more tasteful desires in order not to admit his antisocial ones? Epstein leaves us in the dark on the subject of ambitions that fall this side of the spectacular; he'll have no truck with liberal platitudes about smaller as better. Starstruck as he is with success on the grand scale, he is impatient with the modest strivings of the ordinary life.

Ambition is a little *McGuffy Reader* for intellectuals, consisting of stirring vignettes from the lives of the great, spiced with illuminating quotes from the successful and famous and cautionary admonitions about the flagging of energy in our time. Toynbee-esque in its cyclical view of our history, it suggests that we are now on the downward leg of our cycle. *Das Untergang des Guggenheims*, which Epstein vividly depicts, is something of a metaphor for America itself. America is one vast Faulknerian clan, its vitality running down from one generation to the next, like the South from Sartoris to Snopes. But the book doesn't dwell overlong on the decay of fortunes, for Epstein is more fascinated with their making and with the shaping of America through the accumulation and deployment of capital. Though his meandering tales of great endeavor frequently seem pointless, the same lessons apply to all. One, that the life of a winner is invariably better, more pleasurable, than that of a loser. (Though Epstein probably knows better, he allows his book to give the impression that anyone who is not a big winner is, *ipso facto*, a big loser. The *via media* strikes Epstein as a poor substitute for the big killing.) Two, that the personal ambitions and visions of the Fords, Rockefellers, *et al.* built and gave shape to America. The Captains of Industry are the true Founding Fathers. "Deplorable and self-centered though much of the conduct of the robber-barons generation was, ruthless and rueful though many of its leading figures have come to seem, after all that is bad has been said about them, it needs to be said yet again that they built up the country." They were sons-of-bitches on behalf of the future, and their legacy to all was an American standard of living that was, until lately, second to none in the world. We are all in their debt, and the grumbling of liberals about their social aberrations, such as Ford's anti-Semitism, or about such side-effects of industrial capitalism as inflation, monopoly, alienation, the consolidation of power, the boom and bust cycle, the routine of labor, structural unemployment, and windfall profits is not only gross ingratitude but hypocrisy as well. Notwithstanding his vicious campaigns against the Jews (he is mentioned by name in the American edition of *Mein Kampf*) and his terrible record in dealing with labor, Ford earns Epstein's praise as "The Car Humanitarian."

Epstein does concede a few eidolons of ambition who were not robber barons. As an English professor, after all, he is obliged to defer in some small measure to writers, and he does have some preferences, though not everyone will share them or his reasons for them. Edith Wharton has his approval for having been born into money and having survived the stifling conditions of life at the top to become the novelist of her class. Wallace Stevens managed to combine a lifetime's commitment to poetry with a career in insurance without neglecting his obligations to either. Granting the inner strength implied in both examples, we might nonetheless ask why these writers, of all the examples of triumph over adversity our literature has to offer, should be singled out for special praise. If Stevens is a paragon of ambition for combining poetry and insurance, what of William Carlos Williams, the poet-obstetrician of Paterson? The answer would appear to be that Wharton and Stevens are proof positive that the imagination may thrive in atmospheres dominated by money and business, and that neither the regal salons of Park Avenue nor the bustling offices of the Hartford are, as the liberal imagination would have them, prison houses of the intellect. Williams, only a small-town doctor, would not meet such terms for heroism; he was not ambitious enough to have jeopardized his art with finance and commerce. Moreover, he harbored all kinds of left-wing sentiments, which, for Epstein, would be enough to call both his ambition and his poetry into question.

As for Scott Fitzgerald, who did come into close quarters with big money, his collapse is an exemplary "failure of success," that is, a failure of nerve attendant upon an immature attitude toward money. As Epstein asks, in speaking of the actor Richard Dreyfuss and the writer Michael Harrington, both of whom have confessed to having been thrown off balance by early fame and its rewards, "Is their determination – as well as that of others determined to fail at success – anything more than a grim determination not to grow up?" Neoconservative morality is always on the side of growing up.

Alas for America, the grim determination to remain a child has grown into a national pastime, and the qualms of a Michael Harrington are nothing less than symptoms of a general loss of morale. The will to succeed and the social ambitions that feed it are in eclipse, most notably among the educated classes whose position in society may be due to the very values they now affect to despise.

"Ambition connotes a certain Rotarian optimism, a thing unseemly, in very poor taste, rather like a raging sexual appetite in someone quite elderly." Epstein proposes several "unarguable" theses about contemporary life, the unarguable thesis being to the conservative temper what the non-negotiable demand was to the radical. "To say of a young man or woman that he or she is ambitious is no longer, as it once was, a clear compliment. Rather the reverse. A person called ambitious is likely to arouse anxiety, for in our day anyone so called is thought to be threatening, possibly a trifle neurotic."

For the conservative imagination (the neo makes no useful distinction here), this autumnal mood that has taken hold of us is the very cause of our decline. It suggests "a people that has lost its way, its energy, its dreams – in a word, its ambition." Epstein, citing Durkheim's observation that success is the very basis of our social life, tells us that with the decline of success has come an unraveling of the social fabric. American is fading in the stretch, as its ascendant classes succumb to ennui and the feeling that "the world is pretty well used up." Should one mistakenly ask men of ideas for guidance, one finds among them, save in pockets of neoconservative vigilance, languor and self-indulgence of nearly Proustian proportions.

Anyone who is acquainted with the neoconservative literature of crisis will recognize these sentiments at once. They are as familiar as Milton Friedman and Ben Wattenberg's faces on public television (made possible, of course, by grants from the Mobil Oil company). America has been swallowed up by California – not the California of agribusiness and aerospace but the California of Jerry Brown and inner space, of boutiques and plant shoppes, roller skates, marijuana farms, health foods, hot tubs, zero population growth, sex surrogates, and non-smoking areas in every encounter group. Boutique America, as Epstein calls it in one of his cavalier *American Scholar* essays, has opted out of geopolitics for the nirvanic pools of vacant narcissism. A particularly wacky and colorful version of this thesis is currently being propagated by Lyndon LaRouche, once a Left ideologue, lately a "Democratic" candidate for President. It holds that America's will and resolve are being sapped by an "Aquarian conspiracy" to bliss us right out of the world power game, masterminded by the Tavistock Clinic in London and administered at home by such transparent fronts for therapeutic sabotage as the Trilateral Commission, the Rand Corporation, and Herman Kahn's Hudson Institute.

But where the astrological Right sees empires striking back, the "responsible" Right looks for small perturbations in the *Zeitgeist*: Epstein's version of the American failure of nerve is becoming to an intellectual who is steeped in the great books, has no end of faith in the written word, and takes political guidance from Lionel Trilling. Accordingly, we've come to this sorry pass because *the American novel has sabotaged the American will*. "Although they are not often spoken of thus, novels are among the world's greatest instruments of personal education. People, and especially the young, take from novels a great many things, not all of them what the novelists themselves may have originally intended . . . . It would be naive to assume that many of the notions that Americans hold about ambition do not originate in the novels they have read."

This is not an announcement that fiction in the modern era has been uniformly hostile to the big money, but a claim that the novel has succeeded utterly in reforming the American heart, detaching Americans from the moral equivalents of the gold standard. *The* novel, of all things, turns out to be the *fons et origo* of our failure of nerve; it has so succeeded in putting its message across that it has captured the middle-class, whose social tastes and political habits are now preeminently "adversary culture" phenomena. (This "adversary culture" explanation of our apostasy from the Church of Ambition is not quite the same thing as the "new class" analysis, the one deriving from considerations of the role of art in the formation of culture, the other from a class analysis of contemporary society. But in conservative hands both yield the conclusion that America's leading classes have become spoiled.) "Antisuccess has been perhaps the strongest strain in American literature of the past half-century. And to be against success is to put ambition itself in grave doubt." Since our affliction is patently a failure of nerve, and since, as everyone knows, the native hue of resolution is sicklied o'er by the pale cast of liberal thought, it must be the liberal-modernist complex in our culture that is sapping our will. Our strategic weaknesses are *au fond* cultural failings, since every breach in our geopolitical armor is really a hairline fracture in the American will writ large. Come Election Day, not only is the nerve gap as predictable as the missile or preparedness gaps, it is the very same thing.

This business of demanding affirmative action from our novelists combines the vanity of the professor, who happily discovers in his special field the very fulcrum of the culture, with the zeal of the crusader, who takes literature to be the zone of our affliction. The literary crusader, who cares nothing for the imagination and is indifferent to questions of craft or form, asks only that art be salutary, positive, and morally bracing. Epstein's version of this Sunday service dispenses with the bleakly spiritual side of sanctity in favor of supplications to the local chamber of commerce. Once business is back on its feet and has the moral sanction of the imagination, the spirit will fend nicely for itself.

Literature has always been a whipping boy for apocalypse vendors, especially when they've been English professors, art historians, or literary radicals who've seen the light. From Irving Babbitt's fulminations against Romanticism to Epstein, Podhoretz, and Hilton Kramer's campaigns against the counterculture of the sixties, the business of taking literature to be the enemy of the common man or the life drive or American pluck and know-how or whatever version of the solid life is currently in vogue has been all but an industry. Indeed, were *Ambition* handed to us without a title page we would be justified in mistaking it for a typical product of the 1940s, when American writers were coming off their binge of leftism and taking the pledge of literary nationalism by the wagonload. Best remembered now are Archibald MacLeish's attack on the "irresponsibles," those writers who did not leap to the defense of Western values against Fascist ideology, and Van Wyck Brook's attack on modernist writing as "coterie literature," doomed to triviality for its antipathy to the "life drive." And once Brooks and MacLeish gave the signal, others quickly joined the pack, including Bernard DeVoto, who complained of fiction's neglect of the common life, and J. Donald Adams, who launched weekly raids upon negativism and "the existentialist flubdub" from his command post at the *New York Times Book Review*.

The critic whose arguments most closely resembled Epstein's however, was John Chamberlain, who wrote for the Luce publications after the War and did a piece for *Fortune* in 1948 that made a considerable stink: "The Businessman in Fiction." If one were to believe current fiction, he wrote, the businessman "belonged to a species of indigenous American monster that specialized in subverting the press, bribing the government, shooting it out with labor, and packing the colleges with spineless professors who kowtowed to the monster's least responsible whims." Business deserved a new deal of its own; it was time America's novelists spoke up for its ingenuity, its dynamism, its genius for sharing the wealth. Underlying such enthusiasm was the definitive blend of post-depression optimism and post-Marxist guilt that gave the literary mood of the 1940s its distinctive manic-depressive moodiness. In addition to that there was the spirit of the "managerial revolution," which had replaced the Rasputins of capitalism with modest executives, who were reputed to be the reasonable, self-effacing (even faceless) guys who lived on your block and played on your team. The Henry Fords, John D. Rockefellers, Irving Thalbergs, and Jay Goulds now belonged to the folklore of capitalism, not the actuality of business.

History will record that for all the hectic campaigning by Brooks, MacLeish, Chamberlain, and the volunteers who enlisted in their brigade, fiction was not reformed. Except for John Dos Passos, whose later novels were monotonous efforts to undo the harm he had done in his radical youth, novelists who had had their fill of rebellion in the 1930s did not rush to take communion on Wall Street later on. They drew strength, rather, from the power of negative thinking, showing a decided preference for alienation over boosterism. The efforts to inject a note of celebration into our writing, then, could be virtually dismissed were they not omens of the crusade for political conformity that descended in the 1950s upon Hollywood, where the studio system and heavy capital investment made artists especially vulnerable to the whims and fears of the moguls, who had not yet retired to the Museum of Business History.

Joseph Epstein's *Ambition* is not nearly so ominous. *Kulchubolschewismus*, as Dwight Macdonald called it in the 1940s, is not around the corner this time, except in such a wholly controlled medium as television, whose evil takes the form of unrelieved banality. But contrary to Macdonald's fears about the fate of culture under constant mobilization for war, we've apparently learned to cope with the Cold War without, to take a line from Tom Lehrer, imprisoning an American every time the Soviet Union imprisons a Russian. That Epstein's tastes, however, do not augur an official standard that will soon bear down upon us does not make them any more palatable.

Epstein has correctly noted – how could he not? – that our literature, notwithstanding its own status as a big business, is a holdout against the values of commercial civilization, and he has determined that the stronghold must be taken. Rather than value the pressure that the imagination of life places upon the day to day practice of it and cherish literature as a lonely and rather feeble point of opposition to the idols of the marketplace, he champions the commercial life against the imaginative on the ground that some "adversary culture" of literary parentage has won out over the money culture, and that the latter is now desperately in need of revival, being the very root of our national vitality. Literature has shorn our Samson's locks.

That is the silliest and most dangerous port of Epstein's book, the pretense that the commercial foundations of our society have been undermined by currents of radical chic, as though the chambers of commerce everywhere were occupied by hippies and English majors, bent on greening America at any cost. Unless this world looks a good deal different from Evanston than it does from Buffalo, I fail to see how anyone can blame this winter of our discontent on the alienated views of literary modernism. The prevailing *fleur du mal* in this town is the unemployment of precisely that echelon of Buffalo society that does not read novels.

Yet the illusion that he is holding a tiny beachhead against withering fire has to be defended, lest it dawn on Epstein that his bold counteroffensive may be no more than a mopping-up operation. The pose of embattlement, which sustains the mythos of neoconservatism, serves nicely to mask the self-congratulation of the top dog. More self-assured conservatives, who didn't arrive at the metaphysics of self-interest by tortuous paths from CCNY or its equivalents (for Epstein it was the anti-poverty program in Arkansas), have no need of the excesses of the adversary or counter cultures to justify their principles, which would be quite the same no matter what barbarities were in vogue in Berkeley or at the *New York Review of Books*.

What a dreary spectacle! Here is the Jewish intellectual of our day, the editor of *The American Scholar*, at last free of his own tormented past and so secure in his adjustment to his little room at the top that his *tout pardonner* no longer needs even so meager a rationale as *tout comprendre*. Even Henry Ford is forgiven his trespasses against the Jews. Now the world of our fathers boasts a car humanist.

18
Three Honest Men

In the mid-1970s, Philip French, a film critic for the *Observer* and producer of talks and documentaries for the BBC's Third Programme, now Radio Three, produced three programs on major literary critics, taking Edmund Wilson, F. R. Leavis, and Lionel Trilling as his subjects. Splicing together queries and observations of his own with taped reminiscences by others, French assembled what he called "critical mosaics," in which the outlines of these critics' careers were drawn, to the degree they could be, in miniature. It is the method of oral history brought to the history of ideas, and as any documentarian knows it is no simple matter to select the right commentators and to elicit from them responses that are both exact and mutually complementary.

French did admirably on both counts. Commentaries on Wilson were contributed by Trilling, Stephen Spender, V. S. Pritchett, John Wain, Jason Epstein, Yigael Yadin (Israeli archaeologist and expert on the Dead Sea scrolls), and George Steiner; on Leavis by Steiner, Muriel C. Bradbrook, Denys W. Harding, William Walsh, Roy Fuller, John Gross, Christopher Ricks, Stuart Hall, and Martin Green, and on Trilling by Morris Dickstein, Quentin Anderson,Irving Howe, Norman Podhoretz, Alfred Kazin, Jacques Barzun, Stephen Donadio, Steven Marcus, and Daniel Aaron. Little wonder that French thought to preserve his achievement in print, since what he had captured was a thin but recognizable cross-section of contemporary intellectual history.

The disadvantages of the format, in which disembodied voices are so patently being manipulated by the man at the switchboard, are self-evident. Where respondents are selected for their well-known views, nothing new is likely to be said. Moreover, the brevity of the contributions and the lack of cross-talk has the effect of draining lively issues of much of their heat. But the format also has strengths that a skillful producer can exploit. The way he deploys otherwise predictable remarks may bring about unexpected illuminations, just as ordinary ingredients in the hands of a skilled chef can turn into strange potions. Contributions are expected to be brief, and most of French's contributors, obliged to curb their volubility, proved to be masters of concision. And while no issue could be probed at length, the range of issues briefly touched on is substantial.

French's title, *The Honest Men*, is misleading if it be supposed that he celebrates these critics for their special sincerity and love of truth. He explains that by honesty he means something like intellectual self-reliance, and the conviction, shared in common by all three, that "ultimately men and minds must prevail over methods, and where they do not the insights and judgments will lack savour and intellectual authority." That self-reliance, that dissenter's anathema of system and doxology, runs like a bright thread through all the portraits, and the book might better have been title, without giving offense, *Anglo-Saxon Attitudes* or *Studies in Protestantism* for the temper and method that Wilson, Trilling, and Leavis shared: a mixture of independence and sobriety that bespeaks a heritage of Protestant dissent, of which Trilling's Judaism may be thought a version. The book fairly bristles with imposing phrases like "the right moral framework," "the spiritual conditions of life," "the state of civilization," and "the defense of beleaguered traditions." "Confronted by the page," says George Steiner of Leavis, "he reads with a scruple, with a totality of attention and with such informing power . . . that he elicits from himself, and from all those readers whom he invites to collaborate with him, a response which is also in a full sense responsibility – responsibility, that is, towards literature, towards language, toward the conditions of political society and of education, in which literature can be a human, shaping force, a discipline which makes our feelings richer and more exact." Imposing, to say that least, all that informing power and shaping force. Faced with so stern an example of scruple and responsibility, we might incline to wonder of the individual in question were a critic or a rabbi, and it might be said that the attitude to literature in all three instances is decidedly religious, and that Wilson, Leavis, and Trilling were men who, in less secular ages, might well have found their calling in the ministry or the rabbinate.

Though none had a lasting relation to Marxism, Wilson and Trilling passed briefly through Marxist phases in the 1930s and suffered lingering after-effects that might warrant our thinking of them later as "post-Marxists. All three shared the Marxist's propensity for seeing the world whole, tempered by the Hegelian view of that wholeness as essentially spiritual and therefore uniquely subject to probing by the imagination. They admitted no distinction between literary values and social or spiritual ones, but assumed a single moral universe in which literature, the novel in particular, spoke for the spiritual condition of society. Criticism, then, possessed a quasi-doctrinal value and participated with literature in both the definition of culture and its formation; criticism, as much as literature, performed a duty in the chastening of conduct and the nurturing of the emotions. Steven Marcus calls attention to Trilling's admiration for Freud as a stoic moralist, who gave approval to the renunciation of desire and portrayed civilization as a structure of sublimations. Jason Epstein, commenting on Wilson's stubborn independence of mind, hails him as a "man of the Old Testament." As for Leavis, his stirring rendition of the prophet Jeremiah is everywhere noted. Though only Leavis ever assumed the full Mosaic character of prophet scorned, all three suffered severe dejection, of sometimes bitter depths, in their later years. This books gives us a glimpse of Wilson in the 1950s, squabbling with the Internal Revenue Service over his income tax, which he withheld in protest against the Cold War and the follies of American imperialism, his house a tumult of lawyers, accountants, and canceled checks as he faced the prospect of going to prison. We see Trilling in his gloom over the cultural revolution of the 1960s, which he dubbed "modernism in the streets" and whose local manifestations at Columbia University he felt, as a teacher of modern literature, a modicum of responsibility for. We see Leavis growing every more bitter, immoderate, and dismissive of just about everything modern, including, it seems, Wilson and Trilling. Here, surely, were ministers without a church, except in the Arnoldian sense in which literature itself is a prosthetic, secular church possessing all the customary accouterments of a religion: canons of faith, moral drama, dogma, consolation, schism, and ecclesiastical contention.

But for Wilson and Trilling at least, though not, I think, Leavis, literature was a church of skepticism in which doubts and resistances were honored above doctrines. In such a church could the one's residual Calvinism join hands with the other's threadbare Judaism, both cultural identities that had outlived the religions that had formed them, existing only as isolated habits of being, codes of personal decorum that placed a premium on work, forthrightness, and integrity and set high standards for politics and culture. Cultural Judaism, divorced from the beliefs and ceremonies of Jewish life and the stringent demands and observances of the Jewish religion, maintained only as a discipline of individual nobility, becomes a kind of Protestantism by default, strong in routines of dissent but weak in principles of affirmation. Similarly, Protestantism, released of any conception of heaven and hell and the doctrine of man's salvation through god's sacrifice of his only begotten son, melts into the brand of secular Judaism described by Matthew Arnold as "Hebraism." As the stern and exalted rhetoric that marks these symposia makes plain, the church of literature, in which these three men could pursue their callings at so steep a pitch of moral intensity, is a makeshift parsonage in which lie reconciled and indistinguishable the secularized remains of two-once potent religions: Judaism and Protestantism.

It is such illuminations by juxtaposition that an otherwise scattershot book like *Three Honest Men* is good for. The book is finally and essentially a compendium of commonplaces that some of its readers will be familiar with. But these are vital commonplaces that bear retelling; given what passes for advanced work in the book world, some commonplaces are decidedly welcome and attractive.

19

An American Procession

In 1983, Harcourt, Brace, Jovanovich reissued Alfred Kazin's first book, *On Native Grounds*, in a fortieth anniversary edition, an event that went virtually unnoticed save at Hilton Kramer's *The New Criterion*, where the knives were being sharpened in the wake of Kazin's observations, in *The New York Review of Books* ("Saving My Soul at the Plaza") in March, on the Committee for the Free World's conference on "our country and our culture" at the Plaza. Kazin's strictures on that conference – on the callowness of its prevailing attitudes and its shrillness of tone – earned him a rebuke by *The New Criterion:* a reconsideration of *On Native Grounds* by Kenneth Lynn, who took it to task for its errors of fact (the Manhattan-bound Kazin had thought, as a young man, that there were mountains in Hemingway's northern Michigan) and for its unbridled leftism. Written in the dog days of the depression, *On Native Grounds* was, it seems, unaccountably sour on the prospects for American society and irresponsibly "radical" in its scorn for American business.

That flawed but promising book (Lynn gave it passing grades for style) was, we were told, the high water mark of Kazin's career, and even it has not stood the test of time so well as its contemporary volumes: Perry Miller's *The New England Mind: The Seventeenth Century* and F. O. Matthiessen's *The American Renaissance.* "'No one can tell us,'" Lynn solemnly quoted Kazin, "'all that F. Scott Fitzgerald meant when he said that "there are no second acts in American lives" or why we have been so oppressed by the sense of time, or why our triumphs have been so brittle.' When he wrote those searing words in the preface of the first edition of *On Native Grounds*," Lynn concluded, "the twenty-seven-year-old Kazin was unwittingly composing the epitaph for his own career."

They don't mince words at *The New Criterion*, just reputations, their mission in American letters being to grind literary reputations into rubble. The careful discriminations that once marked T.S. Eliot's original *Criterion* in the 1930s have degenerated into demolitions in

Hilton Kramer's new magazine, whose first criterion of judgment sounds like nothing so much as the slogan of the Republican forces in the Spanish Civil War: *no pasaran*. But even by the lowest *New Criterion* standard, which holds that no career is so exalted that it cannot be blackened, this assault was uncommonly foolish, for it singled out for special reprimand Kazin's "radicalism," a posture so elusive that no one lacking a neo-conservative radar gun can spot it. Kazin, it seems, had fancied himself a radical in *On Native Grounds* and taken the usual swipes at capitalism, and Lynn, sounding quite as if he had just pulled a major cache of microfilms out of a pumpkin, took him at his word. To most readers, on the contrary, Kazin's rhapsodies on America, from *On Native Grounds* to the present time, sound more like the Gershwin brothers than, say, V. I. Parrington, to whom Lynn compares him. As for his failure to come out for the second act, it comes as a distinct surprise to those legions of critics who would gladly swap Kazin's dismal record – seven books since *On Native Grounds* – for their own and be only too happy to take the blame for a vagrant mountain or two in Michigan's upper peninsula as the price of such failure. In our time, which lacks a single great critic to dominate and define the landscape, Kazin is the closest thing we have to a master, a curious master to be sure, caustic and poetic and fonder of rhapsodies than of analyses, but a master in terms that any student of American literature can appreciate. He commands a major literature; he possesses a distinct point of view that charges whatever it touches with meaning, and he writes with a pungency and concision that no other American critic can equal.

An American Procession is the chronicle of a hundred-year period in American literary history, from 1830 to 1930, starting with Emerson and halting abruptly with Eliot, Pound, Faulkner, and Hemingway in mid-career. Kazin begins with Emerson because "Whitman . . . predicted correctly that 'America in the future, in her long train of poets and writers, while knowing more vehement and luxuriant ones, will . . . acknowledge nothing nearer [than] this man, the actually beginner of the whole procession . . . .'" It was Emerson's commanding sense of self that precipitated so much of what was militantly individual in the American character. This God-intoxicated man was the intellectual Godfather of the writers who came after him, even those like Poe, Hawthorne, and Melville, who took a dim view of Emerson's indwelling divinity and held themselves in strict opposition. " . . . What Emerson called his 'one' doctrine – 'the infinitude of the private mind' – nevertheless gave a special radiance to *Nature, Walden,* 'Song of Myself,' and even *Moby Dick,* a radiance that has allowed millions to remember 'morning in America' and that sustains some sense of self in our very different world. The world is always new to those who can see themselves in a new light." This is the sort of aria we have come to expect of Kazin, whose own word-intoxication strikes us as a displacement downward of Emerson's God intoxication.

But *An American Procession* is ruled by darker notes, and it is in the chapters on Melville, Poe, Hawthorne, Henry Adams, Henry James, Emily Dickinson, and T. S. Eliot that Kazin warms to his central theme. Our national penalty for our Emersonian ecstasy and self-exaltation is a trait that de Tocqueville had identified as the isolation of the individual in democratic society, for democracy "throws him back upon himself alone, and threatens in the end to confine him entirely within the solitude of his own heart." (It is no accident that Kazin's history, in its broadest outlines, looks like the manic-depressive cycle on a national scale, as if Kazin himself had discovered in the American procession a map of his own problematic emotions.) Thoreau's isolation found relief only in words, his journal being "the most unflagging example . . . of a man's having to write his life in order to convince himself that he had lived it." Hawthorne's solitude, "in the 'dismal chamber' of the Salem home where he practiced his art, was more than a personal habit; it was a commitment to the wholly mental life of his characters." In Melville we encounter "the peculiar bitterness of a man who has lost everything except the will to survive by writing." But perhaps it was Henry James who spoke for all of them when he confessed in a letter: "The port from which I set out was . . . that of the essential loneliness of my life, and it seems to be the port also, in sooth, to which my course again finally directs itself. This loneliness [is] deeper than my 'genius,' deeper than my 'discipline,' deeper than my pride, deeper, above all, than the deep counterminings of art."

Clearly, a myth is being evoked here, one that will be taken in skeptical quarters as further proof of Kazin's enduring radicalism – the myth of the artist's alienation from and martyrdom by American society. But alienation, in the sense of revulsion, is not what Kazin is driving at: *An American Procession* is anything but a lecture on spirit vs. commerce or the terrible consequences of the artist's pursuit of the Bitch Goddess. Kazin is after something more fundamental: a conception of where the words come from and how art attains *power*. His descant on the American writer's reclusiveness claims only that the imagination grazes in lonely pastures and that without the loneliness there is no art. Melville's "will to survive by writing" is a universal property of the "isolato" (Melville's word), who primes his imagination by sacrificing social relations.

The myth of the artist as the great isolato applies in complicated ways to Henry Adams, who is the focus and hero of this history. He lived, after all, not at Walden Pond but in Washington, the seat of power, where he was the center of a bustling social circle. He was a social gadfly and a public man, boasting two Presidents among his ancestors and diplomats among his intimates. Yet, he also maintained an inviolate interior dimension and was, Kazin calls him, "an immensely private, proud, unfathomably touchy person . . . the most public recluse in Washington." His private sorrow, Kazin claims, was sexual and his famed *Schadenfreude* – his delight in the more dangerous follies of nations – was the projection of his solitude, "his sexual sorrow, and his special dryness of heart and mockery onto a world at war." And yet, despite that dryness of heart, or perhaps because of it, he understood, as did no other writer save Whitman, that sex was power. This theorist of the Virgin and the Dynamo would write with bitter poignancy toward the end of his life: "All one has cared about have been a few women, and they have worried one more than falling empires."

Power is a key term in Kazin's lexicon, one that is as critical to his vision of American literature as isolation. Kazin is attentive to two kinds of power, which gather and fuse in the work of some writers but which are, finally, separate entities: national power which resides in material things, and the power of art. Where they are drawn together, as in Hemingway, whose command of experience "belonged to an imperial race," they create a portrait of the artist as a model of the national character – the brag and bluster of a nation ordaining the self-assurance of the writer. In Adams that confluence of powers operated differently, through the identification of the self with the past, quite as if the interior life were a metaphor for the march of events and one could take the pulse of modern life by simply feeling one's own wrist. The submission of principle to power, which was Adams' great theme in *History of the United States*, was also the very design of his writing: to subordinate the materials of history to the rhythms of myth and the confident order of a lucid, supple, periodic prose.

"The world was running down, and he was going to show why – in prose that would have to do for mathematics, but would be as elegant. Science was the new language. Like his own *History*, his *nuova scienza* would show that necessity unrolls in set quantities and therefore could be fixed in the rhythms of his own prose." For Adams, then, the power of language might thereby be a rival to state power rather than, as it was with Hemingway, merely its unconscious extension – i.e. powerful nations produce powerful men. He was the last of the historians who held history to be a branch of literature and therefore an item of moral education. To Kazin, Adams was *the* great American practitioner of subordinating historical facts to the mythological designs that give pattern to events and world-historical stature to men. As one of the ruling mythographers of American history, "Adams was not interested in telling the 'truth' about himself – whatever that was. His aim was to present himself as History."

Here, as elsewhere in *An American Procession*, the margin blurs and we are no longer certain of what figure is in the carpet, Adams or Kazin. That is intentional, for if Kazin, like Adams, is going to produce a myth of American culture, it shall be one capacious enough to include himself. What are we to make of the fact the Adams, not Twain, not Melville, not Whitman, is the moral center of this book, the single writer in *An American Procession* who was neither a novelist nor a poet, but who wrote histories in which the properties of fiction – style, plot, character, drama, and myth – were all deployed? The historian, in effect, dominates a book on novelists and poets. There is, then, a dramatic element in this book, the drama of the literary historian composing a myth of American consciousness in order to explain it from within.

There is nothing out of order in that: it is what passionate criticism normally does. But what makes it remarkable in Kazin's case is that this testing of literature against the self is so relentless and so public that we are compelled to view Kazin as a product of the history he writes, the history of American individualism and its discontents. In reading *An American Procession*, I find myself underlining those passages in which Kazin, in trying to capture the quintessence of a writer (and Kazin is a maestro of quintessences), sounds like he is composing epigrams about himself. The paean in praise of Henry Adams and his style is the place were Kazin's own style is incited to its fullest exertions. Here Kazin writes competitively, trading Adams sentence for sentence, image for image, cadence for cadence, like a boxer. Kazin's watchwords in this book are intensity, compression, vehemence, energy, style, intoxication, force, avidity, ecstasy, frenzy, acceleration, delirium, relentlessness, power, acceleration, words that channel our attention toward Kazin himself. "The great thing," he quotes James as saying, "is to be *saturated* with something, and I choose the form of my saturation." And that is precisely what we are bound to note of Kazin, his saturation with emotions and words.

We needn't seek far to observe how closely Kazin's thesis expresses his own conception of himself: as an isolate, an ecstatic, a word-intoxicated writer. Throughout his career, Kazin has had a poor instinct for joining up. A New York intellectual in the forties, with all the credentials of the tribe, he was never part of the *Partisan Review* cénacle. Even in his radical days he never joined any Trotskyist group or made party-line pronouncements that had to be later disclaimed with fanfare and regrets. By and large he has sidestepped politics altogether, and there is precious little of it in any of his books, save what has been absolutely essential to characterizing the New York scene. He regards himself first and foremost as a writer who has gone his own way and has brought the resources of his language and his heart to bear on American cultural history, past and present.

It is impossible to ignore Kazin's language, which operates at a pitch of compression beyond what any other critics, and only a handful of novelists, can muster. Kazin is always testing the boundaries of language, straining against its nets and its disabilities, and it is surprising that he does not quote the line from Eliot's "East Coker" about each venture being "a raid on the inarticulate/With shabby equipment always deteriorating," for surely that has been the spirit of his work all his life. These raids on the inarticulate have as their goal a precision of definition and a perfection of style. Only Kazin's is not the transparent, urbane style of a Wilson or a Pritchett, but a more intense and compact style, compressed in places to an epigrammatic concision, elsewhere lambent and lyrical, liquid in its sonorities. There no other American critical writing quite like this. It is not taught in the graduate schools, and not much valued there either, where the most admired styles court a margin of unintelligibility as a token of profundity. The sentence that defies parsing, so the theory goes, points us toward depths beyond language. Unlike those post modernist critics who despair of language by very precept and therefore content themselves with either the stale rites of cliché or the mirthless vanities of "jouissance," Kazin begins his task armed with the conviction that he, and language, can do better; that raids on the inarticulate are bound to yield conquests. That may be a measure of Kazin's naïveté and sentimentality, and Kazin is both a naive and sentimental critic whose prime intellectual equipment is an eager and bursting heart, but therein lies his power too: he approaches writing unencumbered by theories of his own disablement and is always poised to wrest meaning from the miasmas of history and the dark pools of language. Which is another way of saying that Kazin is a romantic.

Still, who is going to read such a book? What teacher is likely to assign it? What graduate seminar is going to heed the words of a generalist who has no method to promote, no great hash to settle, only a code of sensibility, a burden of melancholy to which he assigns responsibility for the universal gift of the poetic, and a style that defies imitation. (The great satraps of our day, after all, are those who shamelessly repeat themselves, who hammer away at banal and repetitive slogans.)

An American Procession broaches no new historical ideas: thematically it is thin. Its integration of history and literary intelligence goes no farther than the commonplaces that are available to any undergraduate in American literature: Emerson and the slavery issue: Thoreau and his poll tax; Whitman's work as a Civil War nurse; Crane's opposition to the Spanish-American War; the sadness of the American artist. Kazin is not interested in new perspectives and new syntheses, and he certainly has no interest in advancing the state of criticism or revolutionizing opinion. Kazin's reader learns little from this book, certainly nothing importable into the classroom. Rather, he enlarges his sympathies and senses and comes away refreshed by evidence of the mind's capacity to define experience by purely verbal means. These essays are character portraits, extended tableaux rather like those Kazin drawn so stunningly in his three volumes of memoirs: *A Walker in the City, Starting Out in the Thirties,* and *New York Jew,* and one is inclined to think of *An American Procession* as an extension of the portraitist's method to the historian's discipline.

An American Procession, then, makes virtually no contribution to our *thinking* about American literature, and yet to say that is to be made aware of Kazin's profound distrust of ideas and their tendency to strangle the imagination. It is of himself and his own sensibility that he speaks in quoting Eliot's remark that Henry James had a mind so fine that no idea could violate it, for if it is possible to construct history, as James constructed fiction, entirely upon sensibility – upon heightened senses and a painter's eye for color and line – then Alfred Kazin's impressionist history of American writing is such a book.

20

The Last Trotskyist

How theatrical a time it was, and if only the dead would rise for one final casting call, what a motion picture it would make! Comedy, of course. You think immediately of Groucho Marx as Max Shachtman and Chico as James P. Cannon, since it should be a brother act, but if they should prove unavailable, then any number of the great comedy teams, from Smith and Dale to Martin and Lewis could capture these squabbling heirs of the revolutionary Trotskyist tradition. And speaking of teams, what about Walter Matthau and George Burns – the sunshine boys – as Philip Rahv and William Phillips of *Partisan Review*?

Norman Podhoretz, I think, should be played as an an ogre, a preening, self-conscious ogre in greasepaint who mugs for the camera while clutching a hapless novelist by the throat, which brings Zero Mostel to mind. Of course, the audience would be alert to the irony of Mostel, whose career was virtually ruined by the blacklist of the fifties, playing the role of a born-again anti-communist. Joan Rivers was born to play Midge Decter as a blunt, abrasive, no nonsense committeewoman for the free world, and a smirking, powdered, lipsticked Peewee Herman would make a most provocative Lionel Trilling. Goldie Hawn is just reckless enough to be the young Diana Trilling, in her revolutionary, Diana Rubin, phase, and Sophie Tucker could strut her stuff as the crusty, dowager Diana. I close my eyes and see Jackie Mason doing send-ups of Sidney Hook, Don Rickles at his most contentious in the role of Irving Howe, baiting the crowd with insults and giving as good as he gets, Woody Allen shrugging his way through *The Saul Bellow Story* (and what a sensitive Herzog he would make!), Lucille Ball as Mary McCarthy, and Dwight Macdonald playing himself. Finally, I like Sid Caesar for the part of Trotsky. He can do a Russian accent, can fly into thundering rages, and has the gift of double-talk. In a white wig and white goatee, pacing the Mexican shore (like Richard Burton in *Night of the Iguana*), hurling anathemas at the Stalinist Moloch across the sea, Caesar would cast a great tragi-comic shadow, a Jewish King Lear without daughters (Trotsky's own daughter committed suicide), abandoned by his revolutionary sons and separated by an evil force from the faithful Cordelia of the revolution, the Russian masses.

As for a script, should anyone but S. J. Perelman be allowed to touch it? Should anyone but Mel Brooks be asked to direct it? Having once done the inquisition as vaudeville, he'd find the Trotskyist slapstick a natural. He wouldn't even need to tamper with the plot much – just play it straight and let the banana peels fall where they may. For a title, of course, there is just one choice: *The New York Intellectuals.*

Alan Wald has the title right and even some of the lines, but not the spirit. How could it escape him so utterly that he was writing Jewish comedy and not, as he took it to be, Jewish soap opera? Where, after all, are the unhappy endings? These aren't the Stalinists he is writing about, many of whom were dragged down and came come to sad endings. Virtually all the Trotskyists, to hear Wald tell it, graduated from the movement to successful careers, substantial fame and occasional wealth. In the New York intellectual melodrama, nobody suffers except the workers and peasants of Brooklyn, and they are marked for hard times anyway.

Is this so outlandish? Note, for one thing, the cast of characters and their social origins. The great majority of the Trotskyist intellectuals in Wald's book shared a social origin with the Catskill comedians and Second Avenue vaudevillians of the 1930s and 1940s. They were either eastern European Jewish immigrants or the children of immigrants; their parents toiled in the same lowly trades and dreamed the same dreams of success; their grandparents read the same Torahs in the same *shuls* of Poland and Russia; they themselves grew up in the same teeming immigrant streets. Only, given the vast freedom of choice in America, they went into different businesses: revolution instead of entertainment. And after the depression, when the bottom fell out of the revolution business, they cut their losses and went into something else. For some, given their years of training in ideology and dialectic, in personal vilification and organizational strategy, and their age – they were too old to start over in retail – they saw their best chance in counterrevolution, where in fact they prospered. But the spirit in which they conducted business on both sides of the barricade was unfailingly theatrical, the comedy of their politics growing out of the absurdity of their crusade enriched by their intuitive sense of the vast comedy of being, with which the culture of Yiddish speaking Eastern European Jewry was deeply imbued.

A friend of mine tells the story of Max Shachtman's visit to Buffalo in the early forties, when founders of the local chapter of the Worker's Party, including Harvey Swados, tried to set up a rally for him in the black community. Only the befuddled Trotskyists got their days wrong and Shachtman came into Buffalo two days before the advertised rally. Up go the hasty posters in the shabby streets around the tavern where the rally is to be held, and Shachtman and his friends sit down to wait for black revolutionaries to show up. Eventually one elderly man, thoroughly drunk, staggers in and takes a seat at the bar, whereupon Shachtman, seeing his chance, treats him to a three hour lecture, at the top of his voice, on the evils of imperial war. Consider the story Wald himself tells of the expulsion of Felix Morrow from James Cannon's Socialist Worker's Party in 1946 for deviationist views. "You can't expel me," he cries at them. "I'll live and die in the movement," and his fellow Socialist Workers, seeing that there are tears in his eyes, take just ten minutes to vote his expulsion, moments after which he is seen "tripping down the stairs of the convention hall with the greatest sense of glee and freedom."

How the humor of all this escapes Wald, who takes this history with leaden solemnity, is hard to fathom. Does he think there was really a revolution at hand, from a movement that was so wedded to faction and expulsion that it regularly decimated its own ranks without the usual nicety of first coming to power? Does he believe that anyone really sold out, except in the sense that a retailer sells out his scorched remnants at ten cents on the dollar after a fire? Compared to even the paltriest of today's television ministries, the Socialist Worker's Party at the apogee of its organizational strength in 1938 was a splinter of a splinter – the Fourth (Trotskyist) International – numbering somewhere in the vicinity of 1,500 members, mostly footloose intellectuals and impecunious teachers, workers, and trade unionists. And even by then the SWP was riven with faction over how to properly define the Soviet regime and whether to "defend the Soviet Union."

This conflict grew sharper in 1939, first over the question how to interpret the war, Stalin-Hitler pact, and then over how to interpret the war, and the Trotskyist movement would be shattered just a year later over the issue of whether the Soviet Union should properly be regarded as a "degenerated workers' state" or a "bureaucratic collectivist" state. The followers of James P. Cannon fought for the former definition and stayed in command of the SWP, while those of Max Shachtman, preferring the latter, broke with the SWP and founded the Workers' Party. Along the way, the Trotskyist movement spun off schismatic Oehlerites, Fieldites (League for a Revolutionary Party), absorbed Musteites (American Workers' Party), and did a "French turn" into Norman Thomas' Socialist Party, from which they would quickly be expelled. After the war, a tiny faction, led by Jean Malaquais, opted for defining the Soviet Union as a "state capitalist" society, and while they did not form a party, they did once influence a novel, Norman Mailer's *Barbary Shore*. The consequences of these tactical marriages and ideological divorces were thought to be shattering, for on them hung the issue of whether this band of 1095 members (the 1940 membership, already down some 500 members from 1938) was prepared to "defend" the Soviet Union. To see the USSR as a "degenerated workers' state" was to see it as a "materially progressive" society whose development toward true socialism had been arrested by the Stalinist aberration but would resume after him, whereas to see the USSR as "bureaucratic collectivist" was to judge the Russian Revolution a failure and the Soviet Union beyond redemption. From this split and from Trotsky's death the same year, the Trotskyist movement never recovered, though for fifty years the products of its fission would continue to leave brilliant traces in the bubble chamber of American society.

The New York intellectuals account for virtually all those traces, for if the Trotskyist movement has mattered to anyone but the participants it has been through the products of its decay, the writers and thinkers who rallied around it in the 1930s and were later propelled from it into the main currents of American intellectual life. Consider this short list of those who were either party members (that is, of either the Communist League of America or the Socialist Workers' Party or the Workers' Party) or sympathetic fellow-travelers: John Dewey, Herbert Solow, Suzanne LaFollette, Saul Bellow, Leslie Fiedler, Philip Rahv, William Phillips, Albert Goldman, Felix Morrow, Sidney Hook, Dwight Macdonald, Mary McCarthy, Meyer Schapiro, Seymour Martin Lipset, Philip O. Selznick, Irving Kristol, Lionel Abel, Elliot Cohen, Irving Howe, and Martin Diamond. What the movement lacked in numbers and resources it made up in words, and it is as a word factory and a school for writers, not a political movement, that American Trotskyism remains spell-binding. It has been said that for every member of the Abraham Lincoln Brigade that fought in Spain during the Civil War there would eventually be three books, either by or about. If so, then for every American Trotskyist there would eventually be five books, one magazine, and two internal bulletins. They lived, it sometimes seems, in order to leave a record of their passing.

The record is being compiled, indeed, with a fury, and as the library shelves sag beneath the weight of memoirs and studies, who isn't weary unto death of hearing how Philip Rahv and William Phillips stole *Partisan Review* from the Communist Party, or how the Trotskyists fertilized the American mind with European ideas to which they, as transplanted Europeans, were uniquely attuned, or how in the long transit from the social margin to the center, the anti-Stalinist left became the backbone of the anti-liberal right? We now have memoirs by Leslie Fiedler, Bernard Wolfe, William Barrett, William Phillips, Irving Howe, Lionel Abel, Sidney Hook, Alfred Kazin – three volumes now – Mary McCarthy, and a *roman fleuve*, two volumes and running, of life in the intellectual trenches by Norman Podhoretz. A memoir by Diana Trilling is in prep-aration, and last year saw the publication of Delmore Schwartz's journals, hot on the heels of his letters just two years before. And as the memoirs pile up, critical histories by Alexander Bloom and Terry Cooney have recently come along to supplement them and update James Gilbert's pioneering study, *Writers and Partisans*. Is there anything left to say? Is anybody paying attention?

Alan Wald believes there is, and his *New York Intellectuals*, the dis-tillation of some eighteen years of research, is his bid to prove it. For one thing, Wald cautions us that the memoirs must be taken with a ton of salt, for they are largely documents of self-congratulation and self-exculpation marked by the "political amnesia" that is the affliction of retreating radicals everywhere. Not only have the writ-ers forgotten their own past, but even what they were fighting for and why. In this charge he finds himself in the surprising company of Hilton Kramer, who has leveled the very same accusation on virtually identical grounds. "Down the memory hole," thundered Kramer in a review of William Phillips's anthology *Writers and Politics: A Partisan Review Reader* in 1983, and "down the memory hole" echoes Wald from a far planet somewhere else in the political universe. Both accuse the memoirists and anthologists of fleeing from their vows of militancy and solidarity made in the days when to be a New York intellectual was to stand for Marxist revolution in the United States. Where Wald and Kramer part company, of course, is over the value and meaning of this revolutionism: for Kramer it was a travesty from which many of the New York intellectuals never recovered; for Wald it was the peak of their moral development, from which all deviation was a fall: a failure of humanity, or of nerve, or of analysis. Lamenting the rightward drift that was paradigmatic of this generation, Wald is moved to announce that "it was the abandonment of an opposition to Stalinism *on anticapitalist premises* (italics mine) that sapped the movement of its most positive qualities in the years following World War II," and the rest of the book is a 440–page footnote to that accusation, a detailed and sometimes wearisome rap sheet on the sins of the old left.

Why should this book be any different from others that document this history and confirm the picture, if not the shame, of this deradicalization? Two things, I think, distinguish Wald's book and single it out for special attention. One: Wald is the unofficial archivist of the American Trotskyist movement. He has interviewed or corresponded with virtually everyone who was in the movement or whose life was touched by it; he has visited most of the libraries; he has collected a vast archive of letters and documents, and has corresponded faithfully with a number of the survivors, especially James T. Farrell, who is the patron saint of this book. Two earlier books, *James T. Farrell: The Revolutionary Socialist Years*, and *The Revolutionary Imagination: The Poetry and Politics of John Wheelwright and Sherry Mangan*, are spin offs of the Trotsky history project, and Wald's papers will support more. *The New York Intellectuals* is an effort to distill this archive, and the problem of organizing, consolidating, and paring down the information at hand is one the book never successfully solves. Two: Wald, a young scholar, declares himself a devoted Trotskyist who is writing his history from within the movement, or rather from within an envelope of memory, since there is no longer a movement. *The New York Intellectuals* is an avowedly sectarian book. Several years ago, when Wald visited Buffalo to interview some of the surviving Trotskyists then living here, I introduced him to my Shachtmanite friend who had been one of the founders of a short-lived Buffalo chapter of the Worker's Party in the 1940s. Several days later I called my friend to find out how the interview went, and he asked in a bemused voice, "How did someone so young get to be such a goddam Cannonite? I haven't met anyone like that in thirty years." They had broached the topic of the Soviet Union, about which they naturally disagreed, and as my friend described the scene to me I caught of glimpse of what it must have been like on the dogmatic left in those days, when differences of interpretation were incitements to denunciation. Forty years ago they'd have spent the afternoon expelling each other from the movement. In the 1980s, they simply disagreed over lunch. *The New York Intellectuals* is a Cannonite's history, in which a heavy burden of villainy falls upon the Shachtmanites.

Wald has two books here, a history and a diatribe. The history, Wald's leaden prose notwithstanding, is a major contribution to our understanding of New York intellectual life, both in the sweep of its conception and the fullness of its documentation. The history, however, is written in the service of a thesis: the basic rightness of the Cannonite line in the 1940s, which Wald is prepared to defend in the very language of Marxobabble that Cannon himself leveled against every doubter and skeptic, every deviant and apostate, every Eastman and Hook, every Burnham and Howe, until one is tempted to believe that it is the language itself that has mesmerized Wald and is the secret to how someone so young gets to be such a goddam Cannonite.

It is no news that the New York intellectuals, or at least that particular herd of independent minds that grazed in the vicinity of *Partisan Review* in the 1940s and 1950s, had their origin in the anti-Stalinist left of the 1930s. Wald's contribution to this history is to displace *Partisan Review* from the center to the wings, in favor of two overlapping groups which he identifies as the seedbed of left anti-Stalinism and the progenitors of the new intellectual-political culture: *The Menorah Journal* and the National Committee for the Defense of Political Prisoners.

The Menorah Journal was a journal of secular Jewish thought dedicated to a "pluralist" conception of society and the participation of Jews in American life as culturally distinct but socially equal. It was the publication of The Menorah Society, which had been founded at Harvard University by Horace Kallen in 1906. Kallen was a spokesman for pluralism: a vision of American society as a "symphony of civilizations" in which individual ethnic groups might preserve their distinctness intact while co-existing under the common rule of mutual tolerance and respect. The pluralist idea, which stands opposed to particularism on the one side and assimilation on the other, idealized difference and posed a *concordia discors*, a harmony of opposites, as an alternative to the melting pot which, in Kallen's view, denatured American society and robbed Americans of their actual past, substituting for real histories an ersatz history of patriotic banalities. Kallen's vision was resonant with that of Randolph Bourne, in recognition of which Bourne published his formulation of the pluralist ideal, "The Jew and Transnational America," in *The Menorah Journal* in 1916.

The Menorah Journal's program for Judaism itself was less clear-cut, and it treated the question of Jewish identity as an historical problem rather than a known quality. Thus the magazine was a forum for raising basic questions, and its pages became home to such historians and explorers of Jewish consciousness as Ludwig Lewisohn, Salo Baron, Maurice Samuel, Waldo Frank, Harry Wolfson, Cecil Roth, and Israel Zangwill. It is not to be wondered that Mordecai Kaplan's project for reconstructing Judaism would be first articulated in the pages of *The Menorah Journal*.

When Elliot Cohen took over as managing editor of *The Menorah Journal* in June, 1925, he brought with him an aggressive agenda for American Judaism that initially seemed consonant with the spirit of the journal's "humanist" and "progressive" bias, which in many Jewish circles was taken to be the cultural component of socialism. As editor, he drew into the magazine writers who were in revolt against the American middle class, and especially against that portion of it they knew best: established Jewry. Among them were Herbert Solow, Felix Morrow, Anita Brenner, Louis Berg, Louis Fischer, Clifton Fadiman, Kenneth Fearing, Isidor Schneider, Tess Slesinger, and a young Lionel Trilling, who published his first short story, "Impediments," in Cohen's first issue and would remain a steady contributor of fiction and reviews so long as Cohen remained editor. Under Cohen, *The Menorah Journal* became a haven for corrosive analyses of Jewish life, and given the politics of the era, this cultural criticism took a radical political turn as the *Menorah* group, under Solow's prodding, moved left. Eventually this would cause a strain between Cohen and his publisher, Henry Hurwitz, who had to face the magazine's wealthy backers and explain his magazine's wayward course, and it was an article harshly critical of Zionism by Solow in 1931 that finally forced the rupture and caused the dismissal of Cohen and his group.

By the time of their dismissal in the Fall of 1931, however, several of the *Menorah* writers had already found their way to the National Committee for the Defense of Political Prisoners, a writers' and intellectuals' auxiliary to the Communist Party – a front, in short

– founded in June 1931 under the chairmanship of Theodore Dreiser, who announced that "the time is ripe for American intellectuals to render some service to the American worker" (57). The service was, as is customary in such cases, legal defense, fund raising, and propaganda, tasks that intellectuals are usually assigned to when pressed into the service of labor. It was a prestigious group, with Dreiser as chairman, Lincoln Steffens as treasurer, and John Dos Passos, Suzanne LaFollette, Franz Boas, Floyd Dell, Waldo Frank, and the ubiquitous Josephine Herbst as endorsers. But as Wald observes, Cohen and several members of his circle, including Solow, Rice, Brenner, Novack, Adelaide Walker, and Diana Rubin ("an aspiring singer" who had married Lionel Trilling in 1929 and was now secretary to the NCDPP's Prisoner Relief Committee) quickly took administrative control of the NCDPP.

Though nominally under CP sponsorship, as an assembly of intellectuals the NCDPP had a will of its own and a desire to conduct its own analyses and direct its own affairs, which did not sit well with the CP, which had a low tolerance for independence. In 1933, after Hitler's seizure of power in Germany, a group from the NCDPP led by Solow, called for a coalition of revolutionary organizations against fascism, an initiative that was rudely denounced by the Communist Party as a Trotskyist tactic. In February of the following year, twenty-five dissident left intellectuals, including many NCDPP members, signed a letter of protest against the Communist Party's breaking up of a Socialist Party rally in Madison Square Garden, which had been called to protest Austrian Chancellor Dolfuss's attack on workers' home in Vienna. Met with storms of slander and invective by the CP, some of the signers – all of them as yet avowed revolutionists – left the NCDPP to form their own organization, the Non-Partisan Labor Defense Committee, and by December, 1934, Solow, Novack, Felix Morrow, and John Macdonald had joined the Trotskyist Communist League of America, and Cohen, Rice, Brenner, and Rubin were in sympathy. So it was that in 1934 the first substantial link between the literary left in New York and the politics of Leon Trotsky was forged.

All this is at odds with the canonical history of the New York intellectuals that begins with the founding of *Partisan Review* as an organ of the John Reed Club in 1934 and the editors' stealing the magazine from the Communists and re-establishing it as an independent organ of the Marxist left opposition to Stalinism. These are in fact parallel histories that, while they frequently intersect, are finally distinct accounts of how the New York intellectuals appeared on the scene. The particular virtue of Wald's history is its comprehensiveness – its view of Marxist revolutionism as an expression of Jewish consciousness in turmoil and therefore as a scenario of self-realization that an entire generation of young Jews was rehearsing in unison. In one sense, what Wald has identified here is that strand of New York intellectual history that leads by commodius vicus of recirculation to *Commentary* magazine, for which a case could be made as the true main line of New York intellectual life, not *Partisan Review*.

Wald is at his most authoritative in excavating the deep past of the New York intellectuals: recalling forgotten events, resurrecting lost careers, and disturbing the historical perspective that the memoirists, eager to place themselves at the eye of history, have been promoting. History is the rhetoric of the winners, and Wald's book has the virtue of bringing back some of the losers, and indeed as Wald traces the odyssey of the *Menorah* group through the NCDPP, the League of Professionals, the Non Partisan Labor Defense Committee, and the Dewey Commission of Inquiry into the Charges Against Leon Trotsky in Moscow, and into their post war fadeout (except for Cohen and the Trillings), he writes a remarkable narrative that is novelistic in its drama and touching in its pathos.

Unfortunately, historian Wald has an alter ego who fancies himself a political philosopher and the prophet of a lost gospel and finds it necessary to join battle with every apostate from the fold, packing his pages with hopeless polemics that do nothing to salvage the Trotskyist wreck but plenty to demonstrate just why it sunk in the first place. Virtually everyone, even Trotsky and Cannon, comes in for a rap on the knuckles, which might be tolerable but that, as every child knows, it isn't the spanking that hurts, it's the lecture.

Some of the lecturing is in the mode of the inspired anathema – Isaiah 1 comes to mind – virtually Mosaic in its scorn for those who forsook the faith of their fathers (or in this case the line of "the old man") and fell to worshipping strange gods: the gods of skepticism and realism, the god of capitalism, the god of neoconservatism, the god of social democracy, the god of imperialism, the god of bourgeois individualism. But Mosaic rage modulates only too readily into sectarian bickering in which old issues are dusted off, old grievances resurrected, and a weary lexicon of damnations brought into play as though charged with some ancient, terrible might.

The particular instance that sums up all that is both vital and chilling about the book is Wald's portrait of Irving Howe. As the great rememberer, Wald holds everyone's follies hostage, and thus he examines in withering detail the record of Howe's life in the Worker's Party, where, as an apprentice revolutionary, he heaped invective upon the very social democracy he later came to embrace, and often in the strange polemical mix of saccharine and bitters that is the hallmark of Leninist language everywhere. Wald quotes with glee a 1947 Howe editorial from the Worker's Party organ, *Labor Action*, attacking the French Social Democratic government for its post war reoccupation of Indo-China.

> We stand squarely by the side of the French Fourth International. They do not bow down before French imperialism; they rather defy it and send their brothers of Indo-China this message: We are with you in the struggle for independence; we are your brothers; we shall fight beside you against the Le Clercs, the Blums, and the Thorez's. (p. 285)

In those days, Howe was a master of phrasebook fanaticism, battling for "independent class action" and scorning "realism" ("the first refuge of scoundrels"), the "intellectual stooges of labor" (retreating radicals like Gus Tyler and Jay Lovestone), "oppositionist liberals supporting the capitalist status quo," and the compulsive Stalinophobia of the *Partisan Review*, which he denounced as "an emotional block to . . . political analysis." Wald's book is quite splendid at such moments, showing us far more about Howe's past as a virtuoso of sectarian combat than we would ever guess from his own recent memoir, *A Margin of Hope*.

But even as he was sharpening his clichés for battle, Howe was entertaining doubts, and by 1947 he was beginning to explore other options, appearing as a literary critic and reviewer in *Commentary* magazine, which the American Jewish Committee founded in 1946 with Elliot Cohen as its first editor. The subsequent vicissitudes of Howe's political career, which Wald traces with malicious detail, describe a jagged curve, as Howe tried, through the founding of *Dissent* in 1953, to chart an independent course as an anti-Stalinist socialist free of all institutional constraints, including the Independent Socialist League, which he finally left in 1953.

As a lifelong socialist who has continued to care about ameliorating the conditions of life, Howe ought to stand as the hero of a book like this, and Wald does grant him a degree of respect as an intellectual engage who didn't follow the ancient footsteps of Eastman, Hook, Burnham, Shachtman, Albert Goldman, Irving Kristol *et al.* into the arms of *Commentary* or *The Public Interest* or *The Reader's Digest.* But Wald remains unforgiving of Howe's failure to take the correct line against the War in Vietnam in the sixties, and it is in taking Howe to the mat over Vietnam that Wald lays his own Trotskyist obsession open for inspection.

Howe stands accused of "[defending] the very stance he had once scorned when it came to the U.S. intervention in Indochina. In 1964 he stated that a pullout of U.S. troops would be 'inhumane.' In 1966 he called simply for a 'cease-fire' and went on to oppose antiwar actions in California that included civil disobedience because they challenged 'the decisions of the democratically elected government.'"

> By giving legitimacy to the American presence in Vietnam, Howe opened himself to the charge of actually defending U.S. imperialism, for he was granting the United States the right to determine the outcome of the struggle by interfering in the internal political life of the Vietnamese nation. While it is important that Howe had criticism of the American role in Vietnam, such criticism cannot be regarded as a substitute for opposing the U.S. presence in that country.

To read Wald only is to be persuaded that Howe was something of a circumspect liberal or even a reluctant apologist for the war, so that it is something of a shock to turn back to *Dissent* itself in the 1960s, to find Howe condemning the war in issue after issue and making plain his scorn for the military planners and social scientists who pursued and defended it. "The record of U.S. intervention in Vietnam is a record of disaster, stupidity, reaction," he wrote in 1966, and one scans the record of the war years in vain for any significant deviation from these sentiments.

The war tormented Howe, as *A Margin of Hope* makes abundantly clear. Opposed, as always, to imperialist wars by western powers, Howe also feared the consequences of a communist victory in Vietnam, a fear which has since proven justified, and yet in calling for a negotiated withdrawal in 1968 on the model of the French withdrawal from Algeria, he concluded that we had no choice but to leave, regardless of the foreseeable consequences. "Almost certainly," he wrote, "there will follow a slide into a Viet Cong dictatorship. But in politics, as in life, there are times when the choices are painful. Better peace with the probability of a Viet Cong take-over than a war which can only go on and on, without resolution, without reason, without honor." This was the same Howe whom Wald charges with "giving legitimacy to the American presence in Vietnam."

Indeed, given the real play of forces in Vietnam, and given Howe's horror of Stalinism, his position as a leading socialist was quite an impossible one. Beset by former allies who had moved far to his right and by a youth movement that refused his counsels of moderation, Howe broke with virtually everyone in the late sixties, and, wearing his anguish on his sleeve, lashed out bitterly at whatever provocateurs came into view: the war and the anti-war movement alike, the counterculture, the New Left, the women's movement, even at the novelist Philip Roth in one famous essay, in spasms that seemed to combine the brimstone of Shachtman with the madness of Ahab. Howe's torment became a public spectacle that one could only watch and wonder at, as he left a trail of scars all over the landscape, but mainly on himself.

In retrospect, however, though many of his judgments now seem excessive and hysterical, he was prophetic about the consequences of America's withdrawal from Vietnam, foreseeing better than the Left the devastation resulting from a communist victory there, fearing, as he wrote in 1966, "the disaster of a re-enactment in the South of the totalitarian terror which followed in the countryside of North Vietnam shortly after Ho Chi Minh took power." He understood that Vietnam was doomed to suffer grievously no matter what the outcome of the war, and it strikes me as a point of decency now, thirteen years after the fall of Saigon and some fifteen to twenty after the peak of anti-war agitation, to honor Howe's scruples as a expressions of humane concern and lessons in reality testing. But Wald will do no better than play the Cannonite game to the comic end, brush off the "degenerated workers' state" thesis, and apply it to Howe's antiquated humanistic qualms. Howe, it seems, had sinned in confusing the Stalinoid regime of North Vietnam with the progressive "post-capitalist" social order it had inaugurated, which would, presumably, outlive the terror, leaving behind after the expropriations, the killings, the re-education camps, and the boats, the residue of a progressive economy. Imagine.

To reductively equate social structure and political regime led Howe to even more errors in his posture toward bureaucratized post-capitalist societies and left-wing political movements around the world. Specifically it led to the equally erroneous identification of a legitimate national liberation movement with its Communist or pro-Communist leadership. The end result led Howe to dismiss entirely the achievements of anticapitalist revolutions because a certain normative stage of democracy had not been reached and to refuse to give support to many struggles because of Communist participation or the acceptance of aid from the Soviet Union.

Irving Howe, for all his rages and instabilities, emerges from this book oddly ennobled, as a man with a strange and volatile heart but one that is at least out in the open where we can see it plain. For what happened to Howe in the mid-forties when he began to question the gospel of the old man was a determination to cast off the sectarian cocoon and emerge as an individual, free to choose his own gospel and his own language and to make his own mistakes. The trouble with Wald is that he is still cocooned in someone else's gospel and language, and seems driven to repeating, like a Sisyphus of lost causes, someone else's mistakes. Small wonder then that he seems bewildered about where all the other Trotskyists disappeared to just as he was getting warmed up.

Index